'This book tackles an important question for international human rights law: how effective is the United Nations Human Rights Council's Universal Periodic Review (UPR) mechanism? It does so in the context of in-depth studies of African states: Nigeria, Kenya, The Gambia, Uganda and South Africa. The book finds that overall the UPR is effective as a non-confrontational system to encourage states to improve their implementation of their international human rights commitments. It also acknowledges many of the limitations and weaknesses of the UPR in practice. The book is a valuable contribution to the literature on the UPR. Its strength lies in its careful analysis and the detail in the case studies. The author has engaged in an impressively close analysis of the way that African states have engaged in the UPR process over its three cycles and the way in which they have responded to UPR recommendations. The author has built on existing methodologies and extended them. The figures presented in the case studies were very effective. A fascinating observation in the book relates to the role of regionalism in the UPR. The author points to the fact that regionalism operates strongly in the African context, with African states much more willing to accept UPR recommendations from other African states. He notes that some scholars have criticised this feature of the UPR, but observes perceptively that the regionalism can also facilitate acculturation to human rights standards. The author displays an excellent knowledge of the relevant literature and he has gone well beyond the legal literature to draw upon studies in international relations, sociology and psychology.'

—**Professor Hilary Charlesworth**, Melbourne Laureate Professor at Melbourne Law School and Distinguished Professor at the Australian National University

The Human Rights Council

This book examines the engagement of African states with the United Nations Human Rights Council's Universal Periodic Review (UPR) mechanism. This human rights mechanism is known for its pacific and non-confrontational approach to monitoring state human rights implementation. Coming at the end of the first three cycles of the UPR, the work offers a detailed analysis of the effectiveness of African states' engagement and its potential impact. It develops a framework which comprehensively evaluates aspects of states' UPR engagement, such as the pre-review national consultation process and implementation of UPR recommendations, which, until recently, have received little attention. The book considers the potential for acculturation in engagement with the UPR and unpacks the impact of politics, regionalism, cultural relativism, rights ritualism and civil society.

The work provides a useful guide for policymakers and international human rights law practitioners, as well as a valuable resource for international legal and international relations academics and researchers.

Damian Etone is a Lecturer at the Division of Law and Philosophy, University of Stirling, United Kingdom.

Routledge Research in Human Rights Law

Indigenous Peoples, Title to Territory, Rights and Resources
The Transformative Role of Free Prior and Informed Consent
Cathal M. Doyle

Civil and Political Rights in Japan
A Tribute to Sir Nigel Rodley
Edited by Saul J. Takahashi

Human Rights, Digital Society and the Law
A Research Companion
Edited by Mart Susi

Criminal Theory and International Human Rights Law
Steven Malby

Women's Health and the Limits of Law
Domestic and International Perspectives
Edited by Irehobhude O. Iyioha

Women and International Human Rights Law
Universal Periodic Review in Practice
Gayatri H Patel

International Law and Violence Against Women
Europe and the Istanbul Convention
Edited by Johanna Niemi, Lourdes Peroni, and Vladislava Stoyanova

The Human Rights Council
The Impact of the Universal Periodic Review in Africa
Damian Etone

For more information about this series, please visit: www.routledge.com/Routledge-Research-in-Human-Rights-Law/book-series/HUMRIGHTSLAW

The Human Rights Council

The Impact of the Universal Periodic Review in Africa

Damian Etone

Routledge
Taylor & Francis Group
LONDON AND NEW YORK

First published 2020
by Routledge
2 Park Square, Milton Park, Abingdon, Oxon OX14 4RN

and by Routledge
52 Vanderbilt Avenue, New York, NY 10017

Routledge is an imprint of the Taylor & Francis Group, an informa business

British Library Cataloguing-in-Publication Data
A catalogue record for this book is available from the British Library

Library of Congress Cataloging-in-Publication Data
Names: Etone, Damian, author.
Title: The Human Rights Council in Africa : the impact of the Universal Periodic Review / Damian Etone.
Description: Abingdon, Oxon ; New York, NY : Routledge, 2020. | Includes bibliographical references and index.
Identifiers: LCCN 2019046975 (print) | LCCN 2019046976 (ebook) | ISBN 9780367182496 (hardback) | ISBN 9780429060304 (ebook)
Subjects: LCSH: United Nations Human Rights Council. | Human rights monitoring—Africa. | Human rights—Africa. | Human rights—International cooperation.
Classification: LCC K3241 .E86 2020 (print) | LCC K3241 (ebook) | DDC 341.48—dc23
LC record available at https://lccn.loc.gov/2019046975
LC ebook record available at https://lccn.loc.gov/2019046976

ISBN: 978-0-367-18249-6 (hbk)
ISBN: 978-0-429-06030-4 (ebk)

Typeset in Galliard
by Apex CoVantage, LLC

Contents

Foreword

This monograph develops an original framework for analysing the effectiveness of African states' engagement with the Universal Periodic Review (UPR) mechanism. It is one that encompasses a theoretical dimension through the use of the theory of acculturation and, in doing so, addresses one of the shortcomings in the existing literature on UPR due to its limited engagement with theoretical frameworks, expands the basis for assessing the efficacy of human rights mechanisms beyond exclusively coercive models and uses the theory to suggest pathways to help close implementation gaps drawing on relevant state practice. The conceptual dimension to the framework draws on work already undertaken on the categorisation of UPR recommendations and the measurement of the implementation of these recommendations but builds on it by developing the four-step approach to evaluating the effectiveness of state engagement with the UPR. The latter broadens the scope of the analysis beyond that which is usually adopted in the existing literature by incorporating the pre-review consultation process and the quality of the UPR delegation. In doing so, it provides a range of useful insights into assessing a state's good faith engagement with the UPR process and the opportunities for greater strategic engagement by NGOs/CSOs with the process.

In terms of making a significant contribution to knowledge, this monograph can be said to do so in several respects. Through its analysis of the four case studies over UPR I, II and III, it demonstrates the evolutionary nature of the UPR mechanism and state engagement with it as well as highlights the importance of the time factor in assessing the value of this mechanism. The empirical analysis of the data, especially when combined with the focus on regionalism, cultural relativism, potential synergies between the UPR and other human rights mechanisms, and NGO/CSO engagement, provides some interesting insights. These include the manner in which regionalism can not only undermine but also enhance state engagement, how issues of cultural relativism can be addressed partly through cognitive reframing and acculturation, the limitations of an exclusively normative approach to certain issues and how NGO/CSO engagement can be harnessed to enhance state engagement with the UPR process, to ensure the relevance of human rights recommendations and to help mitigate human rights ritualism. The latter findings, in particular, emerged as a result of the broadening of the focus of the analysis to include the pre-review stage and the innovative use of the data generated there to explore, for example, the degree of correlation between the recommendations of NGOs/CSOs and states. Significant trends, including those relating to the increasing specificity of the UPR recommendations made by African states and the degree of correlation between membership of the Human Rights Council and engagement with the UPR process, are also set out in the book.

Professor Helen Quane
Head of Research
The Hillary Rodham Clinton School of Law
Swansea University, UK

Preface

This monograph builds on my PhD dissertation which was completed in 2017 at the Adelaide Law School, The University of Adelaide. My interest in the UPR mechanism developed in 2013 during my master's degree at Bangor Law School, Bangor University. After two cycles of the UPR (2008–2016) and midway through the third cycle (2017–2021), questions about the impact of the Human Rights Council's Universal Periodic Review (UPR) mechanism within states have been raised. Scholars and practitioners have generally focused on the nature of the UPR recommendations, the relationship between the UPR mechanism and UN human rights treaty bodies, and the level of politicisation and ritualism within the UPR. However, insufficient attention and consideration have been given to the impact of the UPR within states in terms of implementation of UPR recommendations. This is because, until recently, there was little empirical data to assess the level of state implementation. After ten years of the existence of the UPR mechanism, it is now time to examine the impact of the UPR throughout this time frame. This time period provides a natural opportunity to examine the impact of the UPR mechanism across different regions/states and to use this as a point of reference from which trends could be identified and recommendations for change could be made. This monograph offers not only the prospect of a richer understanding of the current state of affairs in the UPR but also a foundation from which to anticipate the future of the UPR mechanism. It develops an original framework for analysing African states' engagement with the UPR mechanism. This framework encompasses a theoretical dimension through the use of the theory of acculturation and, in doing so, addresses one of the shortcomings in the existing literature on UPR due to its limited engagement with theoretical frameworks. This monograph expands the basis for assessing the efficacy of human rights mechanisms beyond exclusively coercive models and drawing on relevant state practice by African states suggests pathways to help close the UPR implementation gap. The conceptual dimension adopted by this book draws on work already undertaken on the categorisation of UPR recommendations and the measurement of the implementation of these recommendations but builds on it by developing a four-step approach to evaluating the effectiveness of state engagement with the UPR. The latter broadens the scope of the analysis beyond that which is usually adopted in the existing literature by incorporating the pre-review consultation process and the quality of the UPR delegation. In doing so, it provides a range of useful insights into assessing a state's good faith engagement with the UPR process and the opportunities for greater strategic engagement by NGOs/CSOs with the process. Through an illuminating focus on four African states, this book examines themes, including politics, ritualism, regionalism and cultural relativism, influencing the engagement of African states with the UPR mechanism.

Acknowledgements

This manuscript was developed from my PhD project completed in 2017 at the Adelaide Law School, The University of Adelaide. I would like to thank the following people for all their assistance and support throughout the process of completing this manuscript. First, I would like to thank my two terrific PhD supervisors, Assistant Professor Matthew Stubbs and Assistant Professor Laura Grenfell, for their excellent supervision of my PhD project and for their feedback on earlier drafts of this manuscript. My PhD journey was an outstanding experience, and this manuscript is also a product of that journey.

A special thanks to the three anonymous reviewers of the book proposal to Routledge, for their supportive words and their good advice. Thank you to my Adelaide colleagues Dr Mohamed Agal, Dr Rio Maligalig and Dr Samuel Quartey. I would also like to thank my Staffordshire University colleagues, in particular, Dr Gareth Evans, Ayesha Chowdhury, Rhiannon Frost and Tawney Bennett, for inspiring the research culture and creating a supportive work environment that contributed to the successful completion of this manuscript.

I could not have completed this manuscript without the support and encouragement from my family and friends, including Rev. and Mrs Bweh Esembe, Ferdinand Ngale Njume, Bweh Helmuth, Bianca-Love, Sam Paul, Susan-Lucy, Natalie McPhee and Sona Gerald. Now that this task is completed, I promise to become more social and to keep in touch more frequently.

Abbreviations

ACHPR	African Commission on Human and Peoples' Rights
ASEAN	Association of Southeast Asian Nations
CHR	Commission for Human Rights
CSO	Civil Society Organisation
EEG	Eastern European Group
ESC	Economic, Social and Cultural
GRULAC	Group of Latin America and the Caribbean
HRC	Human Rights Council
ICC	International Criminal Court
KSC	Kenya Stakeholders' Coalition
NCF	National Consultative Forum
NGO	Non-Governmental Organisation
NHRC	National Human Rights Commission
NHRI	National Human Rights Institution
OHCHR	Office of the High Commissioner for Human Rights
UDHR	Universal Declaration of Human Rights
UN	United Nations
UNGA	United Nations General Assembly
UPR	Universal Periodic Review
WEOG	Western Europe and Others Group

1 The establishment and operation of the Universal Periodic Review

Contextual background

Monitoring state implementation of human rights treaty standards was pivotal to the UN human rights system at its birth. Specific human rights treaties established mechanisms to monitor state compliance with treaty obligations primarily through the examination of state reports.[1] The hope was that the reports would foster 'constructive dialogue' between states and the various treaty bodies composed of human rights experts.[2] With the competence to examine state human rights reports and consider individual and inter-state complaints, these bodies soon 'evolved into quasi-judicial bodies, displaying a formalised and relatively rigid procedure'.[3] However by 2000, the treaty monitoring system was in crisis as a result of the huge backlog of overdue reports, resource and financial constraints, and limited political support from states to improve the system.[4] While there have been several proposals in recent years to strengthen the human rights treaty body monitoring system,[5] Olivier de Frouville, a member of the UN Human Rights Committee, notes that the development of the treaty bodies has reached its limits.[6] As of September 2019, there was an overall total of 586 overdue treaty body reports and African states represented the majority of the non-reporting states, owing about 39% of the total overdue reports.

1 James Crawford, 'The UN Human Rights System: A System in Crisis' in Philip Alston and James Crawford (eds), *The Future of UN Human Rights Treaty Monitoring* (Cambridge University Press 2000) 1.

2 Ibid.

3 Frans Viljoen, 'Fact-Finding by UN Human Rights Complaints Bodies—Analysis and Suggested Reforms' (2004) 8 *Max Planck Yearbook of United Nations Law* 49, 63.

4 James Crawford, above n 1, 1–12.

5 See Navanethem Pillay, *Strengthening the United Nations Human Rights Treaty Body System: A Report by the United Nations High Commissioner for Human Rights* (OHCHR 2012); Suzanne Egan, 'Strengthening the United Nations Human Rights Treaty Body System' (2013) 13(2) *Human Rights Law Review* 209.

6 Olivier de Frouville, 'Building a Universal System for the Protection of Human Rights: The Way Forward' in M Cherif Bassiouni and William A Schabas (eds), *New Challenges for the UN Human Rights Machinery* (Intersentia 2011) 264.

Furthermore, there has been criticisms from African states relating to the country-specific and special procedures set up by the former UN Commission for Human Rights to deal with gross and systematic human rights violations, addressing thematic and country-specific issues.[7] These procedures were retained under the new Human Rights Council (HRC) established in 2006. As of August 2017, the UN system has 44 thematic and 14 country procedures.[8] However, African states, as well as many non-Western states, have repeatedly condemned findings and resolutions which target the human rights practices of specific states or regions, arguing that they breed selectivity and double standards.[9]

A distinctive addition to the UN human rights system was the Universal Periodic Review (UPR) established by the HRC in 2006 to review the human rights situation in all states.[10] The first cycle of the review (UPR I) spanned from 2008 to 2011, the second cycle (UPR II) from 2012 to 2016 and the third cycle (UPR III) from 2017–2021. The distinctive feature of the UPR, as an approach to monitoring human rights implementation, is that it is based on cooperation and dialogue and is inclusive, collaborative and a process controlled by states. However, some scholars have questioned the efficacy of the UPR, especially the level of state control over the UPR process. Manfred Nowak, former UN Special Rapporteur on Torture, argues that the UPR 'suffers from the disadvantage that states' performance in the field of human rights is assessed by other states rather than by independent experts'.[11] According to de Frouville, the UPR cannot address the compliance problem of the UN human rights system.[12] De Frouville contends that this problem can be effectively addressed by the creation of a World Commission of Human Rights with a strong institutional basis and the powers to issue and enforce binding decisions.[13] Similar desire for stronger and more confrontational approaches to human rights implementation is reflected in the argument that the best final model for securing human rights compliance is the

7 Helen Keller and Geir Ulfstein (eds), *UN Human Rights Treaty Bodies: Law and Legitimacy* (Cambridge University Press 2012) 1–2.

8 Office of the High Commissioner for Human Rights (OHCHR), 'Special Procedures of the Human Rights Council' (2016) available at >www.ohchr.org/EN/HRBodies/SP/Pages/Welcomepage.aspx. There are also several regional monitoring mechanisms across Africa, America, Asia and Europe. At the African regional level, various human rights monitoring mechanisms exist, such as the African Commission on Human and Peoples' Rights, the African Court on Human and Peoples' Rights and the African Peer Review Mechanism. See Frans Viljoen, *International Human Rights Law in Africa* (Oxford University Press 2007) 289–468.

9 Elvira Domínguez-Redondo, 'Rethinking the Legal Foundations of Control in International Human Rights Law-The Case of Public Special Procedures' (2011) 29(3) *Netherlands Quarterly of Human Rights* 261, 274–5.

10 *Human Rights Council,* GA Res 60/251, UN GAOR, 60th sess, 72nd plen mtg, Agenda Items 46 and 120, UN Doc A/Res/60/251 (3 April 2006) ('*Resolution 60/251*') para 5 (e).

11 Manfred Nowak, 'It's Time for a World Court of Human Rights' in M Cherif Bassiouni and William A Schabas (eds), *New Challenges for the UN Human Rights Machinery* (Intersentia 2011) 23.

12 Olivier De Frouville, above n 6, 250–5.

13 Ibid 264–5.

establishment of a world court of human rights.[14] For example, Manfred Nowak argues it is time for a world court of human rights because UN treaty bodies and other monitoring mechanisms have had little impact owing to their inability to issue and enforce binding decisions that would induce state compliance.[15]

The notion that economic sanctions, adjudicative, legalistic and other confrontational approaches can best enforce human rights norms has undermined the potential for more cooperative mechanisms of monitoring human rights implementation. The main argument this book makes is that the above approaches are inherently limited and do not capture the subtle and significant ways in which the UPR, based on cooperation and dialogue, can contribute to human rights changes within states. This monograph situates itself within the academic discourse on international human rights monitoring mechanisms, where the literature on the UPR is minimal. It contends that the UPR mechanism, which relies on cooperation and gives the state some degree of control over the process, can sometimes be at least as, if not more, effective than coercive mechanisms.

The UPR is a unique mechanism of the HRC which adopts a cooperative and inclusive approach to monitoring state implementation of human rights obligations. The review takes place every four and a half years in three main stages: the preparation of state reports, review of the state in Geneva and the implementation stage. The conclusion of UPR III (2017–2021) therefore invites a scholarly examination of the extent to which the mechanism is contributing to human rights implementation within African states. This monograph examines the engagement of four African states (Nigeria, Kenya, South Africa, The Gambia) with the UPR to determine the potential of this cooperative and non-coercive mechanism to improve the human rights situation on the ground. This research limits itself to Sub-Saharan Africa. It measures the effectiveness of the states' engagement with the UPR and analyses the factors impacting on that engagement. In pursuit of this objective, this book examines the following issues:

- i The participation of the states in the pre-review national consultation process, as a state reviewer and as a state under review—to determine their level of engagement with the UPR mechanism;
- ii The extent to which the UPR recommendations were implemented—to determine whether the UPR can contribute to improvement of the human rights situation on the ground;
- iii The potential for the UPR to influence African states over time through the process of acculturation; and
- iv The impacts of politics, regionalism, cultural relativism, ritualism and civil society on the engagement of African states with the UPR.

This research adopts a socio-legal research framework that incorporates a theoretical and empirical analysis of the effectiveness of African states' engagement

14 Andrew Clapham, 'Overseeing Human Rights Compliance' in Antonio Cassesse (ed), *Realizing Utopia: The Future of International Law* (Oxford University Press 2012) 323–4; Manfred Nowak, 'The Need for a World Court on Human Rights' (2007) 7(1) *Human Rights Law Review* 251; Manfred Nowak, above n 11, 26–33.

15 Manfred Nowak, above n 11, 26.

with the UPR mechanism. It examines the impact of factors, including politics, regionalism, cultural relativism and civil society, on the engagement of African states with the UPR mechanism. The unique feature of this approach lies in its ability to create a bridge between the disciplines of law, sociology and political science and has been described as providing the space 'where law meets the social sciences and humanities'.[16] Socio-legal approaches can broaden the scope of legal research by providing conceptual frameworks within which information can be evaluated and exposing power dynamics in a variety of social settings.[17] As such, legal scholars agree that socio-legal approaches are a suitable methodological framework to study international human rights law.[18] This research draws on sociology, socialisation and international law theories such as acculturation, the transnational legal process theory and the five-stage 'spiral model'[19] to determine an appropriate theoretical approach to evaluating state engagement with the UPR and its potential impact. It brings about an awareness of the difficulty in attempting to establish a precise causal link between UPR recommendations and the actions of states, because changes in the human rights practices of states can be motivated by multiple factors. However, the influence of the UPR recommendations is measurable with some confidence by analysing both state and non-governmental organisation (NGO) implementation reports to determine the extent to which the UPR contributed to human rights change within states. Other relevant studies on the UPR accept and use similar methodology.[20]

Background to the HRC and the UPR mechanism

In 2006, UN General Assembly (UNGA) Resolution 60/251 established the HRC as a subsidiary organ of the General Assembly which replaces the Commission for Human Rights.[21] One of the broad mandates of the HRC is to be 'responsible for promoting universal respect for the protection of all human rights

16 See Caroline Hunter, *Integrating Socio-Legal Studies into the Law Curriculum* (Palgrave Macmillan 2012) 2.

17 See Shazia Qureshi, 'Research Methodology in Law and Its Application to Women's Human Rights Law' (2015) 22(2) *Journal of Political Science* 629, 635.

18 Michael Salter and Julie Mason, *Writing Law Dissertations: An Introduction and Guide to the Conduct of Legal Research* (Pearson Education 2007); Mike McConville and Wing Hong (Eric) Chui (eds), *Research Methods for Law* (Edinburgh University Press 2007).

19 See Chapter 3.

20 See Subhas Gujadhur and Marc Limon, *Towards the Third Cycle of the UPR: Stick or Twist? Lessons Learnt from the First Ten Years of the Universal Periodic Review* (Universal Rights Group 2016) 35–7; UPR Info, 'Universal Periodic Review: On the Road to Implementation' (2012) 63 available at <https://bit.ly/2mepWwI> accessed 12/09/2019.

21 *Human Rights Council,* GA Res 60/251, UN GAOR, 60th sess, 72nd plen mtg, Agenda Items 46 and 120, UN Doc A/Res/60/251 (3 April 2006) ('*Resolution 60/251*') para 5 (e).

and fundamental freedoms for all'.[22] The aim was to provide an alternative to the 'politicisation', 'naming and shaming' and practices of selectivity which contributed to the demise of its predecessor, the Commission for Human Rights (CHR).[23] The CHR, during its 60 years of existence, was entrusted with the international promotion and protection of human rights and recorded great achievements.[24] These, among many, included the drafting of the Universal Declaration of Human Rights[25] and a plethora of international human rights treaties.[26] Mandated by Article 68 of the Charter, the importance of the CHR led John Forster to refer to it as the 'soul' of the UN Charter.[27] The extraordinary package offered by the CHR to the international community is summarised to include a universal human rights framework, a unique system of independent and expert procedures and a close engagement with civil society organisations (CSOs) in ensuring human rights compliance.[28]

The CHR fell from grace when allegations of selectivity, double standards and politicisation crippled its operation and accelerated its demise. These allegations can hardly be contested because the wordings of Resolution 60/251[29] acknowledge this fact by explicitly recognising the importance of '. . . the elimination of double standards and politicization'.[30] The criticisms against the CHR heightened and almost became apoplectic when countries like Cuba,[31]

22 Ibid para 2.
23 For a detailed analysis of the failures of the former Commission for Human Rights and the transition to the HRC, see Philip Alston, 'Reconceiving the UN Human Rights Regime: Challenges Confronting the New UN Human Rights Council' (2006) 7(1) *Melbourne Journal of International Law* 185.
24 The CHR was established under Article 68 of the UN Charter to assist the Economic and Social Council in the performance of its functions.
25 The value of this is underscored by the fact that many of its provisions have today crystallised as customary international law or have obtained the status of obligations *erga omnes*, such as protection from racial discrimination and torture or more recently the rights to self-determination. See International Law Association, 'Final Report on the status of the Universal Declaration of Human Rights in National and International law' ILA Report of the sixty-sixth Conference, Buenos Aires 1994, 527; Ian Brownlie, *Principles of Public International Law* (Oxford University Press 2008) 559; *East Timor (Portugal v Australia) (Judgement)* [1995] ICJ Rep 90 para 29.
26 For the functioning of the CHR and the role it played, see Philip Alston, 'The Commission on Human Rights' in Philip Alston (ed), *The United Nations and Human Rights* (Oxford University Press 1992) 126–210.
27 John S Nurser, *For All Peoples and All Nations: The Ecumenical Church and Human Rights* (Georgetown University Press 2005) 11.
28 Report of the Secretary-General, *In Larger Freedom: Towards Development, Security and Human Rights for All*, UN Doc A/59/2005 (21 March 2005) para 181.
29 Resolution establishing the Human Rights Council; see *Human Rights Council*, above n 21.
30 Ibid, preamble.
31 Michael Jordan, 'New Calls for Reform of UN Human Rights Commission: Cuba's Re-Election Last Week to the Commission on Human Rights Is Drawing Criticism from

Sudan,[32] Libya[33] and Zimbabwe[34] were either elected or re-elected as members of the CHR at a time of gross human rights violations within their states. This caused the CHR to be perceived as a shield or sanctuary for violators of human rights.[35] These criticisms of the CHR sparked off a process of reform debates and proposals.

The problems which plagued the CHR had reached a terminal stage, and it was thought that piecemeal reforms will be inadequate to resuscitate it.[36] The Bern Institute of Public Law, Commissioned by the Swiss Foreign Ministry, first came up with the idea of a HRC[37] which gained momentum following the publication of the 2004 report of the UN High Level Panel on Threats, Challenges and Change.[38] Among other things, this report addressed the problems with the CHR and the need for a HRC. Following the Panel's report, negotiations within the UN culminated in the establishment of the HRC as successor to the CHR by GA Resolution 60/251 with 170 states voting in favour, four against and three abstentions.[39] The establishment of the UPR is rooted in one of the following purposes of the HRC.

Rights Groups' *The Christian Science Monitor* (7 May 2003) available at <www.csmonitor.com/2003/0507/p07s02-wogi.html> accessed 05/09/2019.

32 See United States Mission to the United Nations, *Statement by Ambassador Sichan Siv, US Representative to the Economic and Social Council, Regarding the Candidacy of Sudan for the Commission on Human Rights, in the Economic and Social Council* (Press Release, 4 May 2004) available at <https://bit.ly/2kGoX85> accessed 05/09/2019; Colum Lynch, 'US Protests Sudan's Election to Human Rights Panel' *The Washington Post* (Washington, DC, 5 May 2004); Evelyn Leopold, 'Sudan Elected to UN Human Rights Group, US Walks Out' *Reuters News* (5 May 2004).

33 See US Department of State, *US Opposed to Libya Chairing UN Human Rights Commission* (Press Release, 13 January 2003); Reporters without Borders, *UN Commission on Human Rights Loses All Credibility: Wheeling and Dealing, Incompetence and 'Non Action'* available at <www.rsf.org/IMG/pdf/Report_ONU_gb.pdf> accessed 05/09/2019.

34 Eric Green, US Department of State, *Press Freedom Groups Praise Nicaragua, Decry Cuba, Zimbabwe* (2005) available at <https://bit.ly/2lNvL45> accessed 05/09/2019.

35 Paul Gordon Lauren, 'To Preserve and Build on Its Achievements and to Redress Its Shortcomings': The Journey from the Commission on Human Rights to the Human Rights Council' (2007) 29 *Human Rights Quarterly* 307, 325–30.

36 United Nations, *Secretary-General's Address to the Commission on Human Rights* (Geneva, 7 April 2005) available at <www.un.org/sg/statements/?nid=1388> accessed 05/09/2019; attempts by the Commission to bring about institutional change were also futile; see Howard Tolley, *The UN Commission on Human Rights* (Westview Press 1987) 154.

37 Wolfgang A Brülhart, 'From a Swiss Initiative to a United Nations Proposal (from 2003–2005)' in Lars Müller (ed), *The First 365 Days of the United Nations Human Rights Council* (Cambridge University Press 2007) 15–16.

38 High-Level Panel on Threats, Challenges and Change, *A More Secure World—Our Shared Responsibility,* UN Doc A/59/565 (2 December 2004).

39 UN GAOR, 60th sess, 72nd plen mtg, UN Doc A/60/PV.72 (15 March 2006) 6.

The purposes of the HRC

The purposes of the HRC are captured in Resolution 60/251 of the General Assembly. It is within these multiple purposes that the establishment of the UPR mechanism is enshrined. These purposes are:

(a) Promote human rights education and learning as well as advisory services, technical assistance and capacity-building, to be provided in consultation with and with the consent of Member States concerned;
(b) Serve as a forum for dialogue on thematic issues on all human rights;
(c) Make recommendations to the General Assembly for the further development of international law in the field of human rights;
(d) Promote the full implementation of human rights obligations undertaken by States and follow-up to the goals and commitments related to the promotion and protection of human rights emanating from United Nations conferences and summits;
(e) Undertake a universal periodic review, based on objective and reliable information, of the fulfilment by each State of its human rights obligations and commitments in a manner which ensures universality of coverage and equal treatment with respect to all States; the review shall be a cooperative mechanism, based on an interactive dialogue, with the full involvement of the country concerned and with consideration given to its capacity-building needs; such a mechanism shall complement and not duplicate the work of treaty bodies; the Council shall develop the modalities and necessary time allocation for the universal periodic review mechanism within one year after the holding of its first session;
(f) Contribute, through dialogue and cooperation, towards the prevention of human rights violations and respond promptly to human rights emergencies;
(g) Assume the role and responsibilities of the Commission on Human Rights relating to the work of the Office of the United Nations High Commissioner for Human Rights, as decided by the General Assembly in its resolution 48/141 of 20 December 1993;
(h) Work in close cooperation in the field of human rights with Governments, regional organizations, national human rights institutions and civil society;
(i) Make recommendations with regard to the promotion and protection of human rights;
(j) Submit an annual report to the General Assembly.[40]

40 See *Resolution 60/251*, UN Doc A/Res/60/251, above n 21 para 5.

Fundamental principles of the UPR

The principles that guide the UPR aim to address some of the criticisms which were levelled against the former UN Commission on Human Rights. These principles include universality, cooperation, complementarity and the equal treatment of all member states in monitoring human rights compliance.[41] They recognise the 'importance of ensuring universality, objectivity and non-selectivity . . . and the elimination of double standards and politicisation'.[42] These principles, with their principal goal of improving the human rights situation on the ground, reflect a positive continuation of the reformist efforts of the UN to promote human rights while eschewing the 'naming and shaming' strategy.

Universality

The principle of universality is an integral part of the UN human rights system. The notion that human rights are universal is enshrined in the *Universal Declaration of Human Rights* (UDHR).[43] Universality is a key principle of the UPR which is characterised in terms of not only the universality of the process but also the rights covered. This distinguishes it from the human rights treaty bodies. The scope of the work of the treaty bodies is limited only to states that have ratified the specific treaty within their competence and only to the rights specified in each treaty.

In terms of the rights covered, the UPR examines broader obligations under the UDHR and applicable international humanitarian law, including commitments and voluntary pledges made by individual states.[44] It is truly universal because all UN member states are reviewed, regardless of whether the state has ratified any human rights treaties. Except for Israel, which temporarily boycotted its UPR II in January 2013, all UN member states have been reviewed in the first two cycles of the UPR, even North Korea.[45] Israel did not attend its UPR II, which was initially scheduled for 29 January 2013, causing the HRC to postpone Israel's review to 29 October 2013. Israel returned on this new date and undertook its UPR II. The UPR mechanism ensures universal coverage of all states.

Regionalism

Regionalism has an influence on the participation of states in the UPR process, despite the universality of the UPR process. Regionalism generally occurs within

41 *Institution Building of the United Nations Human Rights Council*, HRC Res 5/1, UN HRC OR, 5th sess, Annex [IB], UN Doc A/HRC/RES/5/1, annex (18 June 2007) ('*Resolution 5/1*') para 2.

42 *Resolution 60/251*, UN Doc A/Res/60/251, above n 21, preamble.

43 *Universal Declaration of Human Rights*, GA Res 217 A (III), UN GAOR, 3rd sess, 183rd plen mtg, UN Doc A/RES/217A (III) (10 December 1948).

44 *Resolution 5/1*, UN Doc A/HRC/RES/5/1 para 1.

45 International Service for Human Rights, *Israel: Decision to Boycott Human Rights Review Threatens the Rule of Law* (January 2013) available at <https://bit.ly/2k9DbxU> accessed 12/09/2019.

an international organisation when a group of interdependent states form a sub-group within the main organisation.[46] Rosa Freedman argues that regionalism is detrimental because it polarises and undermines the work of the UN.[47] Bulto argues that the African Group has used its regional alliance to prevent 'real' scrutiny of the human rights situation of their regional peers at the HRC and in the UPR process.[48] However, while there is a risk that regionalism may polarise the UPR and limit its effectiveness by preventing cooperation across regional groups, Bulto and Freedman do not consider the positive outcomes that regionalism can achieve in the UPR process.

Cultural relativism

The principle of universality as articulated in the UPR does not resolve questions which have continuously been raised about the universal application of human rights.[49] The argument of cultural relativism infringes on the notion of universality of human rights. Fernando Tesón appropriately defines cultural relativism in the context of international human rights law as 'the position according to which local cultural traditions (including religious, political, and legal practices) properly determine the existence and scope of civil and political rights enjoyed by individuals in a given society'.[50] Two dominant forms of cultural relativism describe the degree to which culture impacts on the universality of international human rights norms. Strict cultural relativists hold an extreme view that there is no possibility of constructive dialogue between cultural values because belief systems are culturally specific and incomprehensible to one another.[51] This in some way validates arguments by many African scholars in the post-independence period who argued that claims to universal human rights represent cultural imperialism and are a sign of Western hegemony.[52] The Asian region, in particular, has

46 Karl Kaiser, 'The Interaction of Regional Subsystems: Some Preliminary Notes on Recurrent Patterns and the Role of Superpowers' (1968) 21(1) *World Politics* 86.

47 Rosa Freedman, 'The United Nations Human Rights Council: More of the Same?' (2013) 31(2) *Wisconsin International Law Journal* 208, 209.

48 Takele Soboka Bulto, 'Africa's Engagement with the Universal Periodic Review: Commitment or Capitulation' in Hilary Charlesworth and Emma Larking (eds), *Human Rights and the Universal Periodic Review: Rituals and Ritualism* (Cambridge University Press 2015) 250–1.

49 Jack Donnelly, 'The Relative Universality of Human Rights' (2007) 29(2) *Human Rights Quarterly* 281; Christian Tomuschat, *Human Rights: Between Idealism and Realism* (Oxford University Press 2014).

50 Fernando R Tesón, 'International Human Rights and Cultural Relativism' (1985) 25 *Virginia Journal of International Law* 869, 870–1.

51 See W Meyer, 'Toward a Global Culture: Human Rights, Group Rights and Cultural Relativism' (1996) *International Journal on Group Rights* 169, 175; T Spaak, 'Moral Relativism and Human Rights' (2007) 13 *Buffalo Human Rights Law Review* 73, 75.

52 Daniel T Osabu-Kle, *Compatible Cultural Democracy: The Key of Development in Africa* (University of Toronto Press 2000); George B N Ayittey, *Africa Unchained* (Palgrave Macmillan 2005) 422; Korwa G Adar, 'The Wilsonian Conception of Democracy and Human Rights: A Retrospective and Prospective' (1998) 2(2) *African Studies Quarterly* 33–44.

asserted cultural relativism on the premise of 'Asian values' which has continued to influence political and judicial thinking in Southeast Asian states like Malaysia and Singapore.[53] While there is no similar collective approach taken by African states, they have, almost unanimously, opposed same-sex relationship on the basis that it is culturally unacceptable or a form of cultural imperialism. Referring to the issue of gay rights at a debate in the HRC in 2011, the Nigerian delegate on behalf of the African Group (excluding South Africa) stated:

> The heads of states of governments of the African Union . . . resolved not to . . . accept or integrate concepts which have not been universally defined and accepted in international human rights law. The African leaders thereby rescind the obsession by other regions or groups to impose their own value system on other regions.[54]

Therefore, the central belief of strict cultural relativists in relation to human rights is that the existence and scope of human rights are determined by local cultural traditions and 'no transboundary legal or moral standards exist against which human rights practices may be judged acceptable or unacceptable'.[55] This view prioritises adherence to local values over compliance with international human rights law and undercuts the universality of rights espoused by the UPR. However, the widespread adoption of human rights language across different cultures in the world provides prima facie evidence for the cross-cultural validity of human rights norms.

On the other hand, moderate cultural relativists argue that a 'common' culture of universal human rights is attainable because culture is subject to reform and influence due to the porous disposition of cultural boundaries.[56] An-Na'im, one of the leading scholars in this area, argued that, despite peculiar and diverse cultural characteristics, societies 'share certain fundamental interests, concerns, qualities, traits and values that can be identified and articulated as the framework for a "common" culture of universal human rights'.[57] Consequently, a central

53 See Peter R Moody, 'Asian Values' (1996) 1 *International Affairs* 50; Amartya Sen, *Human Rights and Asian Values* (The New Republic 1997); Po-Han Lee, 'LGBT Rights Versus Asian Values: De/re-constructing the Universality of Human Rights' (2016) 20(7) *International Journal of Human Rights* 978.

54 See *Statement by Mr. Ositadinma Anaedu, Representative of the Nigerian Delegation to the United Nations on Sexual Orientation on Behalf of the African Group (Minus South Africa)* (22 March 2011), available at <https://bit.ly/2kwXANS> accessed 12/09/2019.

55 Fernando R Tesón, above n 50, 870–1.

56 Xiaorong Li, *Ethics, Human Rights and Culture: Beyond Relativism and Culture* (Palgrave Macmillan 2006) 11–12; Charles Taylor, 'Conditions of an Unenforced Consensus on Human Rights' in Joanne A Bauer and Daniel A Bell (eds), *The East-Asian Challenge for Human Rights* (Cambridge University Press 1999) 124–46.

57 Abdullahi Ahmed An-Na'im, 'Problems and Prospects of Universal Cultural Legitimacy for Human Rights' in Abdullahi Ahmed An-Na'im and Francis M Deng (eds), *Human Rights in Africa: Cross Cultural Perspectives* (Brookings Institution 1990) 336.

premise of moderate cultural relativism is not to use culture as a tool to reject the universality of human rights but to formulate rights in a way that would be more acceptable and better implemented in various cultures, with the goal to achieving the cultural legitimacy of human rights.[58] Concurring with this view, I argue that the UPR provides a forum for cross-cultural dialogue and can be harnessed to socialise African states through a process of acculturation, by formulating certain rights which are culturally 'radioactive', such as gay rights, in a way that would be more acceptable and incrementally implemented within the African society.

A number of scholars have sought a middle ground between the universal and cultural relativist conceptions of human rights.[59] Jack Donnelly seeks to reconcile the reality of both the universal and contextual elements of human existence by grounding human rights in the concept of 'relative universality' that leaves room for claims of relativism.[60] However, Michael Goodhart argues that the conception of human rights either as universal or relative is unhelpful because it could diminish the value of human rights and that various aspects of human rights can be successfully discussed without resorting to the terms 'relative' and 'universal'.[61] Nevertheless, the UPR mechanism purports to engage with and promote a universal conception of human rights. States that are advocates of cultural relativism in human rights implementation continue to argue that human rights are dependent on the context and respective cultures in which they are applied.[62]

The aforementioned debate highlights the tension between culture and human rights. However, Sally Engle Merry argues that the demonisation of culture by human rights lawyers and the rush to the conclusion that universality is essential while relativism is bad can be attributed to a lack of anthropological understanding of culture.[63] She argues the misreading of culture promotes a loss of tolerance and respect for cultural differences and hinders the global spread and local appropriation of human rights concepts.[64] According to Engle Merry:

> Considering cultures as changing and interconnected, and rights as historically created and transnationally redefined by national and local actors,

58 Ibid 339.

59 Elvira Dominguez Redondo and Edward R McMahon, 'More Honey Than Vinegar: Peer-Review as a Middle Ground Between Universalism and National Sovereignty' (2013) 51 *Canadian Yearbook of International Law*, 61; Michael Goodhart, 'Neither Relative nor Universal: A Response to Donnelly' (2008) 30(1) *Human Rights Quarterly* 183, 187–9; Jack Donnelly, above n 49.

60 Jack Donnelly, above n 49, 281.

61 Michael Goodhart, above n 59, 187–9.

62 For example, Kenya continues to reject gay rights and argue that same-sex unions are culturally unacceptable in Kenya. See Human Rights Council, *Report of the Human Rights Council on Its Eighth Session*, 8th sess, Agenda Item 1, UN Doc A/HRC/8/52 (1 September 2008) ('*Report of the HRC on Its 8th Session*') para 714.

63 Sally Engle Merry, 'Human Rights Law and the Demonization of Culture (And Anthropology Along the Way)' (2003) 26(1) *PoLAR* 55.

64 Ibid 71–2.

> better describes the contemporary situation. It also reveals the impossibility of drawing sharp distinctions between culture and rights or seeing relativism and universalism as diametrically opposed and incompatible positions.[65]

The UPR offers an open platform to identify the cultural relativist players, to contrast their cultural assertions with the universalist view of human rights and also to facilitate the acculturation of states. In each of the case studies examined in subsequent chapters of this book, focus is given to the issue of same-sex relations,[66] which is a culturally sensitive issue in most African states, to examine (i) the extent to which African states invoke cultural relativism in their engagement with the UPR by scrutinising their responses to recommendations calling for the decriminalisation of same-sex relationships; and (ii) whether the UPR can provide an appropriate framework to promote a transformation of the social and political culture against sexual minorities within African states. Examining the response of African states to these recommendations, which are hypersensitive in cultural terms, will contribute to an understanding of the limits of their UPR engagement and the approach needed to better engage African states on such issues.

Cooperation

Cooperation is one of the fundamental principles of the UPR. The UPR recognises that the promotion and protection of human rights should be based on the principles of cooperation and genuine dialogue.[67] This reflects one of the purposes of the UN stated in Article 1 of its Charter 'to achieve international cooperation in solving international problems . . . and in promoting and encouraging respect for human rights and fundamental freedoms'.[68] Many scholars and practitioners were sceptical about a mechanism rooted in cooperation and interactive dialogue. However, others have observed that the cooperative character of the UPR mechanism and the high level of state personnel that engage in it provide a unique context for the 'formation, definition, clarification and consolidation of human rights customary rules'.[69] According to Redondo and McMahon, the

65 Sally Engle Merry, 'Changing Rights, Changing Culture' in Jane K Cowan, Marie Benedicte Dembour and Richard A Wilson (eds), *Culture and Rights: Anthropological Perspectives* (Cambridge University Press 2010) 31, 39.

66 I focus on this issue because Africa is the continent with the highest number of states (33 of 54 as of May 2016) that specifically criminalises same-sex relationships and there have been specific legislations between 2013 and 2014 in countries like Nigeria and Uganda that criminalises same-sex conducts. See Aengus Carroll, *State Sponsored Homophobia 2016: A World Survey of Sexual Orientation Laws: Criminalisation, Protection and Recognition* (ILGA 2016) 57.

67 *Resolution 5/1*, UN Doc A/HRC/RES/5/1, preamble.

68 Charter of the United Nations art 1 [3].

69 Elvira Dominguez Redondo, 'The Universal Periodic Review: Is There Life Beyond Naming and Shaming in Human Rights Implementation?' (2012) 4 *New Zealand Law Review* 673, 706.

UPR mechanism, by relying on cooperation and dialogue, represents an evolving maturity of the international human rights system through its detachment from exclusively legalistic approaches to human rights implementation.[70] Therefore, an important question which this book engages with is whether the UPR, which is based on cooperation, can significantly contribute to improving the human rights situation within African states. If it can, this has the potential to helpfully supplement or reduce the need for more coercive and confrontational mechanisms for human rights implementation.

However, there is evidence of diverging approaches to cooperation in the UPR. African states have adopted a 'soft' approach to the UPR, at least among each other, in contrast to Western states that take a more critical, close to adversarial, approach. The soft approach, which largely produces 'friendly' recommendations, has been criticised for not being sufficiently critical of the human rights situation in states.[71] According to Abebe, this approach results in weak recommendations and tends to ignore serious human rights concerns within states that require immediate attention.[72] Heather Collister notes that 'weaker' UPR recommendations are as a result of the state-centric nature of the mechanism.[73] However, she argues that state control is what induces states to cooperate with the UPR.[74]

Objectivity

In 2006 the UNGA insisted that the UPR be based on 'objective and reliable information'.[75] The first phase of the review is characterised by the gathering of information relevant for the preparation of reports. Information from other sources outside of that provided by the state under review is gathered. Information on the human rights situation of the state under review is derived from three sources. The first source is the national report produced by the state under review. This is limited to 20 pages to guarantee equal treatment of all states and to not overburden the mechanism.[76] This page limit represents a dramatic

70 Elvira Dominguez Redondo and Edward R McMahon, above n 59; De La Vega and Lewis highlight how the UPR transforms human rights monitoring by promoting state accountability for human rights policies and practices. See Constance De La Vega and Tamara N Lewis, 'Peer Review in the Mix: How the UPR Transforms Human Rights Discourse' in M Cherif Bassiouni and William A Schabas (eds), *New Challenges for the UN Human Rights Machinery* (Intersentia 2011) 353–76.

71 Allehone M Abebe, 'Of Shaming and Bargaining: African States and the Universal Periodic Review of the United Nations Human Rights Council' (2009) *Human Rights Law Review* 1, 16.

72 Ibid.

73 Heather Collister, 'Rituals and Implementation in the Universal Periodic Review' in Hilary Charlesworth and Emma Larking (eds), *Human Rights and the Universal Periodic Review: Rituals and Ritualism* (Cambridge University Press 2015) 111–16.

74 Ibid.

75 *Resolution 60/251*, UN Doc A/Res/60/251, above n 10.

76 *Resolution 5/1,* UN Doc A/HRC/RES/5/1 para 15(a).

reduction in the number of pages states can send under the treaty body system and helps to reduce the burden of a state's reporting obligation.[77]

It is a further requirement that the report is prepared through a broad consultation with all relevant stakeholders at the national level.[78] Consulting these stakeholders during the preparation of the report is important because of the usefulness of such engagement in producing a balanced report. Also, the state is required to provide information on the extent of national consultation with UPR stakeholders that took place within the country in the preparation of the national report.[79]

The second source of information is the Office of the High Commissioner for Human Rights' (OHCHR) compilation of UN information. This ten-page report consists of a collation of aspects of the reports of treaty bodies, special procedures and other relevant official UN documents.[80] The last source of information is the OHCHR's ten-page summary of stakeholders' information.[81] These stakeholders include NGOs/CSOs and National Human Rights Institutions (NHRIs) and generally provide information which has the potential to be more critical of a state's human rights commitment than the state report. In 2011, the HRC reviewed the modalities of the UPR. It now requires that the information contained in the OHCHR's summary of stakeholders' information should have a separate section for information by NHRIs accredited in full compliance with the Paris Principles and then information provided by other accredited NHRIs and stakeholders.[82]

Despite these stipulations, international scholars and UPR stakeholders have been critical of the objectivity of the process of gathering information for use in preparing UPR reports. Roland Chauville highlights concerns on the authenticity of domestic NGOs, especially whether they represent the civil society or are agents of their national government.[83] Also, states have at times

77 The report of the treaty bodies can be more than 100 pages in length. For example, in 2010, 30 state party reports to the treaty bodies were between 100 and 200 pages in length and two state party reports were over 200 pages. See Office of the High Commissioner for Human Rights, 'Requirements and Implications of the Ongoing Growth of the Treaty Body System on the Periodic Reporting Procedures, Documentation and Meeting Time' (2011) 12 available at <https://bit.ly/2kHeKZ2> accessed 05/09/2019.

78 *Resolution 5/1,* UN Doc A/HRC/RES/5/1 para 15(a).

79 Human Rights Council, *Decision 6/102: Follow-up to the Human Rights Council Resolution 5/1 Adopted 27 September 2007*, 20th mtg (27 September 2007) ('*HRC Decision 6/102*') para A.

80 *Resolution 5/1,* UN Doc A/HRC/RES/5/1 para 15(b).

81 Ibid para 15(c).

82 UN Human Rights Council, *Review of the Work and Functioning of the Human Rights Council*, HRC Resolution 16/21, HRC 16th sess, Agenda Item 1, A/HRC/RES/16/21 (12 April 2011) ('*Resolution 16/21*') para 9; it is specifically required by the Paris Principles that CSOs have a pluralist representation to gain accreditation. See UN Commission on Human Rights, *National Institutions for the Promotion and Protection of Human Rights*, UN Commission on Human Rights, 48th sess, E/CN.4/RES/1992/54 (3 March 1992) annex.

83 For example, Chauville observed how government-supported NGOs from Cuba and Venezuela flooded the OHCHR with UPR submissions that did not contain any criticism of the

questioned the credibility of the information NGOs provide for the UPR. For example, during its UPR I in 2009, Nigeria characterised the information in some NGO reports as 'preposterous', 'patently false' and 'unhelpful to the UPR process'.[84] Some NGOs have complained about the lack of transparency in the manner in which the OHCHR compiles the summary of stakeholders' information and have raised concerns that the content of their submissions were 'watered down' in the OHCHR's summary of stakeholders' information.[85] However, Julie Billaud examined this transformation process by the OHCHR and found that the discipline and techniques followed by the OHCHR breathe bureaucratic legitimacy into the documents, promote objectivity and impartiality and serve 'to produce "the truth" on the human rights situation in a country'.[86]

Complementarity

The need to prevent duplication of treaty body functions was a great concern during many stages in the negotiations leading to the establishment of the UPR in 2006.[87] The principle of complementarity is reflected in UNGA Resolution 60/251, which provides that the UPR mechanism 'shall complement and not duplicate the work of treaty bodies'.[88] HRC resolution 5/1 reiterates this principle as one of the essential bases of the review and a guarantee that the UPR will add value to the human rights monitoring system.[89] The concept of complementarity is increasingly used in international law to underline the relationship between two or more autonomous organs. It is used by the Rome Statute of the International Criminal Court (ICC) to define that court's relationship with

---

government. See Roland Chauville, 'The Universal Periodic Review's First Cycle: Successes and Failures' in Hilary Charlesworth and Emma Larking (eds), *Human Rights and the Universal Periodic Review: Rituals and Ritualism* (Cambridge University Press 2015) 105–6.

84 UN Human Rights Council, *Report of the Working Group on the Universal Periodic Review—Nigeria*, 11th sess, Agenda Item 6, UN Doc A/HRC/11/26 (5 October 2009) ('*HRC UPR I Report—Nigeria*') para 8; also Morocco condemned a report by Amnesty International (AI) which included Morocco among countries targeted by the anti-torture campaign as 'biased and subjective'. According to Morocco's UPR delegation, this report by AI 'is driven by the will to downplay the current dynamic and the progress achieved in terms of fighting torture, belittling and denigrating the Kingdom'. See Morocco World News, 'Morocco Condemns Biased, Subjective Amnesty International Report' (19 May 2015) available at <https://bit.ly/1e5iYQY> accessed 05/09/2019.

85 See Julie Billaud, 'Keepers of the Truth: "Transparent" Documents for the Universal Periodic Review' in Hilary Charlesworth and Emma Larking (eds), *Human Rights and the Universal Periodic Review: Rituals and Ritualism* (Cambridge University Press 2015) 76–7.

86 Ibid 63–83.

87 For the different draft documents that raised concern on this issue, see Felice D Gaer, 'A Voice Not an Echo: Universal Periodic Review and the UN Treaty Body System' (2007) 7(1) *Human Rights Law Review* 109, 111.

88 *Resolution 60/251*, UN Doc A/Res/60/251 para 5(e).

89 *Resolution 5/1*, UN Doc A/HRC/RES/5/1 para 3(f).

national courts.[90] In the context of the UPR, complementarity regulates the relationship between the UPR mechanism and the UN human rights treaty bodies. This principle aims to ensure consistency and coherence in the operation of the monitoring organs with the goal of avoiding unnecessary duplication of functions which may lead to wastage of resources.

However, there is disagreement among scholars and practitioners regarding the ability of the UPR to complement the work of the human rights treaty bodies. This disagreement has been approached from three viewpoints. The first is duplication, in that the UPR overlaps with the functions of the human rights treaty bodies. Second is that the UPR process has a debilitating effect on existing human rights obligations insofar as it weakens and overshadows treaty body recommendations. The third viewpoint is that the UPR enhances state engagement with treaty bodies.

Nadia Bernaz takes the first perspective by arguing that the UPR encroaches on the work of the treaty bodies resulting in significant overlap between the two mechanisms because of the common features they share.[91] This argument echoes some of the sentiments articulated by Australia and the African Group during the negotiations on the modalities of the UPR in 2006.[92] They argued that a separate report for the UPR will be an unnecessary duplication of the reporting obligations required by the human rights treaty bodies and will represent an additional undue burden for states.[93] This problem was resolved by limiting the state UPR report to a maximum of 20 pages, but the complementarity of the UPR with the treaty bodies was far from being proved.

Sir Nigel Rodley, former UN HRC member, took the second perspective on the relationship between the treaty bodies and the UPR which is that the UPR process has a debilitating effect on treaty body recommendations. He contended that the UPR enables states to evade their obligation to implement recommendations by treaty bodies.[94] According to Rodley, the fact that states have the freedom to reject certain UPR recommendations can negatively impact the work of the treaty bodies because states 'will invoke the gentler diagnosis of the UPR to discredit the harsher diagnosis of the treaty bodies'.[95] For example, he found that by the end of 2009, a total of nine UPR recommendations explicitly quoted recommendations from the Committee against Torture, of which five were rejected.[96] On this basis, Sir Nigel argued that the UPR process presents a risk to the

90 See *Rome Statute of the International Criminal Court* art 1; Jo Stigen, *The Relationship Between the International Criminal Court and National Jurisdictions: The Principle of Complementarity* (Martinus Nijhoff Publishers 2008).

91 Nadia Bernaz, 'Reforming the UN Human Rights Protection Procedures: A Legal Perspective on the Establishment of the Universal Periodic Review' in Kevin Boyle (ed), *New Institutions for Human Rights Protection* (Oxford University Press 2009) 78, 88.

92 Felice D Gaer, above n 87, 122.

93 Ibid.

94 Sir Nigel S Rodley, 'UN Treaty Bodies and the Human Rights Council' in Helen Keller and Geir Ulfstein (eds), *UN Human Rights Treaty Bodies: Law and Legitimacy* (Cambridge University Press 2012) 320–55.

95 Ibid 327.

96 Ibid 329.

work of the treaty bodies as states could use the process to undermine the validity of recommendations from the treaty bodies.[97]

De Frouville criticises the UPR for oversimplifying the hard work of the treaty bodies by summarising their recommendations.[98] According to de Frouville, there is no real interaction between the UPR and other human rights mechanisms because states would only accept UPR recommendations that are consistent with their purpose.[99] He argues that in the worst case, the UPR is overshadowing the work of the treaty bodies by taking away material resources from treaty bodies and attracting more media and public attention.[100] But this raises the question of why the UPR has attracted more state attention and resources than the treaty bodies and whether that could have a positive impact on states' human rights compliance. De Frouville's analysis could not draw a definite conclusion on the impact generated by the interaction between the UPR and the human rights treaty bodies because it was undertaken in 2011 when the first cycle of the UPR was still ongoing.

The work of Helen Quane provides evidence in the case of Association of Southeast Asian Nations (ASEAN) states which supports the third point of view, and it offers a more positive appraisal of the relationship between the UPR and the treaty bodies. Quane demonstrates that the UPR has enhanced the nature and level of the relationship between ASEAN states and the human rights treaty bodies.[101] She argues that by recommending that states enhance their engagement with treaty bodies, submit overdue reports and ratify specific human rights treaties, the UPR has contributed to greater and more constructive engagement between many ASEAN states and the human rights treaty bodies.[102] This book adopts an approach to the relationship between the UPR and the treaty bodies which has received little attention in the literature. This approach considers whether the UPR can potentially create a synergy with other national, regional and international human rights mechanisms by amplifying and reinforcing their recommendations. The potential for this synergy within a cooperative, inclusive and collaborative human rights mechanism can ensure that the recommendations are relevant and that they target the improvement of the human rights situation on the ground.

The participation of CSOs/NGOs and other stakeholders in the UPR process

Ensuring the participation of 'all relevant stakeholders, including non-governmental organisations and national human rights institutions' in accordance

97 Ibid; Heather Collister makes a similar argument when she finds that the UPR contradicts/weakens treaty body recommendations and enables states to use the process as a means of rejecting treaty body recommendations. See Heather Collister, above n 73, 116–9.

98 Olivier de Frouville, above n 6, 251.

99 Ibid.

100 Ibid 250–1.

101 Helen Quane, 'The Significance of an Evolving Relationship: Asian States and the Global Human Rights Mechanisms' (2015) 15 *Human Rights Law Review* 283, 303–9.

102 Ibid 295–309.

with Resolution 5/1 of the HRC is an important principle guiding the UPR.[103] Resolution 60/251 acknowledged that 'non-governmental organisations play an important role at the national, regional and international levels, in the promotion and protection of human rights'.[104] NGOs/CSOs are relevant 'stakeholders' in the UPR but there is no universal understanding of the term 'civil society' as the term means different things in different countries and languages.[105]

The inclusion of NGOs as participants in the UPR process was a compromise which included limiting the extent of their participation in the UPR process. During the negotiations for the modalities of the UPR, the African Group contended that NGOs (including NHRIs) are 'detractors, not peers' and that their role in the UPR should be limited to participation in the preparation of national reports.[106] The Group took this position because its view of the UPR mechanism was one which would avoid confrontation and make the state the exclusive partner in the process.[107] Also, the African and the Arab Groups jointly criticised the procedure adopted by the OHCHR to make the entire texts of NGO contributions available for consideration during the review.[108] The position of the African Group regarding the involvement of NGOs in the UPR is in contrast with that of the European Group (Western Europe and Others Group (WEOG)) that wanted greater NGO involvement in the process.[109] WEOG advocated for a 'full and effective involvement of all stakeholders, including NGOs, as well as openness

103 *Resolution 5/1,* UN Doc A/HRC/RES/5/1 para 3(m).
104 *Resolution 60/251,* UN Doc A/Res/60/251 para 5(h).
105 Defining 'NGO' can be difficult and is sometimes considered an impossible task because many similar or slightly different terms are used to refer to it. Kenya, for example, uses the broad term 'Public Benefit Organisations' to include NGOs, CSOs and other groups that work for the benefit of the public. In this book, I interchangeably use CSOs and NGOs to constitute 'formal (professionalised) independent societal organisations whose primary aim is to promote common goals at the national or international level'. See Kerstin Martens, 'Mission Impossible? Defining Nongovernmental Organizations' (2002) 13 *International Journal of Voluntary and Nonprofit Organizations*, 282; importantly, the UPR mechanism uses the broad term 'stakeholders' to include NGOs and CSOs. See *Resolution 5/1,* UN Doc A/HRC/RES/5/1 paras 3(m) and 66.
106 Algeria's Statement (on behalf of African Group), see Gareth Sweeney, *Human Rights Council Working Group to Develop the Modalities of the Universal Periodic Review, 3rd Session, 11 And 24 April 2007* (International Service for Human Rights 2007) 7. However, South Africa embraced the participation of civil society and NHRIs at the beginning of the negotiations. See Human Rights Council Working Group on the Review of Mandates and Mechanisms, 'Oral Statement by the South African Delegation on the Universal Periodic Review (UPRM)' (12 February 2007).
107 See Human Rights Council Working Group on the Review of Mandates and Mechanisms, 'Oral Statement by Algeria (on behalf of African Group) on the Universal Periodic Review' (UPRM)' (12 February 2007).
108 Allehone M Abebe, above n 71, 27.
109 See Human Rights Council Working Group on the Review of Mandates and Mechanisms, 'Oral Statement by the European Union on the Universal Periodic Review' (12 February 2007).

to the public at large'.[110] It was resolved that NGOs and other stakeholders can attend the review session in the HRC Working Group on the UPR but cannot make statements or pose questions to the state under review.[111] Also, they can participate in the adoption of the outcome of the review during the plenary session of the HRC and make comments.[112]

The limited opportunity for direct NGO participation in the UPR has been criticised by scholars. Abebe notes that the lack of direct participation by NGOs weakens the review process by not granting NGOs an opportunity to express directly their concerns during the interactive dialogue.[113] Bulto argues that by preventing NGOs from participating in the interactive dialogue, the UPR shields African states from open criticism from NGOs.[114] According to McMahon, NGO engagement with the UPR needs to be heightened by giving them a recognised role during the review session in Geneva. In McMahon's view, this would strengthen the UPR mechanism.[115] However, Ben Schokman and Phil Lynch provide pragmatic suggestions on how NGOs can effectively engage in the UPR process even with the institutional constraints noted earlier.[116] These include the formation of NGO coalitions, effective media engagement and a focused advocacy strategy.[117] But they identify three obstacles to effective NGO engagement in the process, namely the political nature of the process, limited formal opportunities for NGOs and the lack of knowledge among NGOs about the UPR process.[118]

The modus operandi of the UPR

The review of each state operates in five phases. The first phase involves gathering and collating information on the human rights situation of the state under review. This process ends with the submission of the three main reports, previously outlined, on the state under review. These are the state report, the OHCHR compilation of UN information and the OHCHR summary of stakeholders' information on the state under review.[119] The guidelines for the preparation of state reports

110 Ibid.
111 See *Resolution 5/1,* UN Doc A/HRC/RES/5/1 para 18(c).
112 Ibid para 31.
113 Allehone M Abebe, above n 71, 29.
114 Takele Soboka Bulto, above n 48, 250.
115 Edward McMahon, 'The Universal Periodic review: A Work in Progress, an Evaluation of the First Cycle of the New UPR Mechanism of the United Nations Human Rights Council' (2012) *Friedrich Ebert Stiftung* 1, 26.
116 See Ben Schokman and Phil Lynch, 'Effective NGO Engagement with the Universal Periodic Review' in Hilary Charlesworth and Emma Larking (eds), *Human Rights and the Universal Periodic Review: Rituals and Ritualism* (Cambridge University Press 2015) 132–44.
117 Ibid.
118 Ibid 144–6.
119 Each of these reports has page limits. The national report by the state is limited to a maximum of 20 pages while the other two reports are limited to a maximum ten pages each. See *Resolution 5/1,* UN Doc A/HRC/RES/5/1 para 15.

provide that such reports should, among other things, contain the legislative background of the state in the promotion and protection of human rights and how the state proposes to overcome challenges and improve the situation of human rights on the ground and follow-up on the previous review.[120]

In the second phase of the review, the state under review presents its national report before the HRC Working Group in a three-and-a-half-hour-long interactive dialogue session in Geneva. During this time, the state under review responds to questions posed by its peers attending that session of the review. The review process in the HRC Working Group is facilitated by the troika. This is a group of three rapporteurs, randomly selected among the members of the HRC and from different regional groups.[121] It is during the review in the working groups that recommendations are made by the peer-reviewing states.

Following the review in the working group of the HRC, a draft 'outcome report' of the state under review is then adopted.[122] It is a summary of the interactive discussion during the review containing the questions and recommendations made by peer-reviewing states to the state under review and the latter's responses. The outcome report is prepared with OHCHR assistance. At this third phase of the review, the state under review has an opportunity to respond or clarify its responses to recommendations made during the review. The state under review provides responses to the recommendations made, by either accepting or rejecting the recommendations from the peer-reviewing states during the adoption of the outcome report of the state's review or prior to the next plenary session of the HRC.[123]

At the fourth phase of the review the final outcome of the report is debated and adopted at the plenary session of the HRC.[124] Each of the 47 member states of the HRC are allowed to express their opinion on the outcome report, and other stakeholders such as NGOs make general comments after which the outcome report is finally adopted.

The fifth and final phase of the review is the follow-up stage where the state is expected to implement the accepted recommendations. This phase of the UPR process provides the pathway to the realisation of the ultimate objective of the UPR process, that is, 'the improvement of human rights situation on the ground'.[125] The responsibility for implementing the outcome of the UPR falls

120 *HRC Decision 6/102*; for the required structure of the state report, see ibid at paras IB, IC, and IG.

121 *Resolution 5/1,* UN Doc A/HRC/RES/5/1 para 18(d); the legal framework for the review are the UN Charter, the UDHR, binding human rights instruments, voluntary pledges and commitments, and applicable international humanitarian law (IHL). For the contentions regarding the inclusion of IHL, see Lijiang Zhu, 'International Humanitarian Law in the Universal Periodic Review of the UN Human Rights Council' (2014) 5 *Journal of International Humanitarian Legal Studies* 186.

122 *Resolution 5/1,* UN Doc A/HRC/RES/5/1 paras 26–32.

123 *Resolution 16/21* para 16.

124 Ibid.

125 *Resolution 5/1,* UN Doc A/HRC/RES/5/1 para 4(a).

Table 1.1 The Five Stages of a UPR Cycle

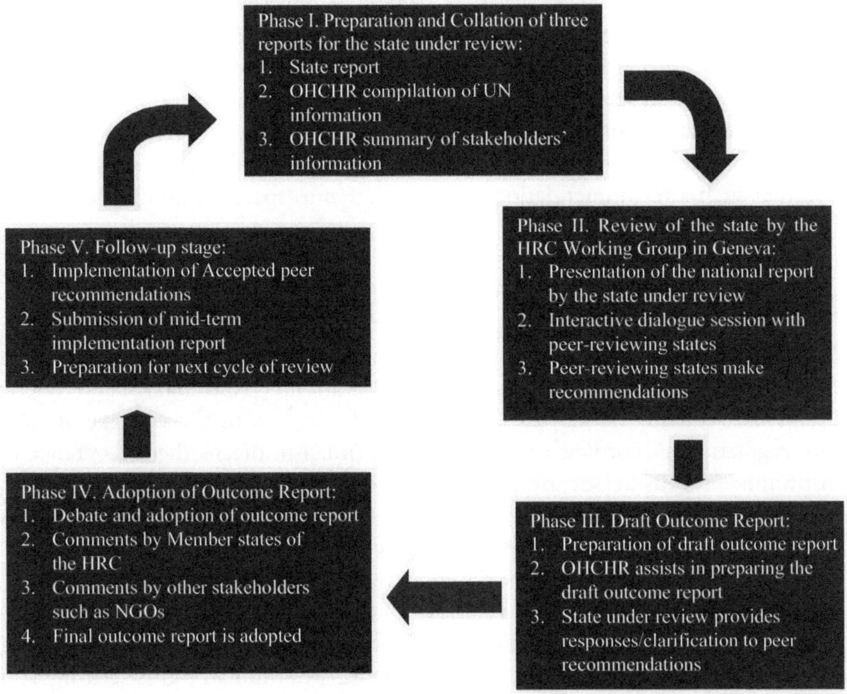

primarily on the state under review with some assistance from the international community on the implementation of recommendations which require capacity building and technical assistance.[126] Many states have provided a mid-term implementation report on the extent to which they have implemented the UPR recommendations. It is required that subsequent reviews focus on the implementation of recommendations given during the previous session. Table 1.1 summarises the various stages of the UPR process.

A sincere and genuine engagement with all the various phases of the UPR is required to make the process effective. However, the interactive dialogue (Phase II) has been criticised for the lack of specificity with regard to state recommendations and the potential for rights ritualism. McMahon's analysis of UPR I recommendations by states indicated that the majority were general recommendations. He argued that such recommendations give the implementing state freedom to determine the mode of implementation which can undermine the utility and impact of the recommendation.[127] Abebe noted that African states often made

126 Ibid paras 33, 36.
127 Edward McMahon, above n 115, 26.

recommendations which were too general to be implemented.[128] There is merit to the above criticisms given that such general recommendations can be frustrating because they are vague in terms of the means of implementation and the difficulties of measuring outcomes. However, it is important to further determine whether the lack of specificity with regard to recommendations by states was only a challenge that featured in the first cycle of the review. Nevertheless, the fact that a recommendation is general does not necessarily imply that it is not relevant and that such a recommendation may translate into specific actions at the point of implementation.

Rights ritualism

Rights ritualism has also been highlighted as one of the core challenges to the central aspect of the UPR process.[129] John Braithwaite, Toni Makkai and Valerie Braithwaite initially developed the concept of ritualism in the context of aged care regulation. According to these authors, ritualism means the 'acceptance of institutional means for securing regulatory goals, while losing all focus to achieving the goals or outcomes themselves'.[130] Hilary Charlesworth draws on this conception of ritualism and applies it to the field of international human rights law. She argues that 'in the field of human rights, rights ritualism is a more common response than an outright rejection of human rights standards and institutions'.[131] According to Charlesworth, 'rights ritualism' is 'a way of embracing the language of human rights precisely to deflect real human rights scrutiny and to avoid accountability for human rights abuses'.[132] In the context of the UPR, Charlesworth and Emma Larking define ritualism as 'participation in the process of reports and meetings but an indifference to, or even reluctance about, increasing the protection of human rights'.[133] They identify elements of cynicism in states' involvement during the interactive dialogue phase of the review.[134] They argue that some states have claimed they recognise certain rights within their states when that is not the case.[135]

In contrast to Charlesworth and Larking, Milewicz and Goodin argue that the UPR is a deliberative success for peer-to-peer accountability because of its insistently

128 Allehone M Abebe, above n 71, 16; Chauville also argues that broad recommendations without reference to specific actions are difficult to interpret. See Roland Chauville, above n 83, 98.

129 See Hilary Charlesworth and Emma Larking (eds), *Human Rights and the Universal Periodic Review: Rituals and Ritualism* (Cambridge University Press 2015).

130 Braithwaite T Makkai and V Braithwaite, *Regulating Aged Care: Ritualism and the New Pyramid* (Edward Elgar Publishing 2007) 7.

131 See Hilary Charlesworth, 'Swimming to Cambodia: Justice and Ritual in Human Rights after Conflict' (2010) 29(1) *Australian Yearbook of International Law* 1, 12.

132 Ibid.

133 Hilary Charlesworth and Emma Larking (eds), above n 129, 16.

134 Ibid 14–15.

135 Ibid.

cooperative and inclusive character which can facilitate a genuine discussion of existing human rights violations.[136] According to Milewicz and Goodin, the interactive dialogue phase involving states, and to a limited extent civil society, effectively induces a cooperative and deliberative culture within the mechanism that encourages states to comply with human rights standards.[137] However, the UPR tends to be inclined towards ritualism because of its political nature as an entirely state-driven process, and the risk of rights ritualism has been found to exist in the review of many diverse states, including Canada, Indonesia and the United States.[138] This book examines the phenomenon of rights ritualism in relation to African states. It argues that such a disingenuous attitude undermines the extent of the states' engagement with the UPR mechanism. In order for the UPR deliberation to be effective, states should genuinely engage in a constructive dialogue, avoid adopting a defensive position and not remain in denial of existing human rights violations.

Is the UPR an effective human rights mechanism?

Some of the literature on the UPR since its inception in 2006 raises scepticism about the ability of a mechanism based on cooperation to act as an effective global mechanism for monitoring the human rights compliance of states. Scholars and UPR stakeholders critique the UPR from different perspectives in an attempt to provide insights into the ability of the UPR mechanism to influence states and improve the human rights situation on the ground. I classify the literature into two main groups—the sceptical group and the evolutionary group.

The sceptical group contends that the UPR mechanism does not add any real value to the human rights system because it is flawed, in that it is dependent on the goodwill of states and has a debilitating effect on other human rights mechanisms. According to the sceptics, the UPR is institutionally weak and needs to be overhauled or replaced by an entirely new institution that will undertake real scrutiny and hold states accountable for human rights violations. For instance, in 2006, UN Watch, one of the earliest critics of the UPR, stated that

> the UN has little need for another toothless mechanism for 'cooperative dialogue'. We call on Council members to fashion a mechanism that will, in a fair manner, apply real scrutiny, to hold governments to account and cite them for violations and abuses.[139]

136 Milewicz and Goodin are both scholars at the University of Oxford and Australian National University respectively. See Karolina M Milewicz and Robert E Goodin, 'Deliberative Capacity Building Through International Organisations: The Case of the Universal Periodic Review of Human Rights' (2016) *British Journal of Political Science* 1–21.

137 Ibid 17.

138 See Hilary Charlesworth and Emma Larking, above n 129, 169–217.

139 UN Watch is an NGO based in Geneva. Its mandate is to monitor the performance of the United Nations by the yardstick of its own Charter. See UN Watch, 'UN Watch Statement

UN Watch made the aforementioned statement during the HRC debate on the modalities for the UPR. It advocated for a 'strong' mechanism that can 'name and shame' state human rights violators and hold them accountable.[140] UN Watch argued that any mechanism based on cooperation and dialogue would be ineffective in scrutinising human rights violations by states.[141]

In 2009, Allehone M Abebe, an Ethiopian diplomat in Geneva and a human rights scholar who participated both in the negotiations on the institution-building text of the HRC and the first two sessions of UPR I, expressed much criticism of the UPR, particularly the participation of African states.[142] He argued that African states have 'deftly manipulated' the system during the formative years to limit NGO participation in the process and have engaged in regional dynamics and the politics of bargaining by not criticising one another during the review of African states.[143] According to Abebe, the tendency of the African Group to use their group alliance to circumvent real scrutiny of their human rights situation signals an ominous sign for the efficacy of the UPR mechanism.[144] Abebe's detailed analysis traces the role played by African states during the negotiations leading to the establishment of the UPR, but on the actual participation of African states during the reviews, his analysis was limited only to the first two sessions.[145] With the end of the first three UPR cycles, a comprehensive analysis of the extent of African states' participation is required to properly assess the efficacy of the UPR mechanism.

Mid-way through the first cycle of the UPR, de Frouville criticised the UPR on three major grounds.[146] According to de Frouville, the UPR 'has failed to live up to expectations' because it overshadows the hard work of the treaty bodies, is wholly dependent upon the goodwill of states and cannot, as a political entity, make a legal assessment or interpretation of the human rights obligations of states.[147] Similarly, Nowak, former UN Special Rapporteur on Torture, argues that the UPR 'suffers from the disadvantage that states' performance in the field of human rights is assessed by other states rather than by independent experts'.[148] For Nowak, the UPR, by not permitting special rapporteurs and treaty body experts to participate in the review, undermines the work of the treaty bodies and special procedures. The general presumption which underlies the criticisms of de Frouville and Nowak is that monitoring human rights implementation is best tackled by human rights expert bodies rather than states. However, their analyses undermine the potential value of the UPR and do not provide empirical data on whether the UPR is effective or not in improving the human rights situation of states.

140 Ibid.
141 Ibid.
142 Allehone M Abebe, above n 71.
143 Ibid 3.
144 Ibid.
145 There were 12 sessions in the first cycle of the UPR and 14 sessions in the second cycle.
146 Olivier de Frouville, above n 6, 250–5.
147 Ibid; for a similar argument, see Nadia Bernaz, above n 91, 79–91.
148 Manfred Nowak, above n 11, 23.

Scholars within the sceptical group generally have based their views on the UPR and its architecture before the actual review started or at best examine a few sessions of the first cycle. Analyses of how the UPR mechanism has operated through the first three cycles will provide a more comprehensive understanding of its effectiveness. However, scholars within this group provide an important contribution to the knowledge regarding the negotiations leading to the establishment of the mechanism, the structure of the mechanism and what must be done or avoided to make it successful.

On the other hand, the evolutionary scholars/commentators view the UPR mechanism more positively. They contend that the UPR is an important and evolving mechanism with considerable potential, albeit that its effectiveness may be limited by factors such as politicisation, regionalism and ritualism. This group of scholars examine the UPR in action, including state practice during the interactive dialogue and the recommendations made during the review process. McMahon undertook one of the first empirical analyses of the UPR.[149] He analysed the first cycle of the UPR focusing on the general quality and quantity of UPR recommendations and the responses by all states. He found that the UPR offers tangible benefits to human rights promotion by attracting universal and high-level state engagement and encouraging dialogue between some governments and civil society.[150] However, he criticised the lack of specificity and the complimentary approach adopted mostly by the African and Asian Groups in the review of their regional peers. Overall, he has expressed optimism that the UPR will evolve into a robust mechanism because states are taking the process seriously.[151]

The analysis of McMahon was ultimately a general evaluation of states' UPR I participation in the interactive dialogue, the quality of state recommendations and the corresponding state response. In 2008, Elvira Dominquez Redondo undertook a similar general assessment to that of McMahon and drew a similar conclusion in relation to high-level state engagement with the UPR.[152] However, she conceded that the effectiveness of the mechanism would only be determined by the extent to which state participation in the UPR process improves the human rights situation on the ground, an assessment which she thought was too early for her to make at that point in time.[153]

---

on the UN Human Rights Council' (2006) available at <https://bit.ly/2mfkqtN> accessed 05/09/2019.

149 Edward McMahon, above n 115.

150 Ibid.

151 Ibid; see also Edward McMahon and Marta Ascherio, 'A Step Ahead in Promoting Human Rights? The Universal Periodic Review of the UN Human Rights Council' (2012) 18 *Global Governance* 231.

152 Redondo's analysis focused on the first session of UPR I. See Elvira Dominquez Redondo, 'The Universal Periodic Review of the UN Human Rights Council: An Assessment of the First Session' (2008) 7 *Chinese Journal of International Law* 726, 729.

153 Ibid 733.

Since 2012, Rhona Smith, Helen Quane and Takele Bulto have analysed the impact of the UPR in different regions.[154] Smith's 2012 case study of Pacific Island states demonstrated that these states actively engaged with the interactive dialogue of their reviews during UPR I and were receptive to UPR recommendations. Smith, however, pointed to the fact that their engagement was limited by their inability to participate in the review of other states due to technical and financial constraints.[155] With regard to states within the ASEAN, Quane argued in 2015 that the UPR mechanism has enhanced the relationship between ASEAN states and the global human rights mechanisms.[156] According to Quane, the UPR impacts other mechanisms by making particular recommendations which have increased their engagement with the UN treaty bodies and special procedures.[157] Quane's case study also highlighted the fact that disagreements on the death penalty and the rights of LGBT persons have limited the engagement of many states in the region.[158]

In Bulto's 2015 general analysis of Africa, he found that African states engage more with the UPR mechanism than with other human rights mechanisms because of the almost complete control they have over the outcome of the UPR process.[159] But he argues that their engagement lacks genuine commitment and is a manifestation of rights ritualism.[160] Bulto supports his claim by the fact that the African Group lobbied for a state-driven system that limits NGO participation and by their failure to be critical of the human rights situation of their peers during the reviews.[161] However, there has been evidence of ritualism and politicisation in the UPR process. While these were not the focus of the analysis in this chapter, they have the potential to undermine the impact of the UPR process and its ability to influence states.[162] But as indicated at the start of this chapter, the UPR is an evolving

154 See Helen Quane, above n 101, 303–9; Rhona Smith, 'A Review of African States in the First Cycle of the UN Human Rights Council's Universal Periodic Review' (2014) 14 *African Human Rights Law Journal* 346; Rhona Smith, 'The Pacific Island States: Themes Emerging from the United Nations Human Rights Council's Inaugural Universal Periodic Review' (2012) 13(1) *Melbourne Journal of International Law* 569; Takele Soboka Bulto, above n 48, 235–55.

155 Rhona Smith, 'The Pacific Island States' above n 154, 594.

156 ASEAN is an inter-governmental Asia regional arrangement comprising of ten member states with the aim of promoting political, economic and social cooperation and regional stability. See Helen Quane, above n 101, 289.

157 Ibid.

158 Ibid 289–95.

159 Bulto's analysis was a general evaluation of the participation of African states during UPR I. He did not engage in any specific case studies in his analysis. See Takele Soboka Bulto, above n 48.

160 Ibid.

161 Ibid 247–51.

162 For evidence of the impact of ritualism and politicisation on state engagement with the UPR, see Damian Etone, 'The Effectiveness of South Africa's Engagement with the Universal Periodic Review (UPR): Potential for Ritualism?' (2017) 33(2) *South African Journal on Human Rights* 258–85.

mechanism with potential for greater state engagement over time and there is some empirical evidence that indicates a more robust engagement from states across UPR I, II and III.[163]

The vast majority of current scholarship focuses solely on the interactive dialogue and covers mostly the first cycle of the UPR (2008–2011). Little consideration has been given to the UPR consultative process and its potential impact on compliance with treaty body reporting obligations. Also, there are few empirical studies that consider the implementation of UPR recommendations by African states or how NGOs in Africa can strengthen state engagement with the UPR mechanism. In addition, little of the existing scholarship takes a theoretical approach to analysing the UPR process.[164] This book seeks to close some of these gaps.

Membership in the UN HRC and compliance

The UN HRC is a subsidiary body of the UNGA and was established in March 2006 by General Assembly Resolution 60/251.[165] In total, 170 states voted in favour, four against and three abstained.[166] It is important to note that no African state voted against or abstained, and African states actively participated in the negotiations leading to the adoption of UNGA Resolution 60/251.[167] Among other things, Resolution 60/251 addressed the HRC's mandate, its interaction with the wider UN human rights machinery, membership and elections.[168] The HRC has the mandate to protect and promote universal respect for human rights.[169] In addition to its promotion and protection mandate, Resolution 60/251 mandates the HRC to undertake a UPR of the human rights performance of all states.[170]

As noted earlier, the work of the HRC is guided by the principles of 'universality, impartiality, objectivity and non-selectivity, constructive international dialogue and cooperation'.[171] However, regional groupings impact on membership

163 Edward McMahon and Ellisa Johnson, 'Evolution Not Revolution: The First Two Cycles of the UN Human Rights Council Universal Periodic Review Mechanism' (2016) *Friedrich Ebert Stiftung* 1, 9.

164 Charlesworth and Larking provide the first sustained analysis of the UPR process that draws on socio-legal theory and underscore the interplay of rituals and ritualism in the UPR. See Hilary Charlesworth and Emma Larking (eds), above n 129.

165 See *Resolution 60/251* above n 21.

166 Belarus, Iran and Venezuela abstained while the United States, Israel, Marshall Islands and Palau voted against the resolution. See UN GAOR, 60th sess, 72nd plen mtg, UN Doc A/60/PV.72 (15 March 2006) 6.

167 For details on the history leading to the establishment of the HRC, see Philip Alston, above n 23, 185; See also Allehone M Abebe, above n 71.

168 *Resolution 60/251*, above n 21 paras 5–9.

169 Ibid para 5.

170 Ibid para 5(e).

171 Ibid para 4.

in the HRC and have an influence on decision-making in the HRC. The five geographical groupings that were established in 1963 continue to be used within the UN system.[172] These are Africa, Asia, Eastern European Group (EEG), Group of Latin America and the Caribbean states (GRULAC), and WEOG. Equitable geographical distribution is a criterion for the distribution of seats in the HRC.[173] Africa has 13 seats, Asia (13), EEG (6), GRULAC (8) and WEOG (7).[174] Africa is the largest regional group in the UN with 54 member states.[175] While these regional groupings ensure full and representative participation by all UN members, such groups promote regional alliances which have generally influenced voting within the HRC and state participation in the UPR mechanism of the HRC.

Does membership in the HRC improve state engagement with the UPR mechanism?

Prior studies have examined whether being a party to international human rights treaties improves states' human rights compliance and why states join international human rights treaties.[176] Few studies have actually examined whether membership in inter-governmental human rights institutions actually influences state compliance with human rights monitoring mechanisms.[177] Emilie Hafner-Burton, Edouard Mansfield and Jon Pevehouse examined the reasons why states join inter-governmental human rights institutions but did not address the issue

172 See *Question of Equitable Representation on the Security Council and the Economic And Social Council*, GA Res 1991 (XVIII), UNGA, 1285 plen mtg (17 December 1963) annex; See also Sam Daws, 'The Origins and Development of UN Electoral Groups' in Ramesh Thakur (ed), *What Is Equitable Geographical Distribution in the 21st Century* (United Nations University 1999) 11–12.

173 *Resolution 60/251*, UN Doc A/Res/60/251, above n 21 para 7.

174 Ibid.

175 The Asian Group has 53 UN member states, 23 from EEG, 33 from GRULAC and 28 from WEOG.

176 See for example Beth A Simmons, 'Compliance with International Agreements' (1998) 1 *Annual Review of Political Science* 75; Eric A Posner, 'Human Welfare, Not Human Rights' (2008) 108(7) *Columbia Law Review* 1758; Oona Hathaway, 'Why Do Countries Commit to Human Rights Treaties?' (2007) 51(4) *Journal of Conflict Resolution* 588; Uta Oberdörster, 'Why Ratify? Lessons from Treaty Ratification Campaigns' (2008) 61 *Vanderbilt Law Review* 681; The impact of human rights treaty membership on state compliance is outside the scope of this book. This focuses on second-order compliance which deals with the institutions that monitor state compliance with human rights obligations, in this case the UPR mechanism.

177 Emilie M Hafner-Burton, Eduard D Mansfield and Jon C W Pevehouse, 'Human Rights Institutions, Membership, and Compliance' (paper presented at Midwest Political Science Association Annual Conference, 2–5 April 2009); Pamela A Jordan, 'Does Membership Have Its Privileges? Entrance into the Council of Europe and Compliance with Human Rights Norms' (2003) 25 *Human Rights Quarterly* 660; Eric Cox, 'State Interest and the Creation and Functioning of the United Nation Human Rights Council' (2010) *Journal of International Law and International Relations* 87, 106–10.

of whether membership improves state respect for human rights.[178] Ryan Goodman and Derek Jinks argue that the ability of these human rights institutions to influence their members would depend on the way in which such institutions are designed.[179] Membership rules are an important aspect in the design of human rights monitoring institutions. This is vital to the theory of acculturation which is 'the general process by which actors adopt the beliefs and behavioural patterns of the surrounding culture'.[180] According to Goodman and Jinks, the membership rules in a human rights monitoring institution can either facilitate or hinder the acculturation process.[181]

Goodman and Jinks identify two types of membership rules—inclusive and restrictive.[182] Inclusive or open membership allows newcomers to join and places negligible conditions for maintaining membership.[183] In contrast, a restrictive membership would condition membership on meeting some prescribed human rights standards and member states could be rejected or expelled if they did not satisfy the prescribed standards.[184] However, inclusive membership could be more beneficial to a cooperative mechanism if it could facilitate the acculturation process.[185] This is because the social and cognitive pressures that are necessary for acculturation can be maximised in an inclusive mechanism.[186] Restrictive membership is punitive and not conducive to acculturation.[187] Goodman and Jinks highlight three important benefits of inclusive membership. These include the production of strong social effects; promoting the idea of universality of human rights norms; and maximising social pressure.[188]

178 Emilie M Hafner-Burton, Eduard D Mansfield and Jon C W Pevehouse, 'Human Rights Institutions, Sovereignty Costs and Democratization' (2015) 45(1) *British Journal of Political Science* 1.

179 Ryan Goodman and Derek Jinks, *Socializing States: Promoting Human Rights Through International Law* (Oxford University Press 2013) 89–109.

180 Ibid 626.

181 See Ryan Goodman and Derek Jinks, 'How to Influence States: Socialization and International Human Rights Law' (2004) 54 *Duke Law Journal* 621, 626.

182 Ryan Goodman and Derek Jinks, above n 177, 101–2.

183 Ibid 91; Emilie Hafner-Burton, *Making Human Rights a Reality* (Princeton University Press 2013); Oona Hathaway, 'Do Human Rights Treaties Make a Difference?' (2002) 111 *Yale Law Journal* 1935, 2024.

184 Oona Hathaway, above n 181, 2024; Ryan Goodman and Derek Jinks, above n 177, 91; Anne Bayesfky, 'Making the Human Rights Treaties Work' in Louis Henkin and John Laurence Hargrove (eds), *Human Rights: An Agenda for the Next Century* (American Society of International Law 1994) 229, 264.

185 Ryan Goodman and Derek Jinks, above n 177, 109.

186 Ibid; See also See Jane K Cowan and Julie Billaud, 'Between Learning and Schooling: The Politics of Human Rights Monitoring at the Universal Periodic Review' (2015) 36(6) *Third World Quarterly* 1175.

187 Ibid 102.

188 Ryan Goodman and Derek Jinks, above n 177, 109.

The HRC is formally restrictive because admission is limited to 47 states and there is a prescribed membership selection and retention criteria.[189] Only states with a commitment to the promotion and protection of human rights can be admitted to the HRC, and members must uphold the highest human rights standards.[190] However, in practice, states with very poor human rights records have been elected to the HRC.[191] In any case, there can only be 47 states in the HRC at any given time. In addition, states stand the risk of losing their membership in the HRC when they commit gross and systematic human rights violations.[192] For example, the UNGA suspended Libya from the HRC in 2011 in response to the gross and systematic human rights violation by the Gaddafi regime.

On the other hand, the UPR mechanism is inclusive. The key principles of universality and equal treatment underpin the inclusive nature of the UPR.[193] The three members of the HRC (the 'troika') that oversee the review of each state only act as facilitators for the review, and a state under review may request that one of the *troika* members be from its own regional group or request the substitution of any *troika* member.[194] Given that the members of the HRC 'shall . . . be reviewed during their term of membership',[195] there is a potential for membership to influence state engagement with the UPR, but the tendency for state behaviour to be influenced by exogenous factors cannot be ignored.

189 The 47 seats in the HRC are geographically distributed across 5 regional groups: Group of African States (13); Group of Asian States (13); Group of Eastern European States (EEG) (6); Group of Latin American and Caribbean States (GRULAC) (8); and Group of Western European and other States (WEOG) (7). See *Resolution 60/251*, UN Doc A/Res/60/251, above n 21 para 7.

190 Ibid para 9.

191 Examples include Libya, Algeria and Saudi Arabia. The restrictive criteria put in place did not effectively act as a filter. See Philip Alston, above, n 23, 196–9; See also UN Watch assessment of the 2016–2018 candidates seeking HRC membership, UN Watch, Human Rights Foundation and Lantos Foundation for Human Rights and Justice, 'Electing the 2016–2018 Members of the UN Human Rights Council' (2015) available at <https://unwatch.org/9128-2/> accessed 12/09/2019; UN Watch and Human Rights Foundation, 'Electing the 2014–2016 Members of the UN Human Rights Council' (2013) available at <https://bit.ly/2kenhT0> accessed 12/09/2019.

192 UN GAOR, 60th sess., 72nd plen mtg, Agenda Items 46 and 120, UN Doc A/RES/60/251 (3 April 2006) [8].

193 *Resolution 5/1,* UN Doc A/HRC/RES/5/1 para 3.

194 Ibid paras 18(d) and 19.

195 UN GAOR, 60th sess., 72nd plen mtg, Agenda Items 46 and 120, UN Doc A/RES/60/251 (3 April 2006) para 9.

2 Theoretical understanding of the UPR

A case for acculturation?*

Introduction

Compliance is a mantra in international law. For many years, scholars have questioned the extent to which states comply with human rights monitoring institutions at the international and regional levels. In most cases these scholars find that human rights monitoring institutions have limited, and sometimes insignificant, impact on the human rights practices of states. At the UN level, Heyns and Viljoen conclude that UN treaty monitoring bodies 'had a very limited demonstrable impact' within states.[1] In 2010, Alebeek and Nollkaemper found only about 12% compliance with the views of the Human Rights Committee, which was declining over time.[2] In 2014, a cross-country study of Finland, the Netherlands and New Zealand found that the concluding observations and recommendations of the human rights treaty bodies have limited influence on the domestic human rights practices of states.[3] At the African regional level, Viljoen and Louw found an overall lack of state compliance with the recommendations of the African Commission on Human and Peoples' Rights.[4]

At the heart of these studies is the question of state compliance with international human rights law and the broader question of how international human rights institutions can influence states. This chapter approaches these questions by reviewing five major theoretical approaches to state compliance to determine which can more appropriately explain the potential impact of state engagement

* First published in the *Journal of Human Rights* (2019) 18 (1), 36–56.

1 Christof Heyns and Frans Viljoen, *The Impact of the United Nations Human Rights Treaties on the Domestic Level* (Martinus Nijhoff Publishers 2002) 6.

2 Rosanne Van Alebeek and André Nollkaemper, 'The Legal Status of Decisions by Human Rights Treaty Bodies in National Law' in Helen Keller and Geir Ulfstein (eds), *UN Human Rights Treaty Bodies: Law and Legitimacy* (Cambridge University Press 2012) 356–7.

3 Jasper Krommendijk, *The Domestic Impact and Effectiveness of the Process of State Reporting Under the UN Rights Treaties in The Netherlands, New Zealand and Finland: Paper Pushing or Policy Prompting* (Intersentia 2014) 368–75.

4 Frans Viljoen and Lirette Louw, 'State Compliance with the Recommendations of the African Commission on Human and Peoples' Rights, 1994–2004' (2007) 101(1) *The American Journal of International Law* 1.

with the UPR mechanism. It considers the best theoretical framework to understand the potential impact of the UPR by reviewing five major theoretical approaches to state compliance with international human rights law. These are the coercive compliance-centred theory, the 'naming and shaming' approach, the transnational legal process theory, the five-stage 'spiral model' and the theory of acculturation. I argue that while these theories are not mutually exclusive, the theory of acculturation provides the best theoretical framework to understand the potential impact of the UPR mechanism. This is because unlike the other theories, the acculturation theory does not incorporate any element of coercion or confrontation. This mirrors the inclusive and cooperative framework of the UPR mechanism which I argue provides important and effective conditions for acculturation. By incorporating a theoretical conception of the potential impact of the UPR process, this chapter contributes to existing scholarship in this area which generally has limited theoretical engagement with the impact of the UPR process.

Theoretical framework

International scholars have extensively engaged with the question of why and when states obey international law. International law and international relations scholars have developed various theories to explain and answer this question, but each arrived at mixed results.[5] At the heart of this discourse is the problem of compliance. In the context of international human rights law, scholars have engaged with the specific question of whether ratification of human rights treaties has any effect on state behaviour. While some studies found that treaties have improved state behaviour,[6] others found that treaties have no positive effect and sometimes even a negative effect.[7] However, Roger Fisher's

5 Laurence R Helfer, 'Overlegalizing Human Rights: International Relations Theory and the Commonwealth Caribbean Backlash against Human Rights Regimes' (2002) 102 *Columbia Law Review* 1834; Harold Honju Koh, 'Transnational Legal Process Theory' (1996) 75 *Nebraska Law Review* 181; Harold Honju Koh, 'Why Do Nations Obey International Law?' (1997) 106 *Yale Law Journal* 2599; Andrew T Guzman 'A Compliance Based Theory of International Law' (2002) 90 *California Law Review* 1826; Andrew T Guzman, *How International Law Works: A Rational Choice Theory* (Oxford University Press 2008); Eric A Posner, *The Twilight of Human Rights Law* (Oxford University Press 2014); Elisabeth Stubbins Bates, 'Sophisticated Constructivism in Human Rights Compliance Theory' (2014) 25(4) *The European Journal of International Law* 1169–82.

6 Beth Simmons, *Mobilising for Human Rights: International Law in Domestic Politics* (Cambridge University Press 2009); Yonatan Lupu, 'The Informative Power of Treaty Commitment: Using the Spatial Model to Address Selective Effect' (2013) 57(4) *American Journal of Political Science* 912–25; Emelie Hafner-Burton, *Making Human Rights a Reality* (Princeton University Press 2013).

7 Oona Hathaway, 'Do Human Rights Treaties Make a Difference?' (2002) 111 *Yale law Journal* 1935–2042; Eric Neumayer, 'Do International Human Rights Treaties Improve Respect for Human Rights?' (2005) 49(6) *Journal of Conflict Resolution* 925–53; Daniel W Hill, 'Estimating the Effects of Human Rights Treaties on State Behavior' (2010) 72 *Journal of Politics* 1161–74; Eric A Posner, above n 5, 69–121.

work differs from these studies by making a distinction between first- and second-order compliance. According to Fisher, 'first-order compliance' relates to compliance with treaties while 'second-order compliance' deals with compliance with the decisions and recommendations of institutions monitoring compliance with international treaties.[8] The aforementioned studies focused on 'first-order compliance', and until recently, little attention has been paid to 'second-order compliance'.[9]

This section reviews five main theories on state compliance with international human rights law—the coercive compliance-centred theory; 'naming and shaming'; the transnational legal process theory; the five-stage 'spiral model'; and the acculturation theory. It critiques each of the theoretical approaches after outlining them in order to justify my preference for the theory of acculturation. This review is not exhaustive in coverage of compliance theories. It rather focuses on the theories that are relevant to my argument and important in framing the debate. The argument here is that the UPR mechanism, which relies on state dialogue and cooperation, embodies a sophisticated human rights approach, whose impact cannot be appreciated by compliance theories that incorporate elements of coercion/confrontation. The coercive compliance-centred theory and other theories that incorporate elements of coercion are not suitable for assessing the UPR or other human rights cooperative mechanisms. Furthermore, this section argues that the acculturation theory provides a more appropriate alternative theoretical framework through which to understand the potential impact of the UPR process. This is because the acculturation theory does not incorporate any element of coercion or material inducement but focuses on the various social and cognitive pressures that influence states. This theory is most suitable in evaluating a monitoring mechanism that tends to be inclusive, cooperative and collaborative. I argue that the UPR is such a mechanism and can influence human rights changes within states in a non-confrontational manner.

The coercive compliance-centred theory

The theoretical starting point of this research follows the argument that human rights compliance mechanisms that rely exclusively on coercive/confrontational approaches are limited and undermine the potential benefit of cooperative mechanisms. Proponents of a coercive compliance-centred theory hold onto the traditional notion that coercive mechanisms are the principal means to induce state compliance with human rights. According to this view, compliance with human

8 Roger Fisher, *Improving Compliance with International Law* (University of Virginia Press 1981) 28–9.

9 Many studies on the impact of the international human rights monitoring bodies generally found low levels of state compliance (second-order compliance). See Jasper Krommendijk, above n 3, 368–75; Van Alebeek and Nollkaemper, above n 2; Frans Viljoen and Lirette Louw, above n 4, 1–34; Open Society Initiative, *From Judgement to Justice: Implementing International and Regional Human Rights Decisions* (Open Society Foundations 2010); Christof Heyns and Frans Viljoen, above n 1.

rights norms occurs when powerful states coerce relatively weak states into complying through sanctions, punitive or other confrontational measures.[10] Many scholars within international relations theory share this view and contend that human rights norms will be enforced only to the extent that it is in the strategic interest of powerful states to enforce them.[11]

While the views of international relations scholars rely on the power of states to enforce human rights norms, international legal scholars generally rely on 'powerful' institutions to coerce states into compliance. According to Henry Steiner, '[i]nstitutions make rights more effective by threatening or taking actions that may lead a state to comply. Institutions with real power cut to the bone of sovereignty'.[12] Based on this view, Steiner argues that the UN Human Rights Committee will require restructuring to address its compliance problem.[13] But the UN treaty bodies in general cannot be characterised as coercive because they do not have the power to compel states to comply with their findings or recommendations. Viewing international monitoring institutions with this compliance-centred optic has led many scholars to regard the monitoring institutions as basically weak and ineffective, underscoring their inability to meaningfully advance human rights.[14] While there have been several proposals in recent years to strengthen the human rights treaty body monitoring system,[15] Frouville argues

10 Oona Hathaway, above n 7, 1934–2034; Elvira Dominguez draws a distinction between confrontational and non-confrontational mechanisms of human rights enforcement. See Elvira Dominquez Redondo, 'The Universal Periodic Review of the UN Human Rights Council: An Assessment of the First Session' (2008) 7 *Chinese Journal of International Law* 726, 681–94.

11 See S P Baumgartner, 'Does Access to Justice Improve Countries' Compliance with Human Rights Norms?—An Empirical Study' (2011) 44 *Cornell International Law Journal* 447; Anne-Marie Slaughter, 'International Relations, Principal Theories' (2011) 4 *Max Planck Encyclopaedia of Public International Law* 1; Andrew T Guzman, 'A Compliance Based Theory of International Law' above n 5, 1826.

12 Henry J Steiner, 'Individual Claims in a World of Massive Violations: What Role for the Human Rights Committee?' In Philip Alston and James Crawford (eds), *The Future of UN Human Rights Treaty Monitoring* (Cambridge University Press 2000) 20.

13 Ibid 15–53.

14 In 2000, James Crawford described the UN human rights monitoring system as a 'system in crises' because of the huge backlog in overdue reports, resource and financial constraints, and limited political support. See James Crawford, 'The UN Human Rights System: A System in Crisis' in Philip Alston and James Crawford (eds), *The Future of UN Human Rights Treaty Monitoring* (Cambridge University Press 2000) 1, 1–12; Andrew Moravsik, 'The Origin of Human Rights Regime: Democratic Delegation in Post War Europe' (2000) 54 *International Organisation* 217, 219; Makau Mutua, 'Looking Past the Human Rights Committee: An Argument for Demarginalising Enforcement' (1994) 4 *Buffalo Human Rights Law Review* 211, 212.

15 See Navanethem Pillay, *Strengthening the United Nations Human Rights Treaty Body System: A Report by the United Nations High Commissioner for Human Rights* (OHCHR 2012); Suzanne Egan, 'Strengthening the United Nations Human Rights Treaty Body System' (2013) 13(2) *Human Rights Law Review* 209–43.

that the development of the treaty bodies has reached its limits.[16] To address the deficiencies of the UN human rights system, Frouville advocates for the creation of a World Commission of Human Rights with a strong institutional basis and the power to issue and enforce binding decisions.[17] The argument that the best and final model for securing human rights compliance is the establishment of a world court of human rights is informed by the desire for more confrontational approaches to monitoring human rights compliance.[18]

The aforementioned arguments are not without merit. They are founded on the premise that human rights norms have a normative force. Hence failure to comply ought to attract a degree of 'penalty'; international human rights monitoring bodies do not have the competence to punish rights violators or provide direct redress to victims of rights violation. It has also been argued that the monitoring process involves legal questions which political bodies like the UPR mechanism are ill-equipped to deal with.[19] This helps explain the earlier call for a judicial articulation of rights by a judicial body, the violation of which should attract punitive sanctions that will secure compliance. However, not all scholars agree. Jill Goldenzeil underscores the need for flexibility in enforcing human rights norms.[20] Goldenzeil, like Laurence Helfer, argues that the 'overlegalisation' of international human rights law through rigid enforcement mechanisms can have a potential backlash.[21] Drawing on the examples of Jamaica, Guyana, and Trinidad and Tobago, Helfer argues that when international human rights law is 'overlegalized' it will create a domestic backlash that may cause states to withdraw from a human rights regime.[22] I argue that the UPR mechanism provides much-needed flexibility through its cooperative, rather than adjudicative, framework and that the potential value of a cooperative mechanism to human rights implementation cannot be underestimated.

Within the governance matrix, Vega and Lewis argue that the UPR has the potential to transform human rights discourse.[23] They take the view that the UPR introduces a distinctive environment that encourages human rights policy

16 Olivier de Frouville, 'Building a Universal System for the Protection of Human Rights: The Way Forward' in M Cherif Bassiouni and William A Schabas (eds), *New Challenges for the UN Human Rights Machinery* (Intersentia 2011) 264.

17 Ibid 264–5.

18 Manfred Nowak, 'It's Time for a World Court of Human Rights' 'in M Cherif Bassiouni and William A Schabas (eds) above n 18, 26.

19 Olivier de Frouville, above n 16, 254.

20 Jill I Goldenziel, 'Regulating Human Rights: International Organisations, Flexible Standards, and International Refugee Law' (2014) 14(2) *Chicago Journal of International Law* 453; Laurence R Helfer, above n 5, 1832.

21 Jill I Goldenzeil, above n 20, 460–1; Laurence R Helfer, above n 5; Guzman and Linos developed the human rights theory of backsliding to explain a related phenomenon. See Andrew T Guzman, 'Human Rights Backsliding' (2014) 102 *California Law Review* 603.

22 Laurence R Helfer, above n 5.

23 Constance de la Vega and Tamara N Lewis, 'Peer Review in the Mix: How the UPR Transforms Human Rights Discourse' in M Cherif Bassiouni and William A Schabas (eds), *New Challenges for the UN Human Rights Machinery* (Intersentia 2011) 353–85.

diffusion and the sharing of best practices among member states.[24] According to Redondo and McMahon, more cooperative and inclusive approaches to human rights implementation can provide a middle ground between universalism and national sovereignty.[25] They argue that voluntary and cooperative approaches if properly utilised can have a 'prophylactic effect' in promoting human rights and help reduce the number of instances that would require 'interventionist' actions.[26] Vega and Lewis described the UPR as a 'soft' accountability mechanism that enables members to adjust their national practices in conformity with shared ideas on how effectively to manage human rights in the 21st century.[27]

Exclusive reliance on 'strong' compliance mechanisms, whether through sanctions or adjudication, not only undermines the potential value of cooperative mechanisms but also has significant limitations and negative impact on human rights. Empirical studies have well documented the adverse impact of economic sanctions on human rights.[28] Empirical analysis from 1981 to 2000 concluded that 'economic sanctions deteriorate citizens' physical integrity rights',[29] especially when directed towards dictatorial regimes.[30] Recent empirical studies equally indicate that even the so-called targeted sanctions have unintended adverse consequences on the respect for human rights.[31] Carneiro and Apolinário

24 Ibid 357.

25 See Elvira Dominguez Redondo and Edward R McMahon, 'More Honey Than Vinegar: Peer-Review as a Middle Ground Between Universalism and National Sovereignty' (2013) 51 *Canadian Yearbook of International Law* 61–97.

26 Ibid 88–97.

27 Constance de la Vega and Tamara N Lewis, above n 23, 363.

28 See Reed M Wood, 'A Hand Upon the Throat of the Nation: Economic Sanctions and State Repression' (2008) 52(3) *International Studies Quarterly* 489–513; Dursun Peksen, 'Better or Worse? The Effect of Economic Sanctions on Human Rights' (2009) 46(1) *Journal of Peace Research* 59–77; Mohamed Bennouna, 'Les sanctions économiques des Nations Unies' (2002-I) 200 *RCADI* 9, 40–7.

29 Dursun Peksen, above n 28, 59.

30 Cristiane Careniero and Dominique Elden, 'Economic Sanctions, Leadership Survival and Human Rights' (2009) 30(3) *University of Pennsylvania Journal of International Law* 969. For a debate on the efficacy of economic sanctions, see, for example, Ella Shagabutdinova and Jeffery Berejikian, 'Deploying Sanctions While Protecting Human Rights: Are Humanitarian "Smart Sanctions" Effective?' (2007) 6 *Journal of Human Rights* 59–74; Daniel Dresner, 'Sanctions Sometimes Smart: Targeted Sanctions in Theory and Practice' (2011) 13 *International Law Review* 96.

31 Cristiane Lucena Carneiro and Laerte Apolinário, 'Targeted Versus Conventional Economic Sanctions: What Is at Stake for Human Rights?' (2016) 42(4) *Journal of International Interaction* 565–89; Emanuel Ingold, 'The Impact of Economic Sanctions on Respect for Human Rights after the End of the Cold War' (APSA 2013 Annual Meeting Paper; American Political Science Association 2013 Annual Meeting 2013); Sylvanus Kwaku Afesorgbor and Renuka Mahadevan, 'The Impact of Economic Sanctions on Income Inequality of Target States' (EUI Working Paper No MWP 2016/04, European University Institute, April 2016); Thomas J Biersteker et al., *The Effectiveness of United Nations Targeted Sanctions: Findings from the Targeted Sanctions Consortium (TSC)* (The Graduate Institute of International and Development Studies 2013) available at <https://bit.ly/2m7enqX> accessed 12/09/2019.

analysed targeted sanctions against African states between the years 1992 and 2008. Their findings indicate that targeted sanctions had similar adverse effects as conventional sanctions and that the level of human rights protection in the country is likely to worsen under an episode of targeted sanction.[32] Africa is the most sanctioned continent in the world, and yet there is little improvement on the human rights situation on the ground.[33] This is an indication that this coercive compliance paradigm has not been effective in the continent. Legal theorists and social psychologists have reasoned that if the ultimate goal of the international human rights system is to improve the human rights situation on the ground, then voluntary obedience, not coerced compliance, must be the preferred mechanism of enforcement.[34]

The analysis in this chapter does not seek to undermine the significance of other human rights mechanism but rather argues that more attention needs to be given to the potential value of cooperative human rights mechanisms, which could complement other existing human rights mechanisms. The UPR mechanism, which relies on cooperation and gives the state some degree of control over the process, can be sometimes at least as, if not more, effective than coercive mechanisms.

The 'naming and shaming' approach

Compliance mechanisms based on the coercion model are unsatisfactory in explaining state engagement with the UN treaty monitoring bodies.[35] This is because the treaty bodies do not have the power to compel states to comply with their findings or recommendations. 'Naming and shaming' is one of the predominant approaches engaged by the UN human rights monitoring bodies.[36] As pointed out by Geir Ulfstein, UN human rights treaty bodies have no coercive power except for 'naming and shaming'.[37] This approach relies on expressing

32 Cristiane Lucena Carneiro and Laerte Apolinário, above n 31.

33 Adrea Charron, 'Sanctions and Africa: United Nations and Regional Response' in Jane Boulden (ed), *Responding to Conflict in Africa: The United Nations and Regional Organizations* (Palgrave Macmillan 2013) 77–98.

34 Harold Honju Koh, 'Why Do Nations Obey International Law' above n 5, 2645. See also different empirical studies by Tom Tyler and Raymond Paternoster et al. which concluded that people obey the law not because of fear of sanctions but because they considered it to be legitimate. See Tom R Tyler, *Why People Obey the Law* (Princeton University Press 2006); Raymond Paternoster et al., 'Perceived Risk and Social Control: Do Sanctions Really Deter?' (1983) 17 *Law and Society Review* 457.

35 For other theories which may best explain state engagement with the UN human rights treaty bodies see Jasper Krommendijk, 'The Domestic Effectiveness of International Human Rights Monitoring in Established Democracies: The Case of the UN Human Rights Treaty Bodies' (2015) 10(4) *The Review of International Organisations* 489–512.

36 Elvira Domlnguez-Redondo, above n 10, 687.

37 Geir Ulfstein, 'Law-Making by Human Rights Treaty Bodies' in Rain Liivoja and Jarna Petman (eds), *International Law-Making: Essays in Honour of Jan Klabbers* (Routledge 2014).

public disapproval of a state's non-compliance with its international human rights obligations and has been used by most of the UN human rights machinery. In the case of the treaty bodies, the sanctions available in the event of non-compliance are limited, for the most part, to 'naming and shaming'.[38] This involves public reporting of the violation and possibly condemnation.[39] While the findings by the relevant experts may be justified, states at the receiving end of the scrutiny tend to perceive such an approach as confrontational, and they dismiss the finding as a foreign imposition. This is, in some way, the result of the fact that mechanisms like the treaty bodies and special procedures rely on human rights experts and engage in a highly technical review process.[40] Even though the independent treaty body experts are nominated by states, the fact that they are not peers sometimes helps create the perception of 'us' as in states versus 'them' as in human rights experts.

Redondo classifies 'naming and shaming' as a confrontational approach, especially when it calls for a country-specific resolution or requests country-specific actions.[41] African states, as well as many other states, have repeatedly condemned findings and resolutions which target the human rights practices of specific states or regions, arguing that they breed selectivity and double standards.[42] For example, South Africa adheres to the belief that 'naming and shaming' is counter-productive and has at various times voted against country-specific resolutions condemning human rights abuses in Myanmar, Sudan and the Democratic Republic of Congo (DRC).[43] In 2006, the African Group in the HRC opposed a strong HRC action on Darfur in favour of a fact-finding mission and wanted the mission to consist of state representatives, reflecting their dislike of independent experts.[44] In March 2009, an attempt by the EU to reinstate the country mandate on the DRC through a draft HRC resolution was opposed by the African Group, which later introduced its own resolution that was eventually adopted.[45]

38 Philip Alston, 'Final Report on Enhancing the Long-Term Effectiveness of the United Nations Human Rights Treaty System' (1996) E/CN.4/1997/74 paras 10–12.

39 Ibid.

40 This has been seen to contribute to low state engagement with human rights bodies and a seemingly low rate of state conformity with their recommendations and findings. See United Nations High Commission for Human Rights, 'Strengthening of the Human Rights Treaty Bodies Pursuant to Assembly Resolution 66/254' (2012) UN Doc a/66/860.

41 Elvira Domlnguez-Redondo, above n 10, 687.

42 Elvira Domínguez-Redondo, 'Rethinking the Legal Foundations of Control in International Human Rights Law-The Case of Public Special Procedures' (2011) 29(3) *Netherlands Quarterly of Human Rights* 261, 274–5.

43 See Edoard Jordaan, 'South Africa and the United Nations Human Rights Council' (2014) 36(1) *Human Rights Quarterly* 90, 100–9.

44 See Statement by Algeria (on behalf of the African Group), 'Human Rights Situation in Dafur' United Nations Human Rights Council, 4th Spec. Sess., 1st plen. Mtg (12 Dec. 2006) available at <https://bit.ly/2lOkkcf> accessed 12/09/2019; International Service for Human Rights (ISHR), 'Human Rights Council 4th Special Session, 12–13 December 2006' (2006) available at <https://bit.ly/2lLgssE> accessed 12/09/2019.

45 International Service for Human Rights (ISHR), above n 44, 7.

The African Group's resolution neither condemned the DRC government nor made any call for the establishment of a country mandate on the DRC.[46]

According to the African Group, the HRC's founding principle of non-selectivity is opposed to selective country-specific resolutions which contributed to the demise of the former Commission for Human Rights.[47] Algeria, on behalf of the African Group, stated that '[o]ne of the reasons why the Commission was not successful was because of the naming and shaming [of states]'.[48] The opposition of African states to 'naming and shaming' through country-specific resolutions partly stems from their view that it is a neo-colonial tool having little to do with human rights concerns.[49] In 2006, James Lebovic and Eric Voeten examined 'naming and shaming' by the former UN Commission for Human Rights from 1977 to 2001.[50] They found evidence of bias as over half of the resolutions condemning human rights abuses only targeted Israel, Chile, South Africa, Equatorial Guinea and Cambodia and avoided public condemnation of politically powerful countries like China and Saudi Arabia.[51]

As argued in this chapter, there is the need for a more inclusive and cooperative approach, and the UPR mechanism provides such a platform. According to Surya Subedi, the UN Special Rapporteur on the situation of human rights in Cambodia, a more constructive approach focusing on cooperation among peers towards improving human rights rather than naming and shaming would help dissipate the perception of "us" versus "them" held by states in relation to human rights experts.[52] This approach, he noted, is supported by developing states.[53]

Moreover, the 'naming and shaming' approach to human rights implementation has largely been seen as a failure.[54] Emilie Hafner-Burton analysed the

46 Ibid.

47 See Statement by Algeria (on behalf of the African Group), 'Implementation of General Assembly Resolution 60/251 of 15 March 2006 Entitled "Human Rights Council"- Darfur' A/HRC/2/L.44 (28 November 2006) available at <webcast.un.org/ramgen/conferences/hrc2006/two/hrc061128pm-eng_part2.rm?start=00:03:30&end=00:10:10>.

48 Ibid.

49 See Rosa Freedman, *The United Nations Human Rights Council: A Critique and Early Assessment* (Routledge 2013) 18.

50 James Lebovic and Eric Voeten, 'The Politics of Shame: The Condemnation of Country Human Rights Practices in the UNHCR' (2006) 50 *International Studies Quarterly* 861–88.

51 Ibid.

52 Surya P Subedi, 'Protection of Human Rights Through the Mechanism of UN Special Rapporteurs' (2011) 33 *Human Rights Quarterly* 228; Former UN High Commissioner for Human Rights, Sergio Vieira de Mello, also observed that 'it is not enough to blame. It is also necessary to help governments or regimes to emerge from their own mistakes or their own contradictions.' See Paulo Sergio Pinheiro, 'Being a Special Rapporteur: A Delicate Balancing Act' (2011) 15(2) *The International Journal of Human Rights* 167.

53 Surya P Subedi, above n 52.

54 See H Richard Friman, *The Politics of Leverage in International Relations: Name, Shame, and Sanction* (Palgrave Macmillan 2015); Fleur Adcock, 'The Limitations of the Current International Human Rights Law System in Regards to Monitoring of Rights? Does It

relationship between 'naming and shaming' and the human rights practices of 145 states.[55] She finds that perpetrators do not change their human rights practices after being shamed and sometimes instead ramp up those abuses.[56] According to Haidi Willmot et al., human rights strategies cannot be limited to 'naming and shaming'.[57] They argue that the limited strategy of blaming the Sri Lankan government for the human rights abuses during the conflict (2002–2009) contributed to the UN's failure to protect the rights of civilians during the conflict.[58] International scholars have underscored the tendency of states to react to threats by redefining 'their interests in the direction of resisting the threat' and that extrinsic incentives in the form of rewards or punishment undermine the intrinsic motivations of states to comply.[59] This trades long-term commitment in favour of short-term compliance.[60]

Many scholars have argued that 'naming and shaming' is less effective today than in the 1970s when it was first used.[61] Roth criticises the 'naming and shaming' methodology of international organisations as ineffective, particularly for addressing violations of economic, social and cultural (ESC) rights because these rights have limited clarity about violation and remedy.[62] Molly Land argues that if 'naming and shaming' is a limited technique, consideration should be given to other approaches 'given the urgency of addressing human rights violations resulting from global inequalities'.[63] These concerns have given rise to calls for new approaches to monitoring human rights compliance, particularly in the

---

Encourage "Rights Ritualism"?' (2015), International Expert Group Meeting—Dialogue on an optional protocol to the United Nations Declaration on the Rights of Indigenous Peoples, UN Doc PFII/2014/EGM, 1–14; Scott Gates and Simon Reich, *Child Soldiers in the Age of Fractured States* (University of Pittsburgh Press 2010) 4; Haidi Willmot et al., *Protection of Civilians* (Oxford University Press 2016).

55 Emilie M Hafner-Burton, 'Sticks and Stones: Naming and Shaming the Human Rights Enforcement Problem' (2008) 62 *International Organisation* 689–716.

56 Ibid.

57 Haidi Willmot et al., above n 54, 369.

58 Ibid.

59 Ryan Goodman and Derek Jinks, 'How to Influence States: Socialization and International Human Rights Law' (2004) 54 *Duke Law Journal* 621, 689; John Braithwaite and Peter Drahos, *Global Business Regulation* (Cambridge University Press 2000) 558.

60 Ibid.

61 Emilie M Hafner-Burton, above n 55, 707–13; Louise Mallinder, 'Law, Politics and Fact-Finding: Assessing the Impact of Human Rights Reports' (2010) 2(1) *Journal of Human Rights Practice* 166, 174.

62 Kenneth Roth, 'Defending Economic, Social and Cultural Rights: Practical Issues Faced by an International Human Rights Organization' in D Bell and J M Coicaud (eds), *Ethics in Action: The Ethical Challenges of International Human Rights Nongovernmental Organisations* (United Nations University Press 2006) 167, 173–4.

63 Molly K Land, 'Democratizing Human Rights Fact-Finding' in Philip Alston and Sarah Knuckey (eds), *The Transformation of Human Rights Fact-Finding* (Oxford University Press 2016) 416.

context of socio-economic rights.[64] Socio-economic rights have figured prominently among state recommendations to their peers in the UPR process. About 10% of the total recommendations made by states during UPR I was on socio-economic rights and more than 12% during UPR II.[65] The UPR provides a new approach to address these issues, and its potential impact cannot be gauged by compliance theories that are confrontational.

Luis Rodrigues-Pinero draws a connection between the general failure of the human rights system to elicit compliance and its predominant naming and shaming approach.[66] He observes 'that the effectiveness of the "name and shame" techniques has long been superseded by crude facts'.[67] Rodrigues-Pinero advocates for a more sophisticated approach to rights implementation which focuses on cooperation, empowers rights-holders, reinforces duty-bearers' capacities and the role of technical cooperation.[68] This chapter argues that the UPR mechanism embodies this sophisticated approach by emphasising state cooperation as the cornerstone of the mechanism. Some may argue that the deliberations that take place during the interactive dialogue phase of the UPR are a form of 'naming and shaming'. However, this does not fully match up with the conventional understanding of the 'naming and shaming' approach, which involves singling out states and publicly condemning their poor human rights record. Most of the state deliberations during the UPR process utilise language which is more encouraging and recommendatory, rather than condemnatory. This to an extent has been a subject of criticism by some scholars. The 'naming and shaming' approach is a particularly unsuitable framework for the UPR because the aim for the establishment of the HRC and its UPR mechanism was to provide an alternative to the 'naming and shaming' and practices of selectivity which contributed to the demise of the former Commission for Human Rights.[69] It would, therefore, be inappropriate to assess the impact of the UPR process by the same framework

64 See A Corkery and S Way, 'Integrating Quantitative and Qualitative Tools to Monitor the Obligation to Fulfil Economic, Social and Cultural Rights: The Opera Framework' (2012) 30 *Nordic Journal of Human Rights* 324, 330; D. Rubenstein, 'How International Human Rights Organisations Can Advance Economic, Social and Cultural Rights: A Response to Kenneth Roth (2004) 26 *Human Rights Quarterly* 845, 849; M. Robinson, 'Advancing Economic, Social and Cultural Rights: The Way Forward' (2004) 26 *Human Rights Quarterly* 866, 870.

65 This included the right to education, health, food, poverty, housing and water. See UPR Info, 'UPR Info's statistics of UPR recommendations' available at <www.upr-info.org/database/statistics/index_issues.php> accessed 12/09/2019.

66 Luis Rodriguez-Pinero, '"Where Appropriate": Monitoring/Implementing of Indigenous Peoples' Rights Under the Declaration' in Claire Charters and Rodolfo Stavenhagen (eds), *Making the Declaration Work: The United Nations Declaration on the Rights of Indigenous Peoples* (IWGIA 2009) 329.

67 Ibid.

68 Ibid 330.

69 See Philip Alston, 'Reconceiving the UN Human Rights Regime: Challenges Confronting the New UN Human Rights Council' (2006) 7(1) *Melbourne Journal of International Law* 185–224; *Human Rights Council,* GA Res 60/251, UN GAOR, 60th sess, 72nd plen mtg,

that it sought to avoid, although the extent to which it has succeeded to avoid 'naming and shaming' may be the subject of debate.

The transnational legal process theory

The transnational legal process theory propounded by Harold Koh holds that the way to achieve compliance with international law is through the repeated participation of states in a variety of law-creating and interpreting fora which results in the internalisation or domestication of norms.[70] Koh makes a distinction between three forms of norm internalisation: social, political and legal.[71] Social internalisation occurs when there is widespread adherence to a norm as a result of that norm acquiring public legitimacy.[72] With political internalisation, the government accepts an international norm as a matter of policy.[73] Legal internalisation occurs when the international norm is incorporated into the domestic legal system via executive action, legislation, judicial interpretation or a combination of the three.[74]

Central to the transnational legal process theory are the successive processes of interaction, interpretation and internalisation. In the context of human rights law compliance, Koh contends that compliance is ultimately achieved as a result of the repeated process of interaction, interpretation and internalisation through which international human rights norms are 'obeyed' (complied with).[75] The interaction and interpretation processes are triggered by non-state actors in an effort to compel the state to implement the findings or recommendations of human rights mechanisms. The treaty monitoring or international adjudicative monitoring bodies then serve as an interpretive community which defines or clarifies the definition of the relevant norms and their violation.[76] The state then achieves legal internalisation through the constitution or other domestic law; political internalisation by incorporating the norm into governmental policy; and social internalisation when the norm acquires public legitimacy.[77]

Agenda Items 46 and 120, UN Doc A/Res/60/251 (3 April 2006) ('*Resolution 60/251*') para 5 (e).

70 See Harold H Koh, 'Transnational Legal Process Theory' above n 5, 181; Harold H Koh, 'How Is International Law Enforced' in Richard Pierre Claude and Burns H Western (eds), *Human Rights in the World Community Issues and Actions* (University of Pennsylvania Press 2006) 305–15.

71 Harold Honju Koh, 'Bringing International Law Home' (1998) 35 *Houston Law Review* 623, 642.

72 Ibid.

73 Ibid.

74 Ibid.

75 Harold H Koh, 'How Is International Human Rights Law Enforced?' (1999) 74(4) *Indiana Law Journal* 1397, 1411.

76 Ibid 1410.

77 Ibid; for an example of a state where the transnational legal process theory was proven to be at work see Caleb J Stevens, 'Hunting a Dictator as a Transnational Legal Process: The

The transnational legal process theory is a comprehensive theory. As Kent argues, it is an inclusive theory in a structural sense because 'it comprehends all levels of state and non-state interaction, influence, and compliance—the international and the domestic, the vertical and the horizontal'.[78] However, the transnational legal process theory is limited in many respects. According to Guzman, the transnational legal theory fails to explain why states comply with international human rights law, but rather it provides an empirical pathway to compliance.[79] While legal internalisation can be achieved through constitutionalisation of human rights norms, Koh's theory does not explain how to ultimately achieve social and political internalisation. It fails to account for the process by which a norm acquires public legitimacy. As argued in the following sections, the theory of acculturation fills this gap by identifying the cognitive and social pressures that drive states to adopt socially legitimate attitudes, beliefs and behaviours (social and political internalisation). Koh acknowledges this limitation of his theory and argues that the theory of acculturation closes the gap by identifying the microprocesses of social influence that affects his process of 'norm internalisation'.[80]

Also, while the UPR provides an interactive process, through a three-and-a-half-hour-long interactive dialogue (Phase II of the UPR), it does not provide a forum for the interpretation of the relevant international law. In the UPR, states only make human rights recommendations to peers and do not undertake a legal interpretation or clarification of the content of those rights. Koh's theory does not explain whether any of the three forms of internalisation (legal, political and social) can occur in the absence of an interpretive community or a law-declaring forum to create, legally interpret or clarify the relevant rights. States tend to be less cooperative with such interpretive and law-declaring fora. This contributes to their limited, and sometimes insignificant, impact on states.

The UPR is a non-adjudicative and non-confrontational mechanism which does not serve as an interpretive community. As such, the transnational legal process theory does not provide a suitable theoretical framework to understand the impact of the UPR process on the human rights situation on the ground. Nevertheless, Koh notes that the various theoretical explanations for compliance are complementary, not mutually exclusive.[81] The process of interaction in the transnational legal process theory which includes the participation of both state and non-state actors is an important component of the five-stage spiral model and underscores the significance of NGO participation in the UPR process.

Internalisation Problem and the Hissènne Habrè Case' (2012) 24(1) *Pace International Law Review* 190.

78 Ann Kent, *Beyond Compliance: China International Organizations and Global Security* (Stanford University Press 2007) 10.

79 Andrew T Guzman, 'A Compliance Based Theory of International Law' above n 5, 1835–6.

80 Harold Hongju Koh, 'Internalisation Through Socialisation' (2005) 54 *Duke Law Journal* 975, 977.

81 Harold Hongju Koh, 'Why Do Nations Obey International Law?' above n 5, 2603, 2649.

The five-stage spiral model

The spiral model was developed by Risse et al. to explain how states ultimately come to comply with human rights norms.[82] The central tenet of the spiral model is that the diffusion of international human rights norms that results in domestic change is dependent on the power of transnational human rights pressures exerted by national and transnational advocacy networks.[83] The spiral model examines the process by which international norms are internalised and implemented domestically, with governments, transnational societies and domestic civil societies as key actors.[84] This theory captures the moral strength of human rights ideas and the central role of domestic and transnational non-governmental actors in shaping the decisions of states to comply with international human rights norms. However, the significance of the spiral model in relation to explaining the potential impact of the UPR is limited by the incorporation of coercion and 'naming and shaming' approaches at some stages of the model.

In the spiral model, there are five phases to human rights change. The first phase of the spiral model begins when there is repression by authoritarian regimes.[85] The situation progresses to the second phase when transnational advocacy groups exert pressure on the state to recognise human rights.[86] This places the state on the international spotlight. In the second phase, once the repressive state has been put on the international agenda, the state, in order to avoid international scrutiny and diffuse pressure, raises the flag of national sovereignty by claiming that its behaviour is not subject to international scrutiny.[87] The target state remains in denial about the validity of human rights norms and rejects the demands of international groups.[88] It is at this phase that coercive strategies in the form of economic sanctions and 'naming and shaming' are employed.

As pressure increases from both domestic and transnational actors, the targeted state enters into the third phase of the spiral model by making some 'tactical concessions' or 'cosmetic' changes such as signing international treaties.[89] This ushers the state into the fourth phase of the spiral model known as 'prescriptive status'. This is characterised by state recognition of the validity of human rights norms through the establishment of human rights institutions and domestic

82 Thomas Risse, Stephen C Ropp and Kathryn Sikkink, *The Power of Human Rights: International Norms and Domestic Change* (Cambridge University Press 1999); Thomas Risse et al., *The Persistent Power of Human Rights: From Commitment to Compliance* (Cambridge University Press 2013).

83 Thomas Risse et al., *The Power of Human Rights*, above n 83, 11.

84 Ibid.

85 Thomas Risse et al., *The Persistent Power of Human Rights: From Commitment to Compliance*, above n 82, 5–6.

86 Ibid.

87 Ibid.

88 Ibid.

89 Ibid.

law reforms.[90] This is a result of state interaction with the interpretive and law-declaring fora at the international law—the first two stages of Koh's transnational legal process theory. By becoming a party to an international human rights treaty, which Risse et al. argue is a consequence of domestic/international pressure and other exogenous factors, the state achieves what Koh refers to as 'legal internalisation'.

The fifth phase is ultimately achieved through the institutionalisation and habitualisation of human rights norms.[91] This is characterised by conformity and sustained compliance with international human rights norms.[92] This is in line with Koh's concepts of social and political internalisation, but while Rise et al. argue from an international relations standpoint of norm socialisation, Koh argues from an international law perspective of norm internalisation. Nevertheless, neither Koh nor Rise et al. address the microprocesses that influence social and political internalisation (socialisation).

The spiral model offers important insights into the process of change in repressive states. It recognises the importance of human rights discourse and the central role of non-governmental actors. It has been tested in over 20 case studies.[93] Jasper Krommendijk argues that, unlike coercion, the spiral model provides a satisfactory theoretical framework to explain the effectiveness of the UN human rights treaty bodies.[94] Based on empirical analysis of the study of the Netherlands, New Zealand and Finland, Krommendijk contends that the greater the level of transnational NGO mobilisation, the higher the effectiveness of the concluding observations of the treaty bodies.[95] Another relevant aspect of this model is the recognition of the significance of civil society/NGO engagement in human rights mechanisms.

However, the spiral model has theoretical shortcomings and is an inappropriate theoretical framework to consider the impact of state engagement with the UPR mechanism. As pointed out by Eran Shor, Risse et al. consider that once the spiral

90 Ibid.
91 Ibid 8.
92 Ibid.
93 For examples on Uganda, Kenya, Morocco, Tunisia, Chile, Guatemala, Indonesia, Philippines and South Africa see Thomas Risse et al., *The Power of Human Rights*, above n 124; for the USA and China see Thomas Risse et al., *The Persistent Power of Human Rights*, above n 83; see also Caroline Fleay, 'Australian Foreign Policy, Human Rights in China and the Spiral Model' (2006) 41(1) *Australian Journal of Political Science* 71–89; Ahmed Shahid and Hilary Yerbury 'A Case Study of the Socialisation of Human Rights Language and Norms in Maldives: Process, Impact and Challenges' (2014) *Journal of Human Rights Practice* 1–25; Alejandro Anaya, 'Transnational and Domestic Processes in the Definition of Human Rights Policies in Mexico' (2009) 31(1) *Human Rights Quarterly* 35–58; Raed A Alhargan 'The Impact of the UN Human Rights System and Human Rights INGOs on the Saudi Government with Special Reference to the Spiral Model' (2012) 16(4) *The International Journal of Human Rights* 598–623.
94 Jasper Krommendijk, above n 35, 492.
95 Ibid 504–8.

process has started, there can be no regression because violations are bound to decrease.[96] According to Shor, Risse et al. fail to closely look into the possibilities of regression and to consider the role of serious conflicts and security threats in shaping states' repressive policies and hindering norm compliance.[97] When conflicts within or between states pose a threat to the nation and/or citizens, governments easily justify repressive measures and human rights considerations are weakened. In 1999, Morocco was transitioning to the fourth phase of the spiral model.[98] However in 2003, it reverted to repression. After the May 2003 terrorist attack in Casablanca, Morocco, the government passed new antiterrorism laws and resumed death sentences and torture (between 2000 to 5000 arrests were carried out and 17 of the 903 persons convicted were sentenced to death).[99] The increased threat of terrorism globally is an issue not addressed by the spiral model, and there has been evidence which proves that terrorism significantly diminishes states' respect for basic human rights.[100]

Moreover, the fact that the spiral model incorporates elements of coercion/confrontation in the second and third phases makes it an inappropriate theory to test the impact of a mechanism based entirely on cooperation. These two phases are characterised by pressure, denunciation and shaming, which, as argued earlier in this chapter, have been proven to be ineffective. In addition, the five-stage spiral model is only focused on civil and political rights and covers a very limited subset of human rights issues. Consequently, the impact of the UPR mechanism with cooperation as its hallmark cannot be adequately explained by the five-stage spiral model, although aspects of the model that underscore the significant role of NGOs/CSOs are relevant when considering the impact of the UPR mechanism.

The theory of acculturation

Theories of human rights compliance which integrate coercive or confrontational strategies do not account for acculturation. Acculturation was first defined in 1936 as 'those phenomena which result when groups of individuals sharing different cultures come into continuous first-hand contact, with subsequent changes in the original culture patterns of either or both groups'.[101] A psychologist's perspective

96 Eran Shor, 'Conflict, Terrorism, and the Socialization of Human Rights Norms: The Spiral Model Revisited' (2008) 55(1) *Social Problems* 5–6.

97 Ibid.

98 Thomas Risse et al., *The Power of Human Rights*, above n 82, 125.

99 Jamil Dakwar, *Morocco: Human Rights at a Crossroads* (Human Rights Watch 2004) 25.

100 See Axel Dreher et al., 'Does Terrorism Threaten Human Rights? Evidence from Panel Data' (2010) 53(1) *The Journal of Law and Economics* 65–93; Eran Shor et al., 'Terrorism and State Repression of Human Rights: A Cross-national Time-series Analysis' (2014) 55(4) *International Journal of Comparative Sociology* 294–317; Eran Shor et al., 'Does Counterterrorist Legislation Hurt Human Rights Practices? A Longitudinal Cross-national Analysis' (2016) 58 *Social Science Research* 104–21.

101 R Redfield, R Linton, and M J Herskovits, 'Memorandum on the Study of Acculturation' (1936) 56 *American Anthropologist* 973–1002.

to the term 'acculturation' was later provided by Graves, who described acculturation as changes to an individual's identity, attitudes and values resulting from his contact with other cultures.[102] In 2004 and 2005, Goodman and Jinks transferred the concept of acculturation to states and international regimes. They define acculturation as 'the general process by which actors adopt the beliefs and behavioural patterns of the surrounding culture, without actively assessing either the merits of those beliefs and behaviours or the material costs and benefits of conforming to them'.[103] Goodman and Jinks argue that their theory of acculturation is 'an extension of Koh's and other's work on transnational norm diffusion' which they intend to supplement by 'isolating the micro processes of social influence'.[104] Acculturation, as used by Goodman and Jinks, therefore draws on a relationship between law and sociology, in contrast to the five-stage spiral model influenced by international relations theory.

The theory of acculturation calls into question the view that compliance with human rights norms is best induced by the exercise of coercive power or by binding decisions emanating from human rights monitoring institutions.[105] Central to the acculturation theory is that power is not merely prohibitive, material and centralised but also productive, cultural and diffuse.[106] Goodman and Jinks argue that mechanisms based on coercion are inadequate because coercion 'fails to grasp the complexity of the social environment within which states act'.[107] Monitoring and reporting are highly effective and important functions in an acculturation-based institutional regime, while sanctions and binding decisions are potentially counterproductive.[108] The acculturation approach shows preference for 'soft law' mechanisms but does not call for a complete abandonment of coercive mechanisms. Rather, it argues that acculturation, like coercion, is more likely to succeed and more likely to fail under certain conditions or when combined with other mechanisms.[109]

The microprocesses of acculturation, which include mimicry, identity and status maximisation, propel cognitive and social pressures which drive a state to adopt socially legitimate attitudes, beliefs and behaviours.[110] By identifying themselves with a reference group, states generate varying degrees of social and

102 Theodore D Graves, 'Psychological Acculturation in a Tri-Ethnic Community' (1967) 23(4) *Southwestern Journal of Anthropology* 337, 338.

103 Ryan Goodman and Derek Jinks, above n 59, 626.

104 Ibid.

105 See the views of Nowak and Frouville discussed earlier. See Manfred Nowak, 'It's Time for a World Court of Human Rights' above n 18, 23; Olivier de Frouville, above n 16, 254.

106 Ryan Goodman and Derek Jinks, *Socializing States: Promoting Human Rights Through International Law* (Oxford University Press 2013) 122.

107 Ryan Goodman and Derek Jinks, above n 59, 625.

108 Ibid 699.

109 Ryan Goodman and Derek Jinks, 'International Law and State Socialisation: Conceptual, Empirical and Normative Challenges' (2005) 54 *Duke Law Journal* 983, 991.

110 Ryan Goodman and Derek Jinks, above n 59, 639–42.

cognitive pressures to conform to the norms of that group.[111] The social environment within which states act propels internal cognitive and social pressures which drive a state to adopt socially legitimate attitudes and beliefs. The adoption of socially legitimate attitudes, beliefs and behaviours by states can contribute to the attainment of what Koh calls 'social and political norm internalisation'. In his review on the theory of acculturation, Koh validates the theory of acculturation as a case study of internalisation through socialisation.[112] He argues that by focusing on acculturation over coercion, Goodman and Jinks unmask a new approach to influence state compliance with human rights law through a 'complex interaction between process and ideas'.[113] Therefore, Koh's transnational legal process theory is not necessarily antithetical to the theory of acculturation as both theories could co-exist and reinforce each other.

Social and cognitive pressures can push the language of human rights into some moral commitments within particular cultures even in terms that challenge one or more aspects of that culture. Benjamin Gregg has employed a cognitive approach rather than a normative one to show how human rights norms can be advanced as rights internal to any given community's culture by means of cognitive reframing.[114] He argues that 'an idea once external can become internal through system-level learning'.[115] While examining the issue of female genital mutilation (FGM) in Africa, he noted that a cognitive rule can be deployed that revises local normative rules that justify FGM but that such a cognitive rule has to be locally owned.[116] For example, reframing FGM as a technical, health issue, rather than a normative human rights concern, can advance the human rights issue as internal to the African culture.

Another example of the potential for social and cognitive pressures in the UPR process to influence states is the problem of cultural relativism to the realisation of human rights. Cultural relativism, in relation to the issue of sexual orientation, is an issue found to have impacted the UPR engagement of African states examined in their participation as a reviewer and as states under review.[117] With the exception of Madagasca, no African state made a recommendation to its African peer on sexual orientation, and an overwhelming majority of the recommendations on the issue made by non-African states to African states were rejected. African states received the highest number of UPR recommendations on the issue of sexual orientation, but the African states rejecting the recommendations often stated that same-sex unions were culturally unacceptable or

111 Ibid.
112 Harold Hongju Koh, above n 80, 975, 977.
113 Ibid.
114 Benjamin Gregg, 'Deploying Cognitive Sociology to Advance Human Rights' (2010) 9 *Comparative Sociology* 279, 289.
115 Ibid.
116 Ibid 304.
117 Damian Etone, 'African States: Themes Emerging from the Human Rights Council's Universal Periodic Review (UPR)' (2017) 6(2) *Journal of African Law* 201–23.

an affront to African values and in some cases an imposition of Western values on them.[118]

Nevertheless, there could be an 'African' way to incrementally realise the rights of sexual minorities within the context of the UPR by focusing on soft recommendations which seek to transform the social and political culture against sexual minorities. Approaches that employ coercion or require immediate normative solutions have either experienced a backlash or have been inadequate. For example, in 2011, Human Rights Watch published a report that found a dichotomy between the constitutional ideals and public attitude towards sexual minorities in South Africa.[119] The report indicated that despite the constitutional protection on the rights of the LGBT community, discrimination against them remained institutionalised in the communities, families and state institutions.[120] There is also evidence that calls for immediate decriminalisation or threats, such as the threat by the British government to withhold UK aid from governments that do not reform legislation banning homosexuality, have been subsequently met with specific legislation further criminalising same-sex unions in some countries like Nigeria and Uganda.[121]

Within the context of the UPR, soft recommendations such as raising public awareness and sensitisation on the need for decriminalisation can help transform the current public support against decriminalisation and subsequently pave the way for normative solutions that would enjoy public support. Also, applying Gregg's cognitive reframing approach, states could find ways to advance the rights of sexual minorities as rights internal to the African culture by means of cognitive reframing. While African states such as Sao Tome and Principe, Ghana, and Cameroon have been receptive to UPR recommendations that require them to condemn, investigate acts of violence against LGBT people or raise public awareness and sensitisation on LGBT rights, they were not receptive to recommendations for immediate decriminalisation, arguably because of the enormous public support against decriminalisation.

The UPR through its social and cognitive pressures can contribute to transform the belief that same-sex relationships are un-African and an imposition of 'white Euro-American sexual norms and gender expressions'.[122] There may be an 'African' way for realising LGBT rights within the context of the UPR by focusing on recommendations which seek to transform the social and political culture against sexual minorities. Such an approach that focuses on transforming the social and political culture through social and cognitive pressures can contribute to incrementally improving the human rights situation on the ground. This

118 An example is Kenya; see Human Rights Council, 'Report of the Human Rights Council on Its Eighth Session' UN Doc A/HRC/8/52 (1 September 2008) [714].

119 Ibid 1.

120 Ibid 14–15.

121 Same Sex Marriage Prohibition Act 2013 (Nigeria); Uganda Anti-Homosexuality Act, 2014 (Uganda).

122 S Ekine, 'Contesting Narratives of Queer Africa' in S Ekine and H Abbas (eds), *Queer Africa Reader* (Pambazuka Press 2013) 77, 78.

can contribute to achieving the social and political internalisation which propels Koh's process of norm internalisation. This is particularly relevant in the context of South Africa where 'the vast majority of South Africans' condemn sexual minorities, despite progressive policies and interpretation of the protection of the rights of sexual minorities in the South African Constitution.[123]

Concluding remarks

The UPR mechanism shows the power of peer pressure and global culture in enforcing human rights law through state influence. Acculturation particularly favours the UPR mechanism because it is based on peer review and not configured to involve a selected group of insiders or experts, examining or reviewing those considered as outsiders or states. This helps to dispel the perception of 'us' versus 'them'. According to Goodman and Jinks, the cognitive and social pressures generated by the acculturation microprocess of identification are more effective when an International Governmental Organisation provides universal membership and subjects all member states to review.[124] Maria Stavropoulou examined the acculturation theory in the context of refugee protection. She finds that refugee protection regimes could explore the benefits of inclusive membership through the creation of additional fora building on acculturation techniques.[125] The UPR mechanism is inclusive, cooperative and collaborative and has in two cycles of the UPR achieved 100% state cooperation rate.[126] These cornerstone principles of the UPR—universality and cooperation—can be effective in harnessing the social and cognitive pressures associated with acculturation which can facilitate the social learning process of African states as they engage with the UPR process.

However, as observed by Goodman and Jinks, acculturation can produce a 'decoupling' situation where public conformity with human rights norms is disconnected from local practice.[127] This is akin to the problem of 'ritualism' identified by Charlesworth and Larking in the context of the UPR.[128] They define

123 See Zahrah Z Devji, 'Forging Paths for the African Queer: Is there an "African" Mechanism for Realising LGBTIQ Rights?' (2016) *Journal of African Law* 1, 4; E Goodsell, 'Constitution, Custom, and Creed: Balancing Human Rights Concerns with Cultural and Religious Freedom in Today's South Africa' (2007) 21 *Brigham Young University Journal of Public Law* 109, 110.

124 Ryan Goodman and Derek Jinks, above n 106, 103.

125 Maria Stavropoulou, 'Influencing State Behaviour for Refugee Protection: UNHCHR and the Design of the Refugee Protection Regime' (UNHCHR Research Paper No. 154, The UN Refugee Agency 2008) 9–15.

126 With the exception of Israel which temporarily boycotted its UPR II in January 2013, all UN member states have been reviewed in the two cycles of the UPR. In October 2013, Israel returned and undertook its UPR II.

127 Ryan Goodman and Derek Jinks, above n 106, 140.

128 Hilary Charlesworth and Emma Larking (eds), *Human Rights and the Universal Periodic Review: Rituals and Ritualism* (Cambridge University Press 2015).

'ritualism' as state 'participation in the process of reports and meetings but an indifference to, or even reluctance about, increasing the protection of human rights'.[129] However, it is plausible that over time acculturation may help narrow the UPR implementation gap through effective NGO participation in the UPR process. This reinforces the significant role of NGOs underscored in the transnational legal process theory and the five-stage spiral model.

Acculturation provides a more suitable theoretical framework to understand the potential impact of the UPR mechanism on the influence of state. The inclusive, cooperative and collaborative framework of the UPR process are important and effective conditions for acculturation. Acculturation is a process, and through this process, continuous engagement with the UPR mechanism can over time transform the shallow human rights commitment of states into a deeper commitment. Charlesworth argues that human rights compliance strategies that focus on a learning culture rather than a culture of blame are useful in achieving improved human rights protection.[130] According to Charlesworth:

> The idea of continuous improvement, which emphasises incremental, constantly monitored step can be achieved by moving from a culture that administers blame to a culture that encourages learning.[131]

The UPR provides such a platform for acculturation that promotes cooperation and encourages continuous improvement of the human rights situation within states. Applying the theory of acculturation contributes to an understanding of the efficacy of human rights strategies based on cooperation. This cooperative mechanism can be beneficial in realising incremental progress in human rights. Notwithstanding, different human rights mechanisms may be more or less effective depending on the political system in the state in question, along with other contextual factors.

129 Ibid 16.

130 Hilary Charlesworth, 'Kirby Lecture in International Law—Swimming to Cambodia: Justice and Ritual in Human Rights After Conflict' (2010) 29 *The Australian Yearbook of International Law* 1.

131 Ibid 14–15.

3 Compliance, implementation and effectiveness

Clarifying the basis for assessing state UPR engagement

Compliance, implementation and effectiveness

Compliance and implementation

Any human rights law study which sets out to evaluate compliance and effectiveness faces measurement problems because compliance and effectiveness are imprecise terms that have been subject to multiple interpretations.[1] It is therefore essential to clarify what it is that this study seeks to measure. The literature on international law makes a distinction between the terms 'compliance' and 'implementation'. Compliance is defined as behaviour or conduct which conforms to the requirements of a specified rule, motivated by factors such as avoidance of sanctions, reputation or obedience deriving from internalisation of the rule.[2] Implementation, on the other hand, is defined as specific action taken by states in response to voluntary international commitments[3] or actions by state and non-state actors which help translate state international commitments into domestic practice.[4] In the context of international human rights law, the OHCHR defines implementation as:

> Moving from a legal commitment, that is, acceptance of an international human rights obligation, to realization by adoption of appropriate measures

1 Benedict Kingsbury argues that there is no single correct definition of the concept of compliance in international law because the different theories of law result in divergent notions of compliance. See Benedict Kingsbury, 'The Concept of Compliance as a Function of Competing Conceptions of International Law' (1998) 19 *Michigan Journal of International Law* 345, 346.

2 See Kal Raustiala and Anne-Marie Slaughter, 'International Law, International Relations and Compliance' in Walter Carlneas et al. (eds), *The Handbook of International Relations* (Sage 2002) 539; Oran R Young, *Compliance and Public Authority, a Theory with International Application* (Johns Hopkins University Press 1979) 4.

3 Kal Raustiala and Anne-Marie Slaughter, above n 2.

4 David G Victor et al. (eds), *The Implementation and Effectiveness of International Environmental Commitments: Theory and Practice* (MIT Press 1998) 3.

> and ultimately the enjoyment by all of the rights enshrined under the related obligations.[5]

Accordingly, implementation is a function of compliance because it deals with the measures adopted by a state to achieve compliance with its international obligations. [6] Implementation is typically a vital step towards compliance.

This research is concerned with the engagement of African states with the UPR mechanism of the HRC. Thus, it envisages specific actions taken by each of the three states under study in relation to recommendations from their engagement with the UPR mechanism. The focus is therefore on implementation and not on compliance. Implementation in this research is defined as actions taken by a state to fulfil the recommendations by its peers during the UPR process and improve the human rights situation on the ground. Subsequent analysis in this book considers whether states took specific actions to fulfil recommendations accepted during UPR I and II. While compliance and implementation are interrelated terms, implementation in the context of this research is more measurable and observable because it connotes state actions in response to accepted UPR commitments.

In analysing the empirical evidence of implementation, this research does not view implementation as necessarily binary—either implemented or not implemented, but rather locates it along a continuum. There are categories of compliance. I borrow and adapt the categorisation of compliance identified by Viljoen and Louw in their study on state compliance with the recommendations of the African Commission on Human and Peoples' Rights (ACHPR).[7] They identified five broad categories of compliance. These are full compliance, non-compliance, partial compliance, situational compliance and unclear cases of compliance.[8] When a state was in full compliance, it meant the state fully implemented the recommendations from the ACHPR or had undertaken significant steps in the process of compliance.[9] Non-compliance occurred when the state did not implement any of the recommendations and at times challenged their legal and factual basis.[10] When part or some of the recommendations were

5 Office of the High Commissioner for Human Rights, *Report of the High Commissioner for Human Rights on Implementation of Economic, Social and Cultural Rights*, UN ESCOR, UN Doc E/2009/90 (8 June 2009) para 3 available at <www.ohchr.org/Documents/Issues/ESCR/E_2009_90_en.pdf> accessed 09/09/2019.

6 Laurence Boisson de Chazournes, *Diplomatic and Judicial Means of Dispute Settlement* (Martinus Nijhoff Publishers 2013) 157.

7 Frans Viljoen and Lirette Louw, 'State Compliance with the Recommendations of the African Commission on Human and Peoples' Rights, 1994–2004' (2007) 101(1) *The American Journal of International Law* 1, 5.

8 Ibid.

9 Ibid.

10 Ibid.

implemented, it amounted to partial compliance. Partial or full compliance which resulted from a transition from a repressive or undemocratic government to a more stable and democratic system of government was known as situational compliance. In other words, the compliance was merely coincidental in the sense that responsive changes occurred not as a result of any deliberate action on the part of the government on the recommendation but as a result of changing circumstances within the state.[11]

This research modifies the above categorisation of compliance to denote implementation and adopts the following three broad categories of implementation:

- 'Fully Implemented' (FI), which connotes that the action taken by the state is to a large extent responsive to the UPR recommendation;
- 'Partially Implemented' (PI), which connotes that the action taken by the state is to some extent responsive to the UPR recommendation but does not implement certain aspects of the recommendation; and
- Not Implemented (NI), which connotes that no action has been taken regarding the particular UPR recommendation or where a contrary action was taken.

When assessing implementation in subsequent chapters, the analysis does not assert a direct causal link between a state's action and specific UPR recommendations. Rather, it considers the extent to which the UPR contributed to the realisation of human rights changes within states. As such, the full or partial implementation of a UPR recommendation could also be 'situational' or 'coincidental'. Consequently, analysis of the question of implementation is limited to the above three categories of FI, PI and NI.

When measuring the level of implementation, reliance is placed on the Implementation Recommendation Index (IRI) developed by UPR Info.[12] The responses used to calculate the IRI of each of the three states under study are gleaned from various UPR reports. These include reports submitted by the state, National Human Rights Commissions (NHRCs) and other UPR stakeholders on the implementation of various UPR recommendations. These can be found in the OHCHR database and the database of UPR Info.[13] This methodology focuses on UN, state and NGO UPR stakeholders' reports on implementation. By using multiple stakeholder information on implementation, the analysis of the extent of state UPR implementation in the subsequent case studies was able to check for ambiguities and disagreements among the UPR stakeholders on

11 Ibid 6.

12 UPR info is a non-governmental organisation with the mission to promote and strengthen the UPR by raising awareness, providing capacity-building tools and bridging the different actors of the UPR process in order to ensure the universal advancement of human rights. See UPR Info available at <www.upr-info.org/en> accessed 12/09/2019.

13 Ibid; Office of the High Commissioner for Human Rights, 'Universal Periodic Review' <>www.ohchr.org/EN/HRBodies/UPR/Pages/Documentation.aspx>.

the outcomes of UPR recommendations. The categories of 'fully implemented', 'partially implemented' and 'not implemented' are applied in the overall analysis of implementation and impact to determine the extent of the actions taken by the case-study states to implement each of the accepted UPR I recommendations.

Effectiveness

Weiss and Jacobson define 'effectiveness' as the extent to which a treaty causes changes in the behaviour of states that further the goals of the treaty.[14] According to Oran Young, it is the degree to which an agreement impacts on states.[15] Consequently, the starting point of this research is the recognition that the 'effectiveness' of state engagement with the UPR mechanism will be determined by the extent or degree to which it contributes to improving the human rights situation on the ground, which is the principal goal of the UPR mechanism. Therefore, while implementation in this thesis only examines specific actions taken by the state in relation to each accepted recommendation, 'effectiveness' considers the overall impact of their engagement and the aggregate number of implemented recommendations. This will determine the extent of the state engagement with the UPR mechanism, which is a fundamental question. The analysis in this book does not equate 'effectiveness' with efficiency, and neither does it refer to the ability of the UPR process to cause immediate implementation of all UPR recommendations. Rather, it examines the degree to which the UPR mechanism has been able to cause observable changes in the domestic human rights situation of states.

To evaluate the 'effectiveness' of state engagement with the UPR, this research develops a four-step approach which is applied in the case-study analysis in subsequent chapters. This approach evaluates 'effectiveness' in terms of the level of state commitment to the UPR national consultation process, representativeness during the review, participation during the review sessions and the aggregate percentage of implemented UPR recommendations. To determine state commitment to the UPR national consultation process, it considers the state's approach to the consultation; the inclusivity of the national consultation process, both in terms of relevant stakeholders and relevant issues; and the time frame utilised for the national consultation. These factors help to determine whether the requirement for the state to undertake a 'broad consultation process' at the national

14 Edith Brown Weiss and Harold K Jacobson (eds), *Engaging Countries: Strengthening Compliance with International Environmental Accords* (MIT Press 1998) 6.

15 Oran R Young and Marc A Levy, 'The Effectiveness of International Environmental Regimes' in Oran R Young (ed), *The Effectiveness of International Environmental Regimes: Causal Connections and Behavioral Mechanisms* (MIT Press 1999) 1. See also Lisa L Martin, 'Against Compliance' in Jeffrey L Dunoff and Mark A Pollack (eds), *Interdisciplinary Perspectives on International Law and International Relations: The State of the Art* (Cambridge University Press 2013).

level was satisfied.[16] The second step of this four-step approach examines the representativeness of a state during its review by considering the level of state representation and whether the requirement to 'fully integrate a gender perspective' in the review, as required by HRC Resolution 5/1, was achieved.[17] This will enable a determination on the competency of the delegation for the review and whether the state views the UPR process as a foreign affairs issue or considers it as a process for internal examination and improvement of the human rights situation on the ground.

The third step to 'effectiveness' considers the extent of state participation in the review sessions as a reviewer and as a state under review. When considering the state as a state reviewer, the state's approach to cooperation, and the quality and relevance of the recommendations it made to its regional peers compared to recommendations made to other groups of states, is examined. As a state under review, this research examines the state receptiveness to UPR recommendations and considers the state's responses to UPR recommendations by determining the percentage of recommendations accepted or rejected within and outside its regional group. The last step analyses the aggregate percentage of the recommendations that were fully, partially or not implemented in each of the three state case studies. This four-step approach is significant because it enables a comprehensive assessment of state engagement with the UPR mechanism by examining state engagement at the key stages of the UPR process.

Categorisation of UPR recommendations

The recommendations made by states during the UPR process are sometimes phrased in a way that makes it difficult to identify the expected outcome of a recommendation. Categorising these recommendations assists the state and other stakeholders to identify whether the expected outcome of each recommendation was achieved at the end of each review cycle. Also, it enables a determination on a state's responsiveness to each of the categories, serves as an indication of its level of engagement and helps identify the category in which the state is more engaged at the implementation stage. McMahon has developed a verb-based action category which provides a semantic analysis of categorisation.[18] This research adopts McMahon's method of categorising UPR recommendations because it has been used successfully by organisations and scholars such as UPR Info, Roland Chauville, David Frazier, Judy McGregor, Sylvia Bell and Margaret Wilson.[19] The

16 *Resolution 5/1,* UN Doc A/HRC/RES/5/1 para 15(a).

17 Ibid para 3(k).

18 See UPR INFO, UPR Info's Database—Action Category' (October 2014) available at <https://bit.ly/2mddHjZ> accessed 09/09/2019; Edward McMahon, 'The Universal Periodic Review: A Work in Progress, An Evaluation of the First Cycle of the New UPR Mechanism of the United Nations Human Rights Council' (2012) *Friedrich Ebert Stiftung* 1.

19 See UPR Info above n 12; R. Chauville, 'The Universal Periodic Review's First Cycle: Successes and Failures' in Hilary Charlesworth and Emma Larking (eds), *Human Rights and the Universal Periodic Review: Rituals and Ritualism* (Cambridge University Press 2015) 98;

Peace, Democracy and Human Rights Directorate of International Organisation of La Francophonie has also found this categorisation very useful to resolve challenges in grouping recommendations and recommends its use.[20]

McMahon ranks the recommendations into five different categories. Rank 1 represents recommendations requiring only minimal action from the state under review. Recommendations under this category call on the state under review to either request technical assistance or share information.[21] States making recommendations which fall under this category use verbs such as 'call on', 'seek' and 'share' when phrasing the recommendations. An example is when Malaysia recommended to South Africa during the second review cycle to '*seek* necessary technical assistance from OHCHR, other relevant UN agencies and funds with a view to effectively implement its key national priorities for 2009–2014 related to health, education, land reform and food security'.[22] This category requires little or no cost on the part of the state under review and can be implemented with minimal effort.

Rank 2 includes recommendations which emphasise continuity. They require that the state under review 'continue' certain actions it had already commenced. In this category, 'continue', 'maintain', 'persevere', 'persist' and 'pursue' are the verbs used in making the recommendations. For example, in Nigeria's second cycle review, Nicaragua recommended that Nigeria '***Continue*** working to harmonise its normative framework with obligations of international instruments recently adhered to'.[23]

In rank 3, the state is required to give consideration to the recommendations made. Key verbs such as 'analyse', 'consider', 'explore', 'examine', 'envisage', 'reflect upon' 'and 'study' are used by states in the construction of the recommendations. Rwanda, for example, recommended to Nigeria during the second cycle review to '*Consider* the abolition of the death penalty'.[24]

Recommendations that are categorised in rank 4 are those that request the state to undertake a general action. Examples of verbs used in their construction include 'accelerate', 'encourage', 'intensify', 'promote', 'strengthen' and 'take

David Frazier, 'Evaluating the Implementation of UPR Recommendations: A Quantitative Analysis of the Implementation Efforts of Nine UN Member States' (August 2011) available at <https://bit.ly/2mfeYHr> accessed 12/09/2019; Judy McGregor, Sylvia Bell, and Margaret Wilson (eds), *Human Rights in New Zealand: Emerging Faultlines* (Bridget Williams Books 2016) 156.

20 International Organisation of La Francophonie, *Universal Periodic Review: Implementation Plan of Recommendations and Pledges* (STIPA 2013) 76–80.

21 See UPR INFO, above n 18.

22 Human Rights Council, *Report of the Working Group on the Universal Periodic Review—South Africa*, 21st sess, Agenda item 6, UN Doc A/HRC/21/16 (9 July 2012) ('*HRC UPR II Report- South* Africa') para 124.59.

23 Human Rights Council, *Report of the Working Group on the Universal Periodic Review—Nigeria*, 25th sess, Agenda Item 6, UN Doc A/HRC/25/6 (16 December 2013) ('*HRC UPR II Report—Nigeria*') para 135.22.

24 Ibid para 137.12.

actions'. Such a verb was used by Australia when it recommended during the first cycle review that Kenya should '*Strengthen* protection for women and children against violence and exploitation'.[25]

Rank 5 recommendations are often those that are most costly for the state under review to implement and require much effort on their part. It is also the most specific recommendation that is made to the state under review (SuR), and it is easy to identify its outcome because it requires specific action to be taken. Recommendations of the specific action category call upon the state to 'eliminate', 'abolish', 'adopt', 'amend', 'accede', 'ratify', 'implement' or 'enforce' such as when Australia recommended that Nigeria should '*Implement* a moratorium on the death penalty'.[26]

In accordance with the principles that guide this categorisation, where there are two different action categories present in a given recommendation, emphasis is placed on the first action.[27] When a recommendation begins with two verbs such as 'continue and strengthen', privilege is given to the second verb and the recommendation categorised in that category.[28] When a recommendation begins in the fourth category (rank 4) but followed by category five verbs, such a recommendation is placed in category five. An example is 'improve women's rights by amending the family code'.

When the recommendations have been classified, it is necessary to determine state responsiveness to the recommendations by classifying their responses into those that were 'accepted', 'noted', 'rejected' and those which received a 'general response'. According to HRC Resolution 5/1, UPR recommendations that do not receive the support of the state under review are 'noted'.[29] For the purposes of this research, when a state clearly uses the word 'accept', the recommendation is considered as accepted. Similarly, when the state clearly uses 'reject', 'noted', 'do not accept' or 'not in a position to accept', the recommendation is classified as 'rejected'. Responses which cannot be placed in the above two classes are classified as a general response. The recommendations are categorised into the above five categories to determine the specificity and relevance of the recommendations and the approach adopted by states. This is significant in examining the nature of the states' engagement with the UPR mechanism as a reviewer and as a state under review.

25 Human Rights Council, *Report of the Working Group on the Universal Periodic Review—Kenya*, 15th sess, Agenda Item 6, UN Doc A/HRC/15/8 (17 June 2010) ('*HRC UPR I—Kenya*') para 101.50.

26 *HRC UPR II Report—Nigeria*, UN Doc A/HRC/25/6 para 137.1.

27 See UPR INFO, above n 18.

28 Ibid.

29 *Resolution 5/1*, UN Doc A/HRC/RES/5/1 para 32.

4 Nigeria's engagement with the HRC's UPR

Potential for acculturation or risk of regression?*

Introductory background

The evolution of human rights in Nigeria can be traced from the pre-colonial, colonial and post-colonial eras. While the existence of human rights in pre-colonial Nigerian society cannot be denied,[1] the catalogue and scope of human rights protected during that era were greatly limited and did not subscribe to the contemporary notion of universality. This is because the rights recognised then were significantly influenced by the laws, customs and beliefs of the individual group or tribe within the society.[2] Many of these customs and beliefs were repugnant to human rights such as human sacrifices, the killing of twins and trial by ordeal.

The colonial era brought about some advancement of human rights within Nigerian society. Nigeria was colonised by Britain for over 60 years. Britain's positive influence on human rights was seen in the enactment of the Native Law Ordinance in 1948, which abolished customary practices that were repugnant to natural justice, equity and good conscience.[3] By abolishing certain objectionable cultural practices, like human sacrifices, the British colonial regime contributed to the progressive development of human rights in Nigeria. However, colonialism is, by definition, the negative of human rights, and the subjugation of people to alien domination and exploitation constituted a very serious denial of human rights.

Upon gaining independence from British colonial rule in 1960, considerable efforts were made to promote and protect human rights in Nigeria. The post-independence Constitutions of Nigeria guaranteed human rights and instituted mechanisms for their enforcement.[4] The Nigerian National Human Rights

* This is the author's accepted manuscript of an article published by Edinburgh University Press in *African Journal of International and Comparative Law* (2020) 28 (2). Forthcoming.

1 Osita Eze, *Human Rights in Africa, Some Selected Problems* (Nigeria Institute of International Affairs 1984) 10.

2 For examples of rights protected in the pre-colonial era in Nigeria, see Jacob Abiodun Dada, 'Human Rights Protection in Nigeria: The Past, the Present and Goals for Role Actors for the Future' (2013) 14 *Journal of Law Policy and Globalisation* 1, 2–3.

3 Native Law Ordinance (Nigeria), cap 211 of 1948, laws of Nigeria, s. 19.

4 See Section 32, 1963; 42, 1979; and 46, 1999 Constitutions of Nigeria.

Commission was established in 1995 and today enjoys an 'A' status.[5] However, from 1966 to 1999, eight military coups destabilised Nigeria and negatively impacted on human rights protection in the country.[6] There has since been a return to civilian rule with some relative gains in the promotion and protection of human rights. However, extrajudicial killings, impunity by security forces and prolonged pretrial detention have remained a human rights challenge.[7] These have become more challenging due to the terrorism activities of *Boko Haram* and the antiterrorism efforts of the government in striking a balance with respect for human rights. Many of these human rights issues have featured prominently in the engagement of Nigeria with the UPR.

Nigeria was one of the 47 members of the HRC for the period 2009–2012 and 2014–2017. It undertook its UPR I in 2009 (when it was a member of the HRC), UPR II in 2013 and UPR III in 2018 (when it was not a member). This chapter provides one of the first comprehensive empirical analysis of Nigeria's engagement with the UPR mechanisms during the first three cycles of the review. To evaluate the 'effectiveness' of Nigeria's engagement with the UPR, this chapter employs an approach which evaluates 'effectiveness' in terms of the level of state commitment to the UPR process, participation during the review sessions and the aggregate percentage of implemented UPR recommendations. The benefit of this approach is that it provides important indicators to a state's level of engagement and enables a comprehensive assessment of that engagement by examining state engagement with the key stages of the UPR process. Also, this chapter considers the potential for acculturation and the impact of conflicts and terrorism on Nigeria's engagement with the UPR.

Commitment to the national consultation process and the quality of Nigeria's UPR delegation

Nigeria's UPR national consultation process

According to HRC Resolution 5/1,[8] states are expected to undertake broad consultation with all stakeholders in the preparation of their national report. This is important because the approach a state takes to the national consultation process

5 It was established by the National Human Rights Commission (Amendment) Act, 1995. In 2010, it was amended by the National Human Rights Commission Act, 2010, to enable it to reattain 'A' Status in accordance with the Paris Principles.

6 Jacob Abiodun Dada, above n 2, 1, 5–6; D O Aihe, 'Fundamental Human Rights and the Military Regime in Nigeria: What Did the Courts Say?' (1971) 15(2) *Journal of African Law* 213.

7 See Nigeria National Human Rights Commission, *The State of Human Rights in Nigeria: 2009–2010* (National Human Rights Commission 2010) 3–40.

8 *Institution Building of the United Nations Human Rights Council, HRC Res 5/1, UN HRC OR, 5th sess, Annex [IB], UN Doc A/HRC/RES/5/1, Annex (18 June 2007) ('Resolution 5/1')* para 15(a).

impacts on its final report and is an indicator of its commitment to the UPR process. Undertaking a broad consultation with all stakeholders will enable the state to have a better understanding of the underlying human rights issues within its jurisdiction.[9] The nature of consultation undertaken by a state in the production of its UPR report is often detailed in the introductory paragraphs of its final report. While there is no requirement on what will constitute 'broad consultation', Gujadhur and Limon have identified a number of characteristics that will form good practice, including the creation of a permanent national coordination and reporting structure for the UPR/international human rights mechanisms; proactive engagement of the executive and legislative branches of government; proactively seek input from the NGOs and CSOs; undertake outreach activities at the national, regional and local levels; and utilise nationwide media campaigns.[10]

In preparation for its UPR I, Nigeria organised a National Consultative Forum (NCF) on 3 and 4 November 2008. This brought together stakeholders from state ministries, human rights NGOs, professional bodies, the NHRC and faith-based organisations.[11] This was organised with the assistance of the NHRC. Chaired by the Director of the Ministry of Foreign Affairs, the two-day workshop produced a draft report to be submitted by the state. The strong support expressed by the government of Nigeria to this consultative process was demonstrated by the participation of the Foreign Minister during the two-day NCF. The inclusion of all human rights issues during the forum's interactive sessions, including sexual orientation,[12] the death penalty and 'traditional practices' like FGM, the rights of widows and child marriage, was an indication of the government's conscientious engagement with the process. Perhaps the fact that Nigeria was a member of the HRC and the Nigerian ambassador, Martin Ihoeghian Uhomoibhi,[13] was at the

9 This is an important indicator of a state's effective engagement because the influence of other stakeholders will help provide (i) a real and comprehensive picture of the actual human rights situation in the country, (ii) the efforts made by the state to progressively improve it and iii) that the proposed recommendations to improve the situation are important, relevant and substantial. See Lisbeth Arne Nordager Thonbo et al., *Universal Periodic Review First Cycle: Reporting Methodologies from the Position of the State, Civil Society and National Human Rights Institutions* (Danish Institute for Human Rights 2011).

10 Subhas Gujadhur and Marc Limon, *Towards the Third Cycle of the UPR: Stick or Twist? Lessons Learnt from the First Ten Years of the Universal Periodic Review* (Universal Rights Group 2016) 22.

11 Working Group on the Universal Periodic Review, *National Report Submitted in Accordance with Paragraph 15 (a) of the Annex to Human Rights Council Resolution 5/1—Nigeria*, 4th sess, UN Doc A/HRC/WG.6/NGA/1 (5 January 2009) ('*HRC UPR I State Report-Nigeria*') para 2.

12 LGBTS issues are rarely spoken of in public gatherings and mostly considered a taboo within Nigeria. Persons found guilty of entering same-sex marriage are sentenced to 14 years imprisonment and persons found to directly or indirectly making show of same-sex relationships in Nigeria are sentenced to ten years imprisonment. See Same Sex Marriage Prohibition Act 2013, section 5 (1) and (2).

13 H E Mr Martin Ihoeghian Uhomoibhi was President of the Human Rights Council in its third session, 2008–2009.

relevant time for UPR I serving as the president of the HRC was an added incentive for Nigeria to actively engage in the pre-review process.

While the two-day workshop was a positive initiative of the government and an indicator of effective engagement at the pre-review stage, it is too small a time period to comprehensively engage with stakeholders such as CSOs and government ministerial departments. More so, judicial personnel were not involved or given any prominent role during the consultation process, limiting the government's ability to address legal and law reform questions which may have arisen from discussions on sensitive subjects. A preferable approach adopted by other states is to set up a national committee with key representatives from across the three branches of government, NGOs/CSOs and the NHRC.[14]

In preparation for UPR II, Nigeria made improvements to the quality of its consultation process and the time frame for the consultation. It set up an Inclusive National Committee on the UPR.[15] The Inclusive National Committee on the UPR comprised eight representatives from various federal ministries and two representatives from NGOs/CSOs.[16] Its primary task was to undertake a national UPR consultation process, prepare the state report and review the UPR outcome on Nigeria. This was chaired by the Solicitor-General of the Federation who by delegation exercises the powers and duties of the Attorney General of the Federation and Minister of Justice. Further, the period of consultation and validation of the UPR state report was extended to 12 months and ran from July 2012 through June 2013, marking a significant improvement from the previous consultation time frame.[17] A similar approach was adopted by the government during UPR III.

Nigeria, therefore, is an example of good practice in relation to the pre-review national consultation process. None of the ten NGO reports on Nigeria during UPR I and the 34 NGO submissions during UPR II questioned the consultative process undertaken by Nigeria during any of its UPR pre-review processes. When the United Kingdom requested information on the consultative process undertaken by Nigeria during UPR I,[18] Nigeria's UPR delegation elaborated on

14 See Working Group on the Universal Periodic Review, *National Report Submitted in Accordance with Paragraph 15 (a) of the Annex to Human Rights Council Resolution 5/1—Kenya*, 21st sess, UN Doc A/HRC/WG.6/21/KEN/1 (6 November 2014) ('*HRC UPR II State Report—Kenya*') paras 1, 2.

15 Working Group on the Universal Periodic Review, *National Report Submitted in Accordance with Paragraph 15 (a) of the Annex to Human Rights Council Resolution 5/1—Nigeria*, 17th sess, UN Doc A/HRC/WG.6/NGA/1 (30 July 2013) ('*HRC UPR II State Report—*Nigeria') para 4.

16 The Inclusive National Committee on the UPR is sometimes referred to as the Inter-ministerial Committee on the UPR Reporting Process, see Federal Ministry of Justice (Nigeria), *Members of Inter-Ministerial Committee on the UN Universal Periodic Review (UPR) Reporting Process* (International and Comparative Law Department 2016).

17 Ibid.

18 OHCHR, 'Questions Submitted in Advance—Nigeria' available at <https://bit.ly/2kc0OpC> accessed 04/09/2019.

the process during UPR I interactive dialogue.[19] The response provided could explain why no state raised an issue on the consultative process during UPR II and III. Algeria during UPR I positively commented on Nigeria's consultative process and recommended that Nigeria consider making the NCF an annual event as a tool to promote dialogue and comprehension in the field of human rights.[20]

This level of engagement with the UPR is in sharp contrast with its engagement with the UN treaty bodies. The pre-review UPR process culminates in the submission of the national report. While Nigeria has submitted all three UPR reports on time, it presently (as of June 2019) has an appalling record of UN treaty body reporting, being the UN member state with the highest number of overdue UN human rights treaty body reports. Nigeria has ten pending reports, three of which are more than five years overdue and four of which are more than ten years overdue.[21] During UPR III, Togo recommended that Nigeria '[i]ntensify its efforts to develop and submit periodic reports to the various treaty bodies. . . .'[22] Also, while the state has been able to satisfy the reporting guidelines under the UPR, it fails to comply with new UN treaty bodies' reporting guidelines and has an underdeveloped primary data collection mechanism.[23]

On the part of NGOs, there was lack of strong mobilisation during UPR I and little effort was made by them to engage the government and raise awareness on the UPR process. In April 2008, Nigeria's CSO Coalition on the UPR was established. However, its membership was composed of only seven organisations,[24] and its most significant activity was the submission of its UPR report which did not comprehensively address the various human rights issues in Nigeria.[25] This is largely because NGOs focusing on issues such as socio-economic rights and the death penalty were not represented in the coalition. It would appear the Coalition disintegrated after UPR I as it neither followed-up on the implementation of Nigeria's UPR I recommendations nor submitted any UPR II report for Nigeria.

19 *HRC UPR I Report—Nigeria,* UN Doc A/HRC/11/26 para 7.

20 Ibid para 27. Other states who appreciated the consultative process included Turkey, Iran, Republic of Korea and Ireland. See ibid paras 60, 47, 89, 83 respectively.

21 See OHCHR, 'Status of Late and Non-reporting by State Parties' available at <https://bit.ly/2kH91T2> accessed 04/09/2019.

22 DRC, New Zealand and Iraq made similar recommendations. See UN Human Rights Council, 'Report of the Working Group on the Universal Periodic Review—Nigeria' 40th sess, UN Doc A/HRC/40/7 (26 December 2018) ('*HRC UPR III Report—Nigeria*') para 148.15–148.18.

23 National Human Rights Commission of Nigeria, *National Human Rights Commission at 20: The Journey So Far, 1995–2015* (NHRC 2015) 46.

24 Constitutional Rights Project (CRP), Access to Justice, Center for Law Enforcement Education in Nigeria (CLEEN), Civil Liberties Organization (CLO), Baobab for Women's Rights, Institute for Human Rights and Humanitarian Law and the Nigerian Bar Association.

25 The report did not address issues on socio-economic rights, the death penalty, sexual orientation and poverty. See Nigeria's Civil Society Coalition on the UPR, 'Universal Periodic Review of Nigeria: A Nigeria Civil Society Coalition Report' (2008) available at <https://bit.ly/2kGjTAB> accessed 05/09/2019.

However, a new national NGO Coalition for the UPR emerged during Nigeria's UPR II alongside other regional and thematic NGO coalitions for Nigeria's UPR. The Coalition of Nigerian Human rights CSOs on UPR (Nigerianhrcsos-UPR) was established after Nigeria's UPR I in 2009 with a goal of monitoring the implementation of the recommendations accepted by Nigeria during UPR I. Nigerianhrcsos-UPR in 2013 released a press statement reminding the government on the implementation of the 32 recommendations accepted during UPR I. In August 2014, the Coalition organised a two-day conference on the national action plan (NAP) and the UPR aimed at strengthening the capacity of human rights advocates to participate in the UPR process and to create awareness about the UPR II recommendations accepted by Nigeria.[26]

While Nigerianhrcsos-UPR has engaged in more activities than its predecessor, the coalition during UPR II lacked a broad and representative mandate. Nigerianhrcsos-UPR had 13 coalition members,[27] eight of whom are from the south-western part of Nigeria and representing very few human rights thematic issues. Such a Coalition could not be considered as broad and representative when considered against the background that Nigeria has more than 1000 active human rights NGOs/CSOs involved in human rights activities. There was observable gain in membership made during UPR III. The UPR III report by Nigerianhrcsos-UPR was authored by 53 members from six geographical regions in Nigeria.[28] Notwithstanding, there was a significant increase in the number of joint submissions from two during UPR I, 14 during UPR II and 18 during UPR III. In addition, two regional coalitions—The Niger Delta UPR Coalition and the UPR Coalition of Southeast Nigeria—submitted reports which addressed human rights issues specific to the relevant parts of Nigeria.[29] There was one other national NGO UPR coalition called 'Civil Society Coalition on Minority Protection, Indigenous Peoples Issues and Children's Rights' (CS-COMIC) which focused on addressing human rights issues affecting minority communities, Indigenous peoples and children.[30] However, each of these regional and

26 Partnership for Justice, '2 Day Zonal Conference (South West) On the National Action Plan and the Universal Periodic Review: 7th–8th August 2014 at the Chesterfield Hotel' (2014) available at <https://bit.ly/2m6gNpM> accessed 05/09/2019.

27 A broad and representative NGO Coalition on the UPR can enhance a state's engagement with the state and influence the outcome of its review.

28 The Coalition on Nigerian Human Rights CSOS on the UPR, *Report on the Human Rights Situation in Nigeria Submitted to the Office of the UN Human Rights Council in Geneva During the 31st Session of the UPR Working Group* (Nigerianhrcsos-UPR 2018) 16.

29 The Niger Delta UPR Coalition, 'Assessment of Nigeria's Implementation Of Previous Review' (2013) available at <https://bit.ly/2m8xAbL> accessed 05/09/2019; UPR Coalition Southeast Nigeria, 'Universal Periodic Review of Nigeria' (2013) available at <https://bit.ly/2ke22kd> accessed 05/09/2019.

30 Civil Society Coalition on Minority Protection, Indigenous Peoples Issues and Children's Rights (CS-COMIC), 'Submission by Civil Society Coalition on Minority Protection, Indigenous Peoples Issues And Children's Rights' (2013) available at <https://bit.ly/2kH9p3W> accessed 05/09/2019.

thematic coalitions only had between three to nine member organisations as part of the coalition. The lack of a broad and representative membership in these NGO coalitions for the UPR limits their ability to effectively engage the government in its review processes. A broad and representative NGO Coalition for the UPR can empower NGOs and enhance their credibility and capacity to influence state engagement with the UPR.

The above analysis therefore indicates that the quality of Nigeria's pre-review consultation process has improved across the three cycles of the UPR, especially in terms of extending the time allocated for the consultation, assigning a legal/judicial personnel to head the consultation and allowing for the inclusion of culturally sensitive human rights issues in the government's deliberation with UPR stakeholders. A broad and representative NGO coalition for the UPR can contribute to achieving a broad and inclusive national consultation process.

The quality of Nigeria's UPR delegation

Another indicator of effective engagement with the UPR is the level of state representation. A high level of participation of state delegates will reaffirm the seriousness with which a state regards the process and provide an opportunity for effective dialogue. It is vital that state delegates are not only present but are able to respond to questions directed to them during the examination of the state report. The quality of the delegates is essential. The African Commission has faced serious problems on this issue. Many African states have sent their reports to the Commission but failed to send representatives during the report examination. For example, the state report of Nigeria was not examined during the 12th session of the African Commission because the state failed to send delegates.[31] In 2017, Nigeria neither submitted the required state report nor sent any government delegation to participate in its review by the UN Committee on Migrant workers.[32]

31 Takele Soboka Bulto, 'Africa's Engagement with the Universal Periodic Review: Commitment or Capitulation' in Hilary Charlesworth and Emma Larking (eds), *Human Rights and the Universal Periodic Review: Rituals and Ritualism* (Cambridge University Press 2015) 243; A similar situation caused the Commission to postpone the examination of the reports of Ghana and Namibia in 2000, during the twenty-seventh and twenty-eighth sessions of the Commission respectively. See Malcolm Evans, Tokunbo Ige, and Rachel Murray, 'The Reporting Mechanism of the African Charter on Human and Peoples' Rights' in Malcolm Evans and Rachel Murray (eds), *The African Charter on Human and Peoples' Rights: The System in Practice 1986–2000* (Cambridge University Press 2002) 42; Another example is Seychelles, see Frans Viljoen, *International Human Rights Law in Africa* (Oxford University Press 2007) 363. A similar attitude on state representativeness is expressed towards the UN treaty bodies, see Andrew Clapham, 'UN Human Rights Reporting Procedure: An NGO Perspective' in Philip Alston and James Crawford (eds), *The Future of Human Rights Monitoring* (Cambridge University Press 2000) 189.

32 UN Human Rights Council, *Compilation on Nigeria: Report of the Office of the United Nations High Commissioner for Human Rights*, UN Doc A/HRC/WG.6/31/NGA/2 (27 August 2018) 1–2.

In contrast, Nigeria has sent a high-level delegation for the UPR during the three cycles. Its delegations in both UPR I and II were represented at the ministerial level and composed of parliamentary representatives, judicial and academic personnel. UPR I delegation for Nigeria was headed by the Minister of Foreign Affairs and composed of 26 members, among which included the Minister of Justice and members of the National Assembly. However, Sweeny and Saito are critical of such a delegation headed by the foreign ministries rather than the ministries of justice or human rights.[33] They argue that the former indicates that the state views the review 'as a foreign affairs rather than a national process for the examination and improvement of human rights protection and promotion'.[34] This argument is valid given that the state delegation should constitute persons empowered to alter the political behaviour of the represented state.

An examination of Nigeria's UPR II delegation indicates that the Nigerian government took the process seriously and did not simply consider the review as a foreign affairs exercise. The delegation was headed by the Attorney General of the Federation and Minister of Justice and composed of 34 representatives. These included the Minister of State for Foreign Affairs, representatives of other ministries, members of parliament and a representative from academia. The inclusion of a representative from academia is significant because it can increase the expert knowledge brought into the review and therefore enhance the quality of the discussions and the outcome of the review. This comprehensive representation is not surprising given that Nigeria is a large and powerful state within the African region and has a permanent mission to the UN in Geneva. However, the contrast in its engagement with the African Commission shows the government's particular preference for the UPR, which is arguably as a result of the inclusive, cooperative and collaborative framework of the UPR. While the same level of representation was maintained during UPR III, the delegation was in this instance represented by the Nigerian UN Ambassador rather than the Attorney General.

The representation of NGOs, by their oral submissions during the plenary session of the HRC, further engaged the government of Nigeria with the UPR. Generally, many states are not self-critical of the negative aspects of their human rights protection. Despite the limitations to NGO participation in the UPR,[35] NGO submissions and intervention during the plenary sessions help to complement the state reports by identifying areas overlooked. During UPR I, ten NGOs submitted written reports in relation to Nigeria and this more than tripled to 34 during

33 Gareth Sweeny and Yuri Saito, 'An NGO Assessment of the New Mechanism of the UN Human Rights Council' (2009) 2 *Human Rights Law Review* 203, 209.

34 Ibid; Dominguez Redondo, 'The Universal Periodic Review of the UN Human Rights Council: An Assessment of the First Session' (2008) 7(3) *Chinese Journal of International Law* 731.

35 NGOs cannot question states during the interactive dialogue and often do not make a very significant contribution to the final state UPR report.

UPR II and 36 during UPR III. Eight NGOs made oral submissions during Nigeria's UPR I plenary session, nine during UPR II and ten during UPR III. There is a general increase in the number of NGO submissions during UPR II and III arguably as a result of increased knowledge about the UPR process among NGOs. The review of other African states such as South Africa and Kenya has witnessed an increase in the number of NGO written submissions as well.

However, there were few domestic NGO reports in the collection of reports submitted by NGOs in relation to Nigeria. A majority of the submissions were made by international NGOs. Only three out of ten submissions during UPR I were from domestic NGOs.[36] Many African countries question the legitimacy of international NGOs and the credibility of the information issued by these NGOs that are not from their respective countries or regions. Nigeria, for example, characterised the allegations in some international NGO's reports as 'preposterous', 'patently false' and 'unhelpful to the UPR process'.[37] However, the number of domestic NGO submissions has increased over UPR II and III. While many domestic NGOs may be able to submit reports, very few are able to participate in the plenary sessions in Geneva. This is explained by the difficult process of obtaining consultative status; the high financial costs and the unavailability of staff to participate in the sessions in Geneva; little familiarity with the HRC's workings and procedure; and the lack of access to information on the review process. None of the domestic NGOs that submitted a written report made oral submissions at Nigeria's UPR I, II and III, further underscoring the limitations to their participation.

Given these challenges, domestic NGOs have tried to be innovative by forming coalitions and making joint submissions.[38] In this way, they can coordinate strategies and develop joint initiatives which will strengthen individual actions, maximise resources and share UPR experiences at home and in Geneva. The formation of NGO coalitions for the UPR can also contribute to enhance their credibility and capacity to engage the state. Nevertheless, the quality of Nigeria's UPR delegation is indicative of the government's commitment to the UPR process, which as highlighted earlier is in contrast with its level of engagement with both the African Commission and the UN human rights treaty bodies.

36 The situation however improved during UPR II with domestic NGO submissions representing more than half of the total NGO submissions. This changed may probably be explained by the fact that domestic NGOs are increasingly gaining knowledge of how the UPR mechanism operate.

37 *HRC UPR I Report—Nigeria,* UN Doc A/HRC/11/26 para 8; Similarly, Morocco has condemned Amnesty International's report as 'biased and subjective' by including Morocco among countries targeted by Amnesty's anti-torture campaign. See Morocco World News, 'Morocco Condemns Biased, Subjective Amnesty International Report' (19 May 2015) available at <https://bit.ly/1e5iYQY> accessed 05/09/2019; It is important to be wary of NGOs that are in reality 'government mouth pieces' or those that prioritise the agenda of their donors which may not necessarily be the priority of the people they claim to serve.

38 There was an increase in the number of joint submissions by civil society from two during UPR I to 13 during UPR II.

Nigeria as a reviewer

An examination of Nigeria's engagement with the UPR as a reviewer indicates that while the government has engaged in the review of various groups of states, it has exercised stronger solidarity with the review of African states. During UPR I, Nigeria participated in all 12 sessions of the UPR Working Group and made a total of 108 recommendations to 60 states. Fifty-one of these total recommendations were made to 26 African states, and 86% of these recommendations were accepted. During UPR II, Nigeria participated in 11 of the 14 UPR sessions and made a total of 182 recommendations to 70 states. Fifty-two of its 55 UPR II recommendations to African states were accepted. Similar level of engagement was evident mid-way UPR III (May 2017–June 2019) where Nigeria made 103 recommendations to 50 states. During UPR I, 86% of the 51 recommendations by Nigeria to African states were accepted compared to 53% of the recommendations accepted by states in WEOG. Similarly, during UPR II, 94% of the total 55 recommendations made by Nigeria to its African peers were accepted, compared to 60% of the total 23 recommendations Nigeria made to WEOG states. During UPR I, Nigeria made more recommendations to African states (47%) than to Asian (19%), WEOG (14%) and EEG (5%) combined. Nigeria made more recommendations to African states during UPR II and III than to any other group of states (see Figures 4.2 and 4.3). This echoes the theme of regionalism.

In addition, Nigeria adopted a cultural relativist approach in its review of African states, an attitude embraced by many African states.[39] While most of the Western states in their review of African states focused on the rights of sexual minorities,[40] none of the 54 African states (with the exception of Madagascar during UPR II) made any recommendation on sexual orientation. Figures 4.1, 4.2 and 4.3 provide an overview of Nigeria's engagement with both cycles of the UPR as a reviewer.

Figures 4.1, 4.2 and 4.3 indicate that Nigeria engaged as a reviewer during the first three cycles of the UPR and made several recommendations to its peers. However, the extent of its engagement as a reviewer is not determined solely by the quantity of recommendations but also by the extent of its participation, the specificity and the relevance of such recommendations.

The extent of Nigeria's participation as a reviewer

Some states either do not attend the review sessions of their peers or are very selective in reviewing their peers. This raises questions on the universality of the UPR process and allows states to rely on their regional groupings to shield themselves

39 This is in relation to their receptiveness to recommendations on sexual orientation. Except for Madagascar, no Africa state made a recommendation on sexual orientation to its regional peer during both cycles of the UPR.

40 One reason why so many Western states focused on this could be because of the low level of tolerance towards sexual minorities in this region. See Neville Hoad, *African Intimacies: Race, Homosexuality, and Globalization* (University of Minnesota Press 2007); See recent example in Nigeria, Same Sex Marriage Prohibition Act 2013, section 5 (1) and (2).

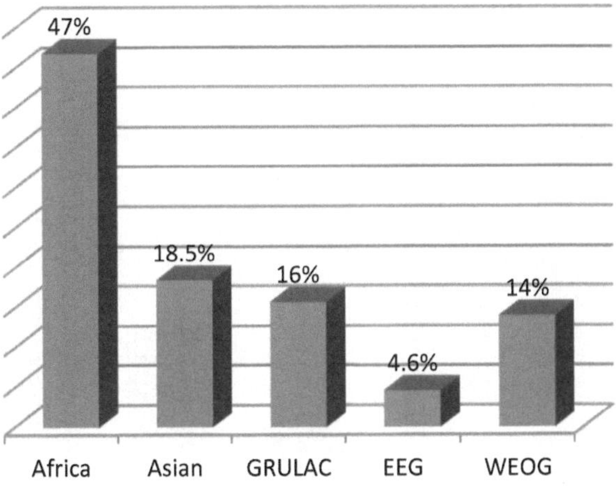

Figure 4.1 UPR I recommendations by Nigeria

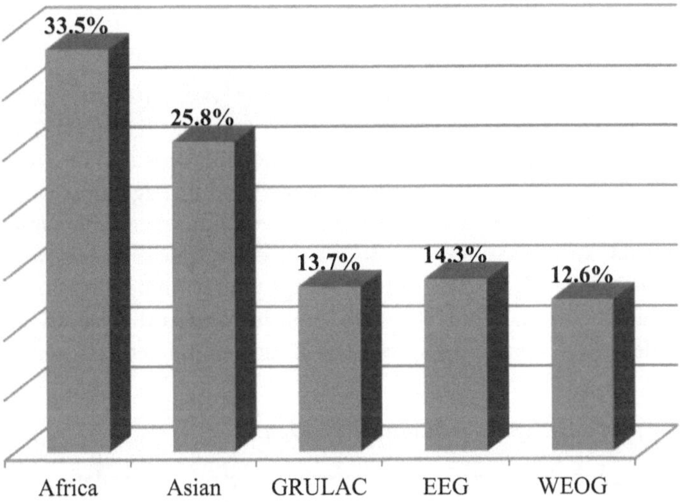

Figure 4.2 UPR II recommendations by Nigeria

from proper scrutiny, where such a review is dominated exclusively by states from the same region. Kenya is an example of a state that did not participate as a reviewer during UPR I. As indicated in Figures 4.1, 4.2 and 4.3, Nigeria actively engaged within and outside the African regional group. The majority of UPR recommendations across the three cycles of the UPR (about 47%, 34% and 38% respectively) by Nigeria were made to its African regional peers. Nevertheless, it made recommendations across GRULAC, EEG and WEOG regional groups.

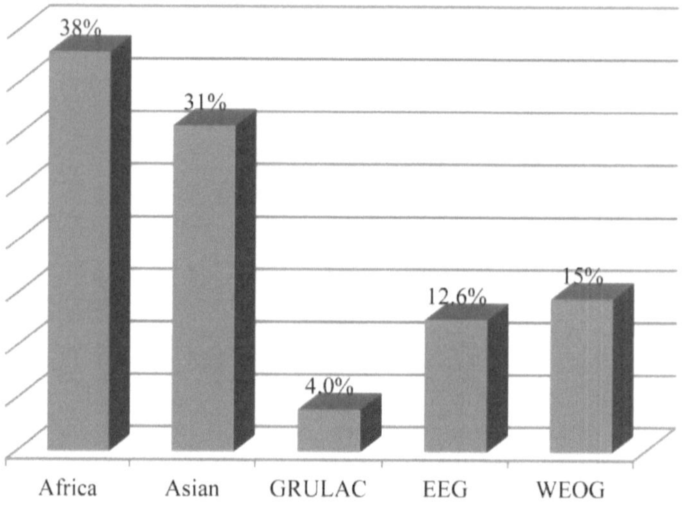

Figure 4.3 UPR III recommendations by Nigeria

While Nigeria may be actively engaging as a reviewer, it has exhibited a double standard in its engagement with other states. For example, during UPR I it recommended that Argentina '[r]atify the Second Optional Protocol to the International Covenant on Civil and Political Rights already signed by Argentina, aiming at the abolition of the death penalty'.[41] Argentina accepted this recommendation. However, when the same recommendation was made by Brazil and Montenegro to Nigeria during UPR II, Nigeria did not accept the recommendation.[42] Notwithstanding this double standard, the state implicitly asserts the validity, legitimacy and relevance of the human rights invoked in each recommendation it makes.

Specificity and relevance of recommendations

Abebe has argued that African states largely make recommendations which are at times too general (R4) to be implemented.[43] However, they have in some

41 UN Human Rights Council, 'Report of the Working Group on the Universal Periodic Review—Argentina' 8th sess, UN Doc A/HRC/8/34 (13 May 2008) ('*HRC UPR I Report—Argentina*') para 64.21.

42 *HRC UPR I Report—Nigeria*, UN Doc A/HRC/11/26 para 137.5 read alongside with UN Human Rights Council, 'Report of the Human Rights Council on Its Twenty-fifth Session' 25th sess, UN Doc A/HRC/25/2 (27 May 2014) ('*Report of the HRC on its 25th Session*') paras 466–467.

43 Allehone M Abebe, 'Of Shaming and Bargaining: African States and the Universal Periodic Review of the United Nations Human Rights Council' (2009) *Human Rights Law Review* 1, 16. The pacific approach adopted by most African states to the UPR largely prompts them to make general recommendations.

cases not hesitated to make specific recommendations (R5), even to their African peers. Also, the fact that states make general recommendations does not necessarily imply that such recommendations are not valuable, and they may sometimes translate into specific actions at the point of implementation. Figures 4.4, 4.5 and 4.6 below provide an analysis of the various categories of recommendations to determine the quality of recommendations Nigeria engaged its peers with. Although these recommendations were largely 'friendly recommendations', they cut across the five categories of recommendations, from those requiring minimal actions (R1) to the more specific ones (R5).

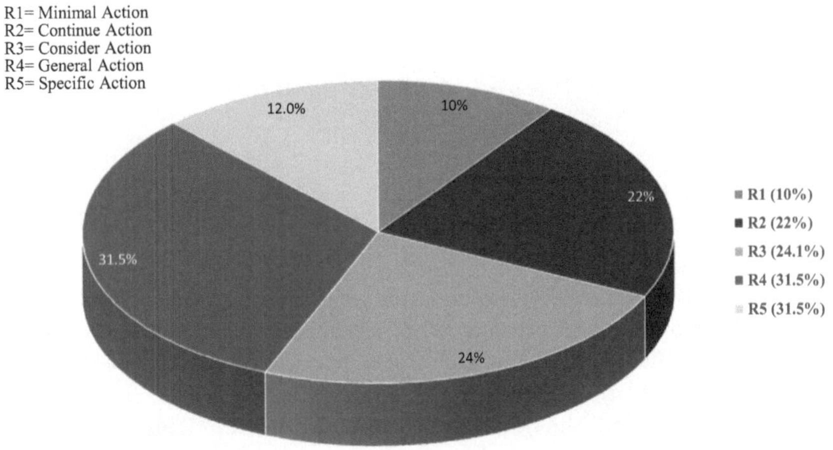

Figure 4.4 UPR I recommendations made by Nigeria in categories

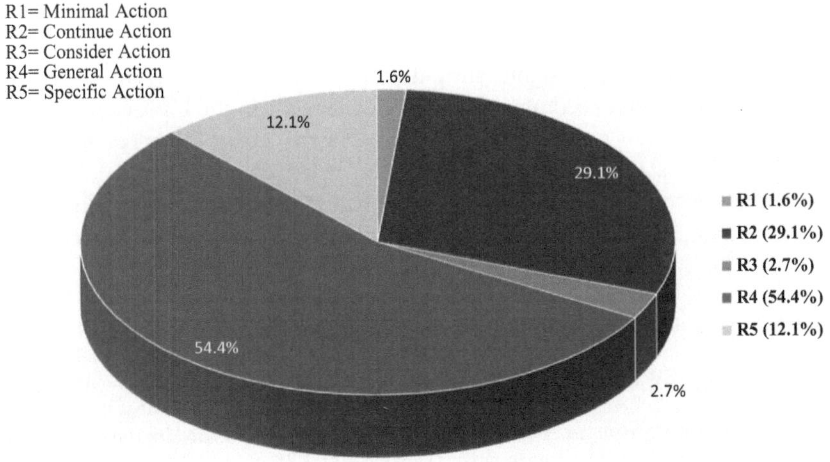

Figure 4.5 UPR II recommendations made by Nigeria in categories

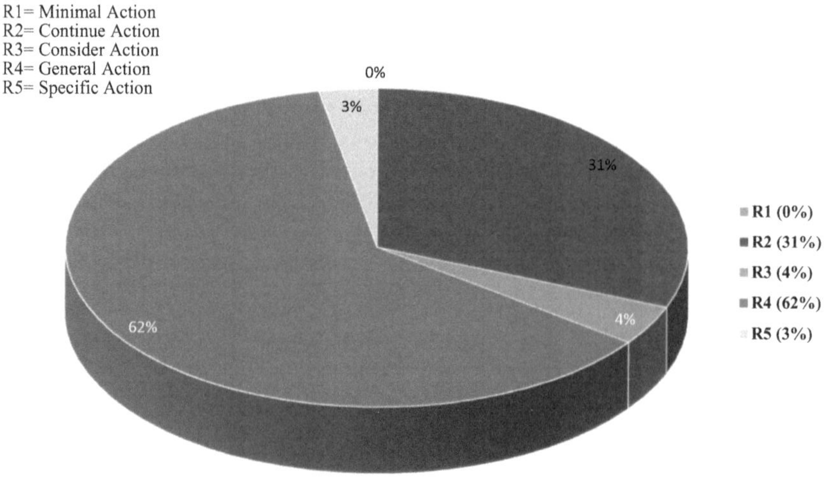

Figure 4.6 UPR III recommendations made by Nigeria in categories

As indicated in Figures 4.4, 4.5 and 4.6, Nigeria engaged its peers with various categories of recommendations. While it made more general (R4) than specific (R5) recommendations, this does not necessarily undermine the relevance of such recommendations. For example, Nigeria made a general recommendation (R4) that Burundi should reform the judicial system.[44] This is particularly relevant given that reports from Amnesty International and other NGO studies indicate that Burundi's judiciary is weak, under-resourced and suffers from political interference and allegations of corruption.[45] Nevertheless, the recommendation would have been more meaningful if it identified specific actions Burundi could take to reform their judicial system.

Nigeria equally engaged its peers with specific recommendations (R5) across the three cycles of the review. However, the percentage of specific recommendations by Nigeria dropped significantly during UPR III from 12% to 3%). Also, majority of the specific recommendations Nigeria made in the UPR were directed towards non-African states. During UPR I, Nigeria made more recommendations to African states (about 47% of the total 108 recommendations), but only one of these recommendations was a specific recommendation (representing only 2% of the total 51 recommendations to African states). Comparatively, about 24%

44 UN Human Rights Council, 'Report of the Working Group on the Universal Periodic Review—Burundi' 10th sess, UN Doc A/HRC/10/71 (8 January 2009) para 20.

45 Human Rights Watch, 'World Report 2014: Burundi' (2014) 1 available at <https://bit.ly/2lNrc9X> accessed 05/09/2019; Tracy Dexter and Philippe Ntahombaye, *The Role of Informal Justice Systems in Fostering the Rule of Law in Post-Conflict Situations the Case of Burundi* (The Centre for Humanitarian Dialogue 2005) 28.

of the total recommendations made by Nigeria to states within GRULAC during UPR I were specific recommendations. Out of a total of 112 recommendations made by Nigeria to African states during UPR I and II, only 7% were specific recommendations. In contrast, 24% of the 38 recommendations made to states within the WEOG in the first two cycles of the UPR were specific recommendations. This indicates that Nigeria adopts a softer approach in addressing human rights issues within its regional group and a tougher approach outside the African Group. Having said this, based on Abebe's observation, this tendency may not only exist within the African Group as 'groups never issue statements that are critical of one of their own', including WEOG.[46]

Nigeria as a state under review

Nigeria was reviewed by the UPR Working Group (WG) in February 2009 (UPR I), October 2013 (UPR II) and November 2018 (UPR III). As a result of its membership of the HRC, the Nigerian government entered voluntary pledges and commitments which are included as part of the assessment basis for its review. Fifty-two states made recommendations to Nigeria during UPR I, 13 of which were African states. Out of a total of 32 recommendations,[47] 30 were accepted by the government of Nigeria. It accepted all the recommendations from African states. During UPR II, states made a total of 219 recommendations to Nigeria, of which it accepted 84%. In the third cycle of the review, Nigeria received 290 recommendations, of which it accepted 79%. The high acceptance level evident in all three UPR cycles indicates an active engagement with the recommendations. Some states like Botswana, China and South Sudan did not accept more than 50% of recommendations made to them during UPR I. South Sudan in particular did not accept more than 85% of the recommendations made to it during UPR I.[48] Figures 4.7, 4.8 and 4.9 provide an analysis of Nigeria's engagement as a state under review. It depicts its review by African states compared to other groups of states.[49]

46 Allehone M Abebe, above n 43, 19.

47 These recommendations were gleaned from the WG reports. See UN Human Rights Council, *Report of the Working Group on the Universal Periodic Review—Nigeria*, 11th sess, Agenda Item 6, UN Doc A/HRC/11/26 (5 October 2009) ('HRC UPR I Report—Nigeria') paras 18–24; several of these recommendations include more than one category of recommendation covering one or more issue(s). In the analysis in Figure 4.5, these recommendations were separated to identify each in its own category and to easily identify implementation level. This totalled 115 recommendations. This total corresponds with that stated by UPR info. See UPR Info <http://s.upr-info.org/1G1cXQV> accessed 05/09/2019.

48 UN Human Rights Council, *Report of the Working Group on the Universal Periodic Review—Sudan: Addendum- Views on Conclusions and/or Recommendations, Voluntary Commitments and Replies Presented by the State Under Review*, 18th sess, UN Doc A/HRC/18/16/Add.1 (16 September 2011) paras 1–35; During UPR II, states like Republic of Korea and Australia only accepted about 51% and 52% of recommendations respectively.

49 There are five regional groups in the HRC: Group of African States; Group of Asian States; Group of Eastern European States (EEG); Group of Latin American and Caribbean States (GRULAC); and Group of Western European and other States (WEOG). See Human

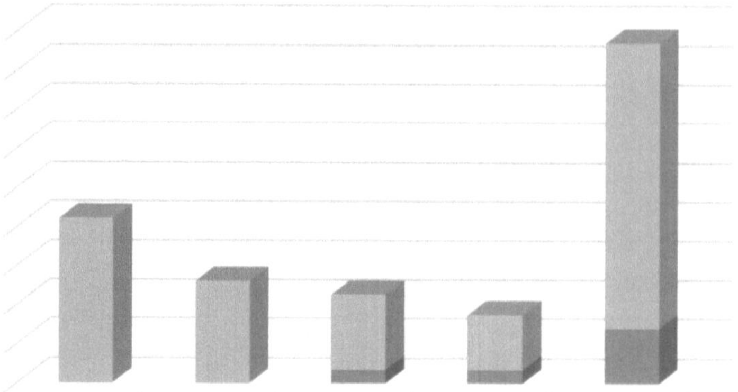

	Africa	Asia	EEG	GRULAC	WEOG
Accepted	21%	13%	10%	7%	37%
Rejected	0%	0%	2%	2%	7%

Figure 4.7 Nigeria UPR I percentage of recommendations accepted

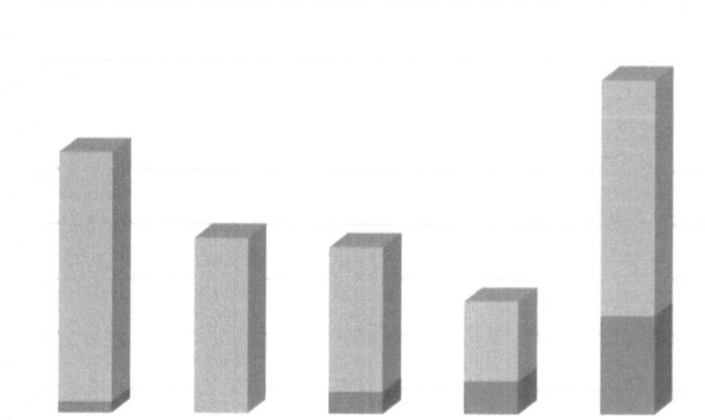

	Africa	**Asia**	**EEG**	**GRULAC**	**WEOG**
Accepted	**23%**	**16%**	**13%**	**7%**	**22%**
Rejected	**1%**	**0%**	**2%**	**3%**	**9%**

Figure 4.8 Nigeria UPR II percentage of recommendations accepted

Figures 4.7, 4.8 and 4.9 indicate that Nigeria engaged with recommendations within and outside its regional group. However, it maintained a stronger engagement within its African and Asia-Pacific regional groups. As seen in Figure 4.7, Nigeria accepted all the recommendations from African states during UPR I. This

Rights Council, *GA Res 60/251, UN GAOR, 60th sess, 72nd plen mtg, Agenda Items 46 and 120,* UN Doc A/Res/60/251 (3 April 2006) ('Resolution 60/251') para 7.

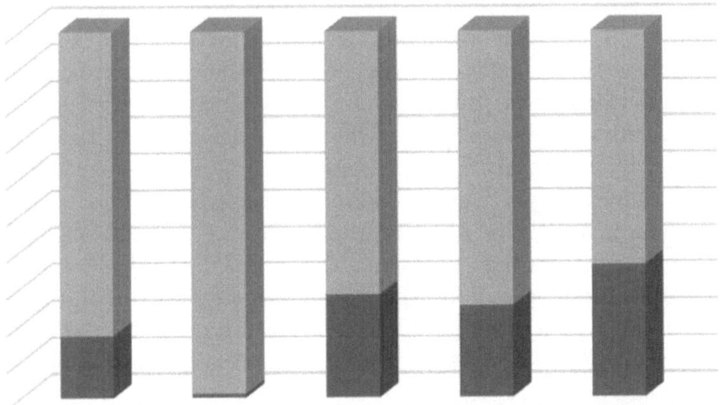

	Africa	Asia	EEG	GRULAC	WEOG
Accepted	83%	99%	72%	75%	64%
Rejected	17%	1%	28%	25%	36%

Figure 4.9 Nigeria UPR III percentage of recommendations accepted

constituted 21% of the total recommendations made to Nigeria during UPR I. Figures 4.8 and 4.9 show that during UPR II and III, Nigeria rejected fewer recommendations from the African (1% and 17% respectively) and Asian (0% and 1% respectively) regional groups compared to about 9% and 36% of the recommendations rejected from WEOG during the respective UPR cycles. This finding would indicate that Nigeria is more receptive of intra-African and Asia-Pacific recommendations and more likely to reject recommendations from Western states.

There was a remarkable increase in the total number of recommendations made to Nigeria across UPR I and II, from 32 during UPR I to 219 during UPR II. The increase in the number of recommendations made to Nigeria may reflect the general increase in the number of recommendations which was evident during UPR II.[50] However, there may be other particular factors which may explain the rise in the number of recommendations to Nigeria. These are the escalation of the conflict between the government and *Boko Haram* after UPR I,[51] the enactment of the Same Sex Marriage Prohibition Act in 2013 and the resumption of the death penalty in Nigeria.[52] Thirty-eight recommendations during UPR II were dedicated to addressing these three issues. The last two issues constituted the total 35 recommendations which were rejected by Nigeria during UPR II

50 Edward R McMahon, Kojo Busia, and Marta Ascherio, 'Comparing Peer Reviews: The Universal Periodic Review of the UN Human Rights Council and the African Peer Review Mechanism' (2013) 12 *African and Asian Studies* 266, 280–2.

51 Two bombings in the capital, Abuja in 2011 resulted in this escalation of violence. See Simeon H O Alozieuwa, 'Contending Theories on Nigeria's Security Challenge in the Era of Boko Haram Insurgency' (2012) 7(1) *Peace and Conflict Review* 1.

52 About 600 people in early 2015 were on death row; see Roger Hood and Carolyn Hoyle, *The Death Penalty: A Worldwide Perspective* (Oxford University Press 2015) 274.

and the two rejected during UPR I. Of the recommendations rejected by Nigeria during UPR III, 65% focused on the abolition of the death penalty and discrimination based on sexual orientation. During all three UPR cycles, no recommendation on sexual orientation and gender identity was made by an African state (except for Madagascar) and none of the recommendations made by non-African states on this issue was accepted by the Nigerian delegation. These recommendations were found by many African states to be 'hyper-sensitive in political, social and/or cultural terms'[53] and 'contravened deeply held beliefs or policy positions of governments'.[54] Five African states made recommendations relating to the abolition of the death penalty across the three UPR cycles.[55] While Nigeria did not accept recommendations which related to the abolition of the death penalty, it surprisingly made a similar recommendation to Argentina during UPR I.[56]

Figures 4.10, 4.11 and 4.12 examine the categories of recommendations and issues raised during Nigeria's UPR I, II and III.

As Figures 4.10, 4.11 and 4.12 indicate, Nigeria was receptive to both general (R4) and specific (R5) recommendations across UPR I, II and II. A majority of the recommendations accepted by Nigeria were general recommendations (R4),

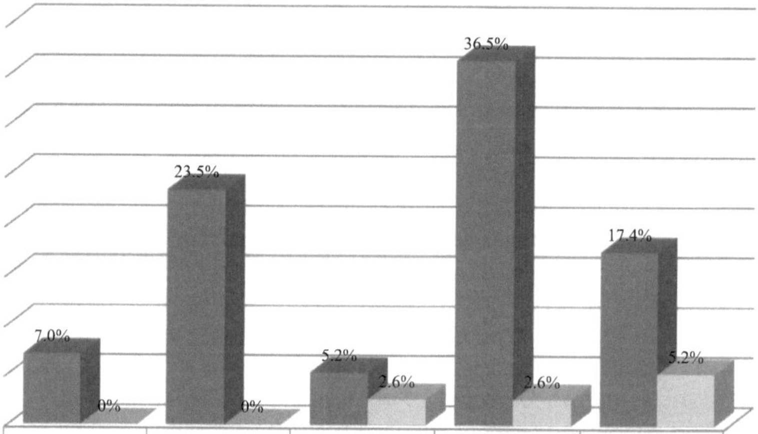

	R1	R2	R3	R4	R5
Accepted	7.0%	23.5%	5.2%	36.5%	17.4%
Rejected	0%	0%	2.6%	2.6%	5.2%

Figure 4.10 UPR I acceptance level by category

53 Edward McMahon, 'The Universal Periodic Review: A Work in Progress, An Evaluation of the First Cycle of the New UPR Mechanism of the United Nations Human Rights Council' (2012) *Friedrich Ebert Stiftung* 1, 18.

54 Ibid.

55 The recommendations were made by Togo, Benin, Cape Verde, Mozambique and Rwanda.

56 UN Human Rights Council, '*Report of the Working Group on the Universal Periodic Review—Argentina*' 8th sess, UN Doc A/HRC/8/34 (13 May 2008) para 64.21.

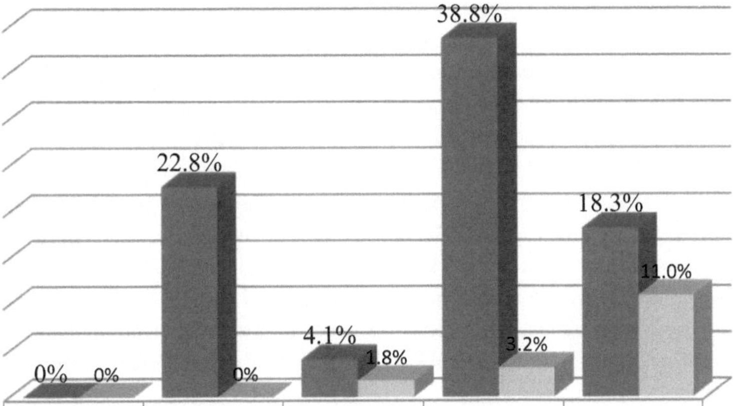

	R1	R2	R3	R4	R5
Accepted	0%	22.8%	4.1%	38.8%	18.3%
Rejected	0%	0%	1.8%	3.2%	11.0%

Figure 4.11 UPR 1I acceptance level by category

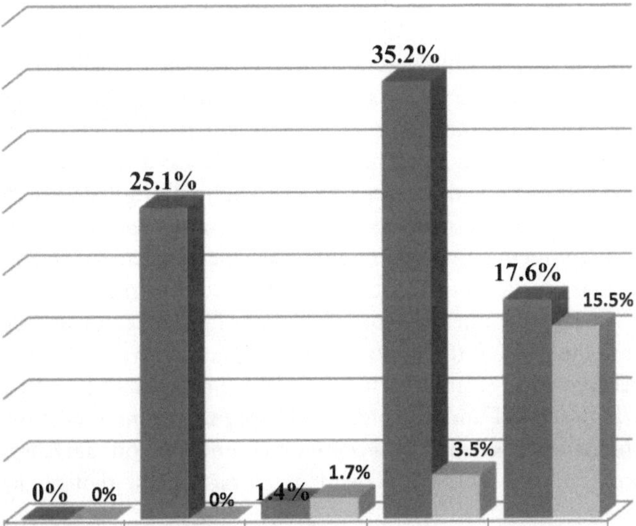

	R1	R2	R3	R4	R5
Accepted	0%	25.1%	1.4%	35.2%	17.6%
Rejected	0%	0%	1.7%	3.5%	15.5%

Figure 4.12 UPR 1II acceptance level by category

and this constituted about 37%, 39% and 35% of the total recommendations during UPR I, II and III respectively. As pointed out earlier, the fact that such recommendations are general does not mean that they are meaningless. Nigeria also engaged with a good number of specific recommendations but only to the extent that they did not involve issues of the death penalty and sexual orientation which have tended to be politically contentious in social-cultural terms within Nigeria. About 23% of the 26 specific recommendations (R4) rejected by Nigeria during UPR I were on the death penalty and discrimination based on sexual orientation. Similarly, during UPR II, recommendations on the death penalty and sexual orientation accounted for 95% of the 24 specific recommendations rejected by Nigeria; 67% of the recommendations rejected during UPR III by Nigeria were on these two issues. This indicates a cultural relativist tendency in the engagement of Nigeria with the UPR. This theme of cultural relativism is reinforced in subsequent chapters.

However, while the Nigerian government was not receptive to recommendations on the above two issues, it was receptive to other human rights issues that dominated both cycles of its review. Table 4.1 lists the top 15 issues that received recommendations during Nigeria's UPR I, II and III. The human rights issues in Table 4.1 are clustered based on the frequency with which states made recommendations. A similar classification has been used by UPR Info and by the Nigerian National Human Rights Commission.[57]

As indicated in Table 4.1, the three issues which came up prominently during the UPR I of Nigeria were women's rights, torture and detention, and justice, impunity and rule of law. All the recommendations on these three categories of issues were accepted by Nigeria. The NGO UPR I Coalition of Nigeria prioritised similar recommendations, including women and children rights, torture and extrajudicial execution.[58] During UPR II and III, women's rights remained the dominant issue. Other issues including 'healthcare and education', 'justice, impunity and rule of law', 'death penalty' and 'children's rights' were also predominant recommendations by states to Nigeria. Recommendations on the issue of 'business, environment and human rights' have increased across the three cycles of the UPR from two recommendations (UPR I) to four recommendations (UPR II) and then 11 recommendations (UPR III). This indicates an increasing recognition among states of the importance of these issues. The government of Nigeria was receptive to recommendations on these prominent issues that arose during UPR I, II and III and accepted many specific recommendations on the dominant human rights issues. It accepted recommendations such as to '[c]riminalize torture and establish an independent monitoring system of detention places',

57 UPR Info, 'Issue Categorisation' available at <https://bit.ly/2lSPwab> accessed 12/09/2019; The National Human Rights Commission of Nigeria, *Report on State of Compliance with International Minimum Standards of Human Rights by Nigeria Under the Universal Periodic Review Mechanism* <https://bit.ly/2kGqICb> accessed 12/09/2019.

58 Nigeria's Civil Society Coalition on the UPR, above n 25, 1–5.

Table 4.1 List of Thematic Issues Raised During Nigeria's Review Cycles

UPR I				*UPR II*				*UPR III*			
Rank	*Issue*	*No. of Recom. (UPR I)*	*% of 115 Recom. (UPR I)*	*Rank*	*Issue*	*No. of Recom. (UPR II)*	*% of 219 Recom. (UPR II)*	*Rank*	*Issue*	*No. of Recom. (UPR III)*	*% of 290 Recom. (UPR III)*
1	Women's Rights	17	14.8	1	Women's Rights and Gender Equality	32	14.6	1	Women's Rights	45	15.5
2	Torture and Detention	14	12.2	2	Healthcare and Education	29	13.2	2	Justice, Impunity and Rule of Law	38	13.1
3	Justice, Impunity & Rule of Law	13	11.3	3	Children's Rights	24	11	3	Healthcare and Education	29	10
4	Death Penalty	11	9.6	4	Death Penalty	24	11	4	Terrorism and Human Rights	22	7.6
5	Healthcare and Education	10	8.7	5	Justice, Impunity & Rule of Law	18	8.2	5	Children's Rights	21	7.2
6	Cooperation with Human Rights Mechanisms	10	8.7	6	Religion, Civil Society & Political Participation	15	7	6	Death Penalty	21	7.2
7	Religion, Civil Society & Political Participation	8	7	7	Torture and Detention	13	6	7	Institutional Reform	21	7.2
8	Trafficking and Sexual Exploitation	7	6.1	8	Treaty Ratification	12	5.5	8	Trafficking and Sexual Exploitation	17	6
9	Rights of the Child	6	5.2	9	Sexual Orientation	12	5.5	9	Treaty Ratification	15	5.2
10	Minorities	5	4.4	10	Cooperation with Human Rights Mechanisms	8	3.7	10	Sexual Orientation	12	4.1

(*Continued*)

Table 4.1 (Continued)

UPR I				*UPR II*				*UPR III*			
Rank	*Issue*	*No. of Recom. (UPR I)*	*% of 115 Recom. (UPR I)*	*Rank*	*Issue*	*No. of Recom. (UPR II)*	*% of 219 Recom. (UPR II)*	*Rank*	*Issue*	*No. of Recom. (UPR III)*	*% of 290 Recom. (UPR III)*
11	Institutional Reform	5	4.4	11	Institutional Reform	8	3.7	11	Religion, Civil Society & Political Participation	11	3.8
12	Treaty Ratification	4	3.5	12	Housing, Poverty and Adequate Living Standards	6	2.7	12	Business, Environment and Human Rights	11	3.8
13	Sexual Orientation	2	1.7	13	Trafficking and Sexual Exploitation	6	2.7	13	Housing, Poverty and Adequate Living Standards	9	3.1
14	Business, Environment and Human Rights	2	1.7	14	Disability Rights	5	2.3	14	Torture and Detention	7	2.4
15	Disability Rights	1	0.9	15	Business, Environment and Human Rights	4	2	15	Disability Rights	6	2.1
16					Terrorism and Human Rights	3	1.4	16	Cooperation with International Mechanisms	5	1.7

'[e]nact legislation to prohibit FGM', 'Fully implement its national action plan . . . to meaningfully involve women in peace process and to combat gender-based violence and discrimination' and '[s]ign and ratify the Optional Protocol to the ICESCR and the Optional Protocol to the Convention on the Rights of the Child on a communications procedure'.[59] Such an outcome shows that states are willing to rethink their policies and consider and commit to adopting international human rights treaties as a result of constructive dialogue and their participation in a cooperative mechanism. The key question would be whether many of these recommendations were subsequently implemented.

Recommendations on the issue of sexual orientation, specifically calling for the decriminalisation of same-sex relationships, have increased across the three cycles from two during UPR I to 12 during UPR II and III. Nigeria has not been willing to accept any of these recommendations. Recommendations calling for either the abolition or a moratorium on the death penalty came up among the top six issues raised during each cycle of Nigeria's review. Recommendations on the death penalty represented about 10% of the total recommendations made during UPR I, about 11% during UPR II and 7% during UPR III. This underlines the importance of the death penalty in the review of Nigeria. The Nigerian UPR delegation rejected all the recommendations on the issue except the UPR I recommendations by Argentina and Benin that Nigeria 'considers' the possibility of abolishing the death penalty in the near future.[60] This shows limits to Nigeria's receptiveness on this important UPR recommendation.

Overall, it is observable from the above analysis of Nigeria's engagement that Nigerian, as a reviewer, participated and made recommendations across the various regional groups thereby demonstrating the universality principle underlying the UPR mechanism. In terms of the relevance and specificity of the recommendations made by Nigeria, it was evident that the Nigerian government engaged the various regional groups with the various categories of recommendations. However, it made fewer specific recommendations to its African regional peers compared to other groups of states. But the fact that a recommendation is non-specific does not undermine the relevance of such a recommendation. Nevertheless, it provided evidence of a diverging approach to reviewing states, with Nigeria adopting a softer approach in reviewing its regional peers compared to the approach adopted in reviewing Western states. As a state under review, Nigeria was generally receptive to various categories of recommendations from its peers, evidenced by the high acceptance level across all three cycles of the UPR. There is evidence of regionalism in terms of Nigeria's receptiveness to recommendations across the various regional groups, with particular preference for intra-African and Asian recommendations. Also noteworthy is that cultural relativism, in relation to issues of sexual orientation, has limited Nigeria's engagement at this stage of the review.

59 *HRC UPR II Report—Nigeria,* UN Doc A/HRC/25/6 paras 135.73, 135.56, 135.1.
60 *Report of the HRC on its 25th Session*, UN Doc A/HRC/25/2 paras 1, 14.

Implementation of Nigeria's UPR recommendations

Implementation is an important component to evaluating state engagement with the UPR. State engagement with the UPR process will not be effective if it does not result in the implementation of recommendations that would contribute to the improvement of the human rights situation on the ground. This section examines the extent to which Nigeria implemented its UPR recommendations and the gap between the accepted and the implemented recommendations. It argues that the number of fully and partially implemented recommendations underscore the potential of the UPR process to contribute to human rights changes within states through a cooperative and collaborative process. While the gap between the accepted and implemented recommendations signals that the government needs to engage more effectively with implementation, it is arguable that the implementation gap can potentially narrow over time through the process of acculturation and by effective NGO engagement.

The IRI is used to measure state implementation of UPR recommendations. The IRI is an index developed by UPR Info which brings together an average of stakeholders' responses.[61] The value of this index is that it considers the comments of both states and stakeholders on the implementation of UPR recommendations. A major challenge in measuring state UPR implementation is that the UPR is a dynamic and ongoing process. As such, recommendations which this index may classify as implemented or not implemented may have at the conclusion of this research changed status. To control the changes which may subsequently occur, the implementation measured is restricted to the implementation time frame allocated for each review. It is also difficult to draw a direct causal link between UPR recommendations and the actions of states.

The implementation time frame for Nigeria to implement its UPR I recommendations ran from February 2009, when the UPR working group adopted its UPR report, till July 2013, when it submitted its UPR II report. Nigeria's UPR III implementation time frame was between December 2013 and August 2018.[62] About 43% of the UPR I recommendations were either fully or partially implemented. Some of the pledges made by Nigeria to the HRC when it sought membership during UPR I were also implemented. From among the stakeholders, only the Nigerian NHRC in its UPR II report[63] directly addressed the level of

61 When all stakeholders agree that a recommendation was fully implemented the recommendation is scored 1. Whenever a stakeholder claimed that no aspect of a recommendation was been implemented, the index score is 0. The score is 0.75 when the state under review claims that the recommendation has been fully implemented but a stakeholder says it has only been partially implemented. The average of the scores is then transformed into an implementation level where 0–0.32 = Not Implemented, 0.33–0.65 = Partially Implemented and 0.66–1 = Fully Implemented. For more details on the IRI methodology see UPR Info, 'Universal Periodic Review: On the Road to Implementation' (2012) 63–4 available at <https://bit.ly/2mepWwI> accessed 05/09/2019.

62 Since UPR III implementation stage was still ongoing, I limited the analysis on implementation to UPR I and II.

63 See National Human Rights Commission of Nigeria, 'Report on State of Compliance with International Minimum Standards of Human Rights by Nigeria Under the Universal

implementation. Some of the pledges and commitments made by Nigeria corresponded to some of the recommendations made by states during Nigeria's UPR I review.[64] Other stakeholders indirectly provided responses to the pledges in their reports on Nigeria's implementation of UPR recommendations. To implement some of the pledges made, Nigeria ratified the International Convention on the Protection of the Rights of All Migrant Workers and Members of Their Families (ICRMW); deposited its NAP which amended the National Human Rights Commission Act to grant the NHRC independence, investigative and enforcement powers; and diplomatically intervened to restore peace and democracy in Guinea, Guinea Bissau and Mali.[65]

Regarding the UPR I state recommendations to Nigeria, the government of Nigeria triggered actions on some of the recommendations at the end of UPR I implementation period. Out of a summary of 30 recommendations accepted by Nigeria, 10% were fully implemented (FI), about 33% were partially implemented (PI), about 53% were not implemented (NI) and about 3% of the recommendations were not assessed because UPR stakeholders did not provide any information in relation to their implementation. At the end of Nigeria's UPR II, 35% of the total recommendations made were either fully or partially implemented. Figures 4.13 and 4.14 represent percentages of the recommendations that were FI, PI and NI during UPR I and II.

As indicated in Figure 4.13, about 43% of the UPR I recommendations Nigeria accepted were either fully or partially implemented while about 53% were not implemented. Figure 4.14 indicates 35% of the UPR II recommendations were either fully or partially implemented compared to 47% not implemented. On the FI UPR I recommendations, the state, the NHRC, domestic and some international NGOs agreed on the full implementation of some of these recommendations. For example, the state,[66] NCHR[67] and Amnesty International[68] were

Periodic Review Mechanism' (2013) 2 available at <https://bit.ly/2kGqICb> accessed 05/09/2019.

64 For example, Nigeria undertook to accelerate the process full domestication of international human rights treaties and this correspond to its second UPR I recommendation made by Ghana, Norway, Niger, Algeria and Brazil. For details on the pledges and commitments made by Nigeria see OHCHR, 'Human Rights Council: Nigeria's Voluntary Pledges and Commitments' available at <www.un.org/ga/60/elect/hrc/nigeria.pdf> accessed 05/09/2019.

65 See National Human Rights Commission of Nigeria, 'Report on State of Compliance with International Minimum Standards of Human Rights by Nigeria Under the Universal Periodic Review Mechanism' (2013) 2 available at <https://bit.ly/2kGqICb> accessed 05/09/2019.

66 *HRC UPR II State Report*—Nigeria, UN Doc A/HRC/WG.6/NGA/1 para 32.

67 National Human Rights Commission of Nigeria, 'National Human Rights Commission Table of Commentary on 2009 UPR recommendations and the extent of Compliance' available at <https://bit.ly/2mbANaB> accessed 12/09/2019.

68 Amnesty International (AI), 'Universal Periodic Review of Nigeria: Submission by Amnesty International, 17th Session of the UPR Working Group, October 2013 (July 2013) IOR 41/011/2013, 2 available at <https://uprdoc.ohchr.org/uprweb/downloadfile.aspx?filename=557&file=EnglishTranslation>.

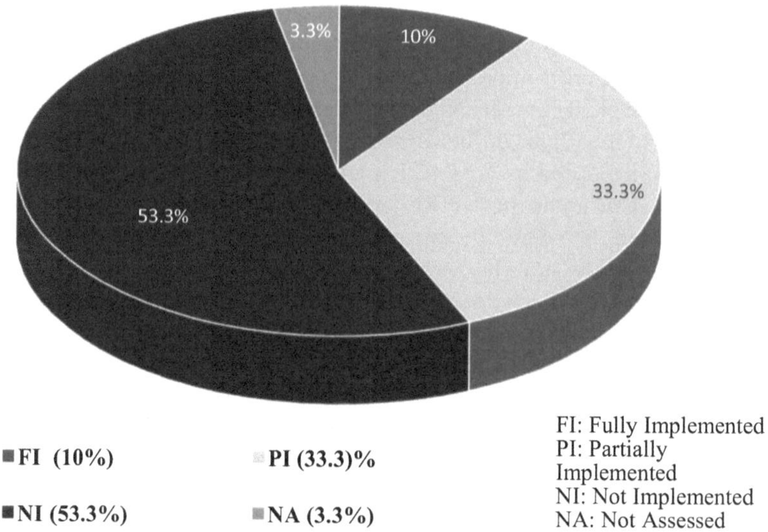

Figure 4.13 Nigeria UPR I—implementation of recommendations

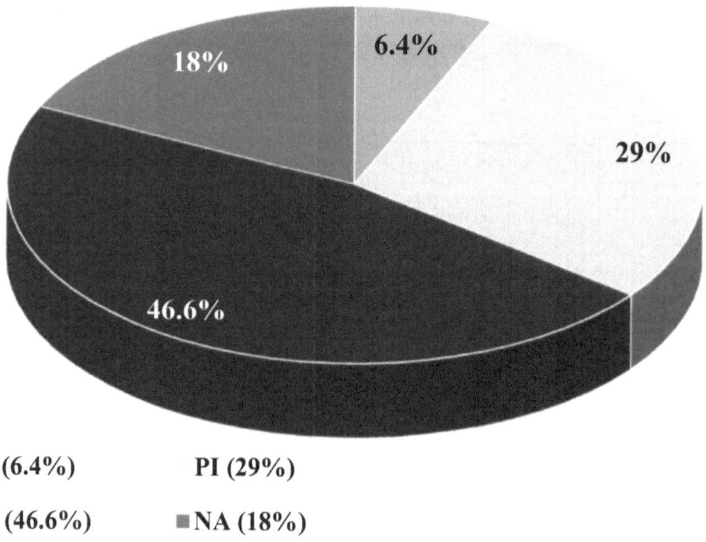

Figure 4.14 Nigeria UPR II—implementation of recommendations

in agreement that recommendation 4 relating to the amendment of the Human Rights Commission Act to grant the NHRC independence, investigative and enforcement powers had been fully implemented. This greatly contributed to the Commission attaining an 'A' status at the International Coordinating Committee of Human Rights a year after. Similarly, the response of Human Rights Agenda Network (HRAN), a leading domestic NGO,[69] did not dispute that the government had continued to invest in education within the relevant time. As such, the recommendation in this regard was fully implemented.[70] Regarding some of the fully implemented UPR II recommendations, stakeholders agreed that the recommendations for the government of Nigeria (to extend a standing invitation to UN human rights mechanisms, to continue to follow-up on requests by special procedure mandate holders and to continue efforts to eradicate polio in Nigeria) had been fully implemented.[71]

On the partially implemented recommendations, the government of Nigeria had triggered the process of implementation on some of the recommendations from both cycles of the review even though not yet completed. In some of the recommendations, both the state and the stakeholders agreed that the recommendation had only been partially implemented. On others there were disputes not only between the state and the stakeholders but equally among the stakeholders. For example, HRAN,[72] NHRC[73] and the government of Nigeria[74] all accepted that UPR I recommendation relating to accession to human rights instruments to which Nigeria was not yet a party had only been partially implemented. This featured among the top five recommendations that were made to Nigeria. UPR I Recommendation 28 required the government to take steps to bolster the national health system. While the NHRC[75] and the state[76] agreed that steps have been taken in this regard, HRAN's response was not in agreement with this.[77] Relevant studies on the Nigerian health system indicated that the

69 A coalition of 39 domestic NGOs. See Human Rights Agenda Network (HRAN) 'Written Submission to Universal Periodic Review of Nigeria, Oct-Nov 2013' (2013) 8 available at <https://bit.ly/2lKCM5I> accessed 12/09/2019.

70 Other recommendations that were fully implemented during UPR I covered issues on the National Human Rights Institution, education and raising awareness among cultural and religious leaders.

71 See Office of the High Commissioner for Human Rights, *Compilation on Nigeria: Report of the Office of the High Commissioner for Human Rights,* Un Doc A/HRC/WG.6/31/NGA/2 (27 August 2018) para 6; Edmund Rice International, 'Universal Periodic review: Mid-Term Implementation Report of Nigeria' (2016) 6 available at <https://bit.ly/2kwzaUJ> accessed 05/09/2019.

72 Ibid 2.

73 National Human Rights Commission of Nigeria, 'National Human Rights Commission Table of Commentary on 2009 UPR recommendations and the extent of Compliance' above n 67 para 1.

74 *HRC UPR II State Report*—Nigeria, UN Doc A/HRC/WG.6/NGA/1 para 22.

75 The National Human Rights Commission of Nigeria, above n 67, [28].

76 *HRC UPR I Report—Nigeria,* UN Doc A/HRC/11/26, [102].

77 Human Rights Agenda Network (HRAN), above n 69, 7.

system was deplorable and the attitude of healthcare workers towards patients was very poor.[78] During Nigeria's UPR II, recommendations on women's right and gender equality were predominant (see Table 4.1). In terms of implementation of some of these recommendations, Nigerianhrcsos-UPR, OHCHR and Partnership for Justice agreed that many of them had only been partially implemented, including recommendations to curb gender-related violence, address gender disparities in education and socio-economic empowerment of women.[79] There was consensus among various stakeholders that the recommendations for the government of Nigeria to enact a national law prohibiting the practice of FGM had only been partially implemented through the enactment of the Violence against Persons (Prohibition) Act 2015.[80]

Many of the recommendations which had not been implemented concerned issues such as justice, rule of law and detention, women's rights, torture and extrajudicial executions, the death penalty and the rights of sexual minorities. Most of these issues were among the five prominent issues that received the most recommendations during Nigeria's UPR I and II (see Table 4.1). The relevance and effects of the non-implementation of some of these recommendations are examined in the following sections. While the state took some steps towards implementation outside the implementation time frame, these issues still raise serious human rights concern in Nigeria.

Justice and detention

Access to justice and detention conditions have been persistent problems in Nigeria. Mary Robinson, former UN High Commissioner for Human Rights, pointed out that the 'way in which justice is administered is a key benchmark of a country's commitment to human rights'.[81] The right to fair trial and freedom from arbitrary arrest are enshrined in sections 35 and 36 of the 1999 Constitution of Nigeria, but these provisions have largely not been implemented.[82] In its 2010 report on the state of human rights in Nigeria, the Nigerian NHRC recommended that the justice administration should be overhauled.[83] A 2012 national

78 See Ajovi Scott-Emuakpor, 'The Evolution of Health Care Systems in Nigeria: Which way Forward in the Twenty-First Century' (2010) 51(2) *Nigerian Medical Journal* 53; Nigeria National Human Rights Commission, *Research Study on Human Rights and Maternal Mortality: Pilot Study on Women's Access to Health Care Facilities in the Six Area Council of the Federal Capital Territory (FCT), Abuja* (National Human Rights Commission 2015) 29–30.

79 The Coalition on Nigerian Human Rights CSOS on the UPR, above n 28, 3; Office of the High Commissioner for Human Rights, above, n 71 para 67; Partnership for Justice, 'Report on the Human Rights Situation in Nigeria' (2018) 3 available at <https://bit.ly/2ke3Rxz> accessed 08/07/2019.

80 Ibid.

81 Mary Robertson, *A Voice for Human Rights* (University of Pennsylvania Press 2010) 255.

82 Nigeria National Human Rights Commission, above n 7, 60.

83 Ibid.

prison audit undertaken by the Nigerian NHRC highlighted major issues. The prisons were old and dilapidated, congested and appalling prison facilities.[84] More than 18,000 detainees had spent a long time awaiting trial, with some having spent up to 16 years awaiting trial.[85] Another prison audit exercise undertaken by the NHRC in 2014 at the Kuje Medium Security Prison, Abuja, reported that 86 detainees have been awaiting trial for at least three years.[86] In 2010 there were 479 cases of unlawful arrest and detention reported by the NHRC. This number rose to 2,560 in 2011, 3,642 in 2012[87] and 5,294 in 2016.[88] While this increase in numbers may simply reflect an increase in reporting rather than occurrences, they do unveil the underlying problem and underscore the relevance of the recommendations which states made during Nigeria's UPR I and II. France recommended during UPR I and II that Nigeria should '[i]mprove the conditions of detention within prisons, access to health and the respect for the most elementary rights of detainees'[89] and '[e]stablish a procedure for providing immediate registration of arrest and detention of people'.[90] The United Kingdom recommended during UPR I that Nigeria '[t]ake action to tackle the backlog of prisoners who have been detained without trial or beyond the end of their sentence',[91] and Belgium recommended that Nigeria '[t]ake specific measures in order to address the dis-functioning of the judicial system and the lack of internal and external monitoring of the police'.[92]

However, in terms of implementation, very little progress was made by the state within the implementation period. There were efforts to reform the criminal justice system with new judges appointed at all levels.[93] However, according to the NHRC, Nigeria's pretrial system continues to violate human rights, the prison system is below UN Standard Minimum Rules for the Treatment of Prisoners and police oversight bodies remain weak and unable to monitor the excesses of the police.[94] Amnesty International reported in its 2018 UPR report that between 2014 and 2017, the military has continued to illegally detain people

84 The audit report revealed that out of 50,645 persons detained, about 70% were awaiting trial. See The National Human Rights Commission Nigeria, *National Prison Audit 2012* (The National Human Rights Commission 2014) 3–11.

85 The audit report revealed that out of 50,645 persons detained, about 70% were awaiting trial. See The National Human Rights Commission Nigeria, *National Prison Audit 2012* (The National Human Rights Commission 2014) 5, 17.

86 The National Human Rights Commission Nigeria, *Annual Report 2014* (National Human Rights Commission 2014) 87–8.

87 After 2012, there was decline in the number of cases reported. See ibid 52.

88 The National Human Rights Commission Nigeria, *Annual Report 2016* (National Human Rights Commission 2016) 134–5.

89 *HRC UPR I Report—Nigeria,* UN Doc A/HRC/11/26 para 41.

90 *HRC UPR II Report—Nigeria,* UN Doc A/HRC/25/6 paras 135.109.

91 Ibid para 25.

92 Ibid para 64.

93 See The National Human Rights Commission of Nigeria, above n 86.

94 Ibid.

in some parts of Nigeria for up to two years without access to trial.[95] Nevertheless, in 2015, the Administration of Criminal Justice Act was enacted to reform the criminal justice sector.[96] While this falls outside the implementation period for UPR I, it underscores the potential for the UPR to, over time, influence changes within states. Six new recommendations were made on this issue during UPR III.[97]

Women's rights

According to the Nigerian NHRC, reports of violence against women grew by alarming proportions within the first cycle of the UPR. In 2010, the NHRC received 323 reported cases of domestic violence.[98] In 2012, this number rose to 2,656, and in 2016, there were over 24,000 reported cases of domestic violence.[99] In 2017, the Nigerian NHRC received over 250,000 complaints on the issue of women's rights and gender equality, and over 33,000 of the complaints were on the domestic violence.[100] Also, Nigeria has the highest number of reported FGM cases in the world, accounting for about one-quarter of the estimated 115–130 million circumcised women worldwide.[101] Therefore, states were justified to place women's rights issues at the top of Nigeria's UPR I, II and III recommendations, accounting for approximately 15% of the recommendations made in each cycle of the review (see Table 4.1). Many of these recommendations required the Nigerian government to implement legislation against sexual and gender-based violence, undertake awareness raising campaigns to eradicate FGM and enact legislation to prohibit FGM.[102]

Implementing these recommendations within the UPR I implementation period proved challenging for the state. As observed by the NHRC, few state governments within Nigeria enacted laws on FGM, but there was no federal legislation on FGM, discrimination against women, child marriage and betrothal

95 Amnesty International, 'Nigeria: Amnesty International Submission for the UN Universal Periodic Review 31st Session of the UPR Working Group' (2018) 3 available at <https://bit.ly/2kwUppq> accessed 05/09/2019.

96 Administration of Criminal Justice Act, 2015 (Nigeria).

97 See UN Human Rights Council, *Report of the Working Group on the Universal Periodic Review—Nigeria*, 40th sess, Agenda Item 6, UN Doc A/HRC/40/7 (26 December 2018) 148.153–148.157.

98 This continues to prevail despite section 46 (1) of the 1999 Constitution of Nigeria which protects women against violence and discrimination. See The National Human Rights Commission Nigeria, *Annual Report 2014*, above n 86, 52.

99 Ibid 52.

100 The National Human Rights Commission Nigeria, *Annual Report 2017* (National Human Rights Commission 2017) 177–81.

101 NPC and UNICEF Nigeria, 'Children's and Women's right in Nigeria: A wake up call—Situation Assessment and Analysis of Harmful Traditional Practice (FGM)' (Abuja 2001) 195–200.

102 *HRC UPR I Report—Nigeria*, UN Doc A/HRC/11/26 paras 18, 62, 71, 77, 83.

or gender-based violence.[103] Many of these recommendations which were not implemented were vital in improving the human rights situation on the ground. However, as noted earlier, over time some of these recommendations have been implemented, even though outside the UPR I implementation time frame. In 2015 (within UPR II implementation time frame), the Violence against Persons Prohibition Act was passed into federal law. This Act specifically addresses violence against women, including FGM in Article 6, and prescribes a penalty of up to four years imprisonment and/or a fine.[104] While the Act can be criticised for its failure to recognise the particular vulnerability of women to violence by replacing the word 'women' with 'persons', it nevertheless demonstrates a positive move by the government of Nigeria in fighting violence against women and other vulnerable persons. This is supplemented by a four-year National Policy and Plan of Action for the Elimination of FGM in Nigeria which identifies and engages key stakeholders at the federal, state and community levels.[105] However, there has been no evidence of their enforcement, and reports indicate that the practice of FGM 'remain widespread, with low rates of reporting'.[106] Various UPR stakeholders in their UPR III report expressed disappointment that this legislation is not being implemented.[107]

Torture, cruel, inhuman and degrading treatment

In 2006, the UN Special Rapporteur on Extrajudicial, Summary or Arbitrary Executions observed that torture was an intrinsic part of law enforcement methods in Nigeria.[108] Section 34 (1) of the 1999 Constitution of Nigeria expressly provides that 'no person shall be subjected to torture or to inhuman or degrading treatment'.[109] Furthermore, Article 4 of the Convention against Torture (CAT) provides that '[e]ach state party shall ensure that all acts of torture are offences under its criminal law'.[110] This is a non-derogable right and a peremptory norm

103 See The National Human Rights Commission of Nigeria, above n 86 para 18.

104 *Nigeria: Violence Against Persons (Prohibition) Act, 2015 (VAPP)* [Nigeria] (25 May 2015).

105 Federal Ministry of Health Abuja, *National Policy and Plan of Action for the Elimination of Federal Genital Mutilation in Nigeria* 2013–2017 (Federal Ministry of Health Abuja 2013).

106 Immigration and Refugee Board of Canada, 'Nigeria: Prevalence of female genital mutilation (FGM) among the Urhobo, including the consequences for refusing to undergo this procedure, particularly pregnant women; state protection available (2014-March 2015)' (2015) available at <www.refworld.org/docid/56498d834.html> accessed 05/09/2019.

107 Partnership for Justice, above n 79; The Coalition on Nigerian Human Rights CSOS on the UPR, above n 28, 6.

108 UN Human Rights Council, *Report of the Special Rapporteur on Torture and Other Cruel, Inhuman or Degrading Treatment or Punishment, Manfred Nowak: Addendum: Mission to Nigeria (4 to 10 March 2007)*, UN Doc A/HRC/7/3/Add.4 (22 November 2007) para 40.

109 Constitution of the Federal Republic of Nigeria (1999), s 34 (1).

110 *Convention Against Torture and Other Cruel, Inhuman or Degrading Treatment or Punishment*, opened for signature 10 December 1984, UNTS 1465 (entered into force 26

of international law. Despite these, the number of cases reported to the Nigerian NHRC between 2009 and 2012 was on the rise. In 2009, the number of reported cases was at 94, but in 2010 the number had risen to 1,403 and in 2016 the number stood at 2,544.[111] States, including Benin, Ukraine, the Netherlands and Denmark, recommended that Nigeria should 'establish a national preventive mechanism to align itself with its neighbours positive practices'; '[s]tep up its efforts to halt torture and ill-treatment'; adopt legislative measures to prevent and prosecute acts of torture and other ill treatment;[112] and '[c]riminalise torture and establish an independent monitoring system of detention places'.[113]

With regard to their implementation, in 2009, Nigeria set up the National Committee against Torture (NCAT) as a national preventative mechanism.[114] The NCAT was mandated among other things to receive and consider complaints on torture; conduct visits to places of detention and examine allegations of torture therein; review the treatment of persons in detention with a view to prevent torture; develop a national anti-torture policy; and propose anti-torture legislation.[115] The NCAT has partnered with the NHRC to organise training workshops and sensitise relevant actors on the UN CAT and its Optional Protocol.[116]

Despite these efforts, torture continues to persist. The Nigerian Criminal and Penal code does not explicitly prohibit torture, and the NCAT does not have investigatory or prosecutorial powers.[117] This is arguably inconsistent with the constitutional provision and international obligation earlier mentioned. Force Order 237 of Nigeria's Police Regulations contributes to the ongoing use of torture by permitting police officers to shoot detainees and suspects who attempt to escape or avoid arrest, regardless of whether they pose a threat to life.[118] Nevertheless, the work undertaken by the NCAT is a significant step. But Nigeria is yet to recognise the competence of the Committee against Torture to receive communications from individuals under Article 22 of CAT.

June 1987); Nigeria ratified the Optional Protocol of the Convention against Torture (OPCAT) in 2009. See also Article 5 of the African Charter on Human and Peoples' Rights.

111 The National Human Rights Commission Nigeria, *Annual Report 2013* (National Human Rights Commission 2013).

112 *HRC UPR I Report—Nigeria,* UN Doc A/HRC/11/26 para 103.1.

113 *HRC UPR I Report—Nigeria,* UN Doc A/HRC/11/26 para 103.1, 103.22, 103.40, 103.42.

114 Federal Ministry of Justice (Nigeria), 'Mandate of the National Committee on Torture' (2010) available at <https://bit.ly/2lMchN6> accessed 05/09/2019.

115 Ibid; National Committee against Torture, 'Fourth Quarterly Report of the National Committee against Torture to the United Nations Sub Committee against Torture in Geneva, Switzerland' (2015) available at <https://bit.ly/2keddJP> accessed 05/09/2019.

116 See The National Human Rights Commission of Nigeria, above n 86, 63–4.

117 Ibid para 22.

118 See Federal Ministry of Justice (Nigeria), 'Mandate of the National Committee on Torture' (2010) available at <https://bit.ly/2lMchN6> accessed 05/09/2019.

Narrowing the UPR implementation gap: acculturation and the internal/external audience effects

Nigeria has made major commitments in its UPR engagement and is a party to major international human rights instruments. Despite this, implementation has often proved problematic. As the aforementioned findings indicate, the majority of the recommendations made during UPR I and II were not implemented by Nigeria despite the high percentage of acceptance of recommendations. Narrowing the gap between a government's human rights rhetoric and its human rights actions is crucial for the human rights situation on the ground to be improved. But can this gap be narrowed?

The gap between compelling human rights rhetoric and meaningful political change is often a sizeable one.[119] However, it is arguable that over time shallow or rhetorical human rights commitments will resonate to deeper commitments through a process that Jon Elster refers to as the 'civilizing force of hypocrisy'.[120] Elster reasoned that rhetorical commitments, though hypocritically made, can lead to some positive outcomes over time because an actor would hardly deviate from the principled position to which he has publicly committed himself.[121] States respond to global cultural forces just like individuals, and organisations respond to cultural forces within their wider environment. By identifying themselves with a reference group, states generate varying degrees of social and cognitive pressures to conform to the norms of that group.[122] Identification as a microprocess of acculturation has been exploited to drive states to make human rights commitments. Identification occurs 'when an individual accepts influence because he wants to establish or maintain a satisfying relationship with another person or group'.[123] The social environments within which states act propel internal cognitive and social pressures which drive states to adopt socially legitimate attitudes and beliefs.[124] The interest of Nigeria to identify itself with the cooperative and inclusive UPR mechanism can over time facilitate its acculturation.

119 Emilie M Hafner-Burton, 'Human Rights Institutions: Rhetoric and Efficacy' (2007) 44(4) *Journal of Peace Research* 379, 382.

120 Jon Elster, 'Deliberation and Constitution Making' in Jon Elster (ed), *Deliberative Democracy* (Cambridge University Press 1998) 111.

121 Ibid 104.

122 Ibid 4.

123 Herbert C Kelman, 'Compliance, Emulation, and Internalization: Three Processes of Attitude Change' (1958) 51(2) *Journal of Conflict Resolution* 53.

124 For example, within the framework of the UPR, even though China rejected all its UPR I recommendations relating to the abolition of the death penalty, it thereafter reduced the scope of its application by excluding 13 non-violent economic crimes. See Dui Hua, 'NGO Submission for the Universal Periodic Review of the People's Republic of China' (March 2013) para 16; It is however important to note that the scope of the application of the death penalty in China is still very high.

In the analysis of Nigeria's UPR engagement, acculturation through identification was evident in several ways. The act of identifying itself with the African Group generated internal social and cognitive pressures which induced Nigeria to accept a high percentage of recommendations from its referenced group.[125] While acceptance of UPR recommendations does not yield automatic implementation, it is a positive step towards implementation. While some may see the existence of this regional alliance as detrimental to the UPR process,[126] it arguably could favour the process of acculturation. States may tend to be more receptive to sensitive recommendations coming from the regional group they identify with than from other groups. An example of the power of identification was evident during Nigeria's review. During UPR I, Nigeria accepted a general recommendation (R4) touching on the death penalty from Benin[127] but rejected similar general recommendations from Western states such as the United Kingdom and Sweden.[128] Also, during UPR II, Chad accepted a recommendation from Cape Verde (on violence against women, FGM and forced marriages) but rejected a similar recommendation from Italy, even though both recommendations addressed the same issues and fell in the same action category.[129] This provides evidence of the positive outcome of identification as a microprocess of acculturation by causing recommendations made by states within a regional block, which otherwise may not have been accepted, to be accepted by members of that regional block. However, the extent to which the UPR could transform the culture on the rights of sexual minorities within African states through acculturation remains to be seen, but the cognitive pressures associated with acculturation are an important part of the process.

Cognitive pressures associated with the acculturation microprocess of identification can push the language of human rights into some moral commitments within cultures even in terms that challenge one or more aspects of that culture. Benjamin Gregg employed a cognitive approach rather than a normative one to

125 See Figure 4.2.

126 Allehone M Abebe, above n 43, 19–21; Dominguez Redondo, 'The Universal Periodic Review of the UN Human Rights Council: An Assessment of the First Session' (2008) 7(3) *Chinese Journal of International Law* 731; Edward McMahon, above n 53, 1, 19–25.

127 *HRC UPR I Report—Nigeria*, UN Doc A/HRC/11/26 para 14.

128 Ibid. Another example of the positive impact of regionalism in the UPR, with regard to Africa states, was evident in the review of Chad. During Chad's UPR II, Togo and the Czech Republic recommended that Chad 'Ratify the Optional Convention against Torture and Other Cruel, inhuman or Degrading Treatment or Punishment.' Even though both recommendations were of the same action category of specific recommendations (R5), Chad refused to accept the same recommendation from the Czech Republic because it added 'without delay'. See UN Human Rights Council, *Report of the Working Group on the Universal Periodic Review—Chad*, UN Doc A/HRC/25/14 (3 January 2014) para 110.18, 110.120.

129 UN Human Rights Council, 'Report of the Working Group on the Universal Periodic Review—Chad: Addendum' UN Doc A/HRC/25/14/Add 1 (3 January 2014) 2. See ibid paras 110.107, 110.110, read together with *Report of the HRC on its 25th Session*, UN Doc A/HRC/25/2 paras 110.107, 110.110.

show how human rights norms can be advanced as rights internal to any given community's culture by means of cognitive reframing.[130] He argued that 'an idea once external can become internal through system-level learning'.[131] While examining the issue of FGM in Africa, he noted that a cognitive rule can be deployed that revises local normative rules that justify FGM but that such a cognitive rule has to be 'indigenized'.[132] For example, reframing FGM as a technical, medical issue rather than a normative human rights concern can advance the human rights issue as internal to the African culture.[133] Such an approach can be equally beneficial to other cultural aspects affecting the engagement of Nigeria with the UPR.

As the acculturation process progresses, it will be difficult for a state to sustain purely rhetorical commitments because of external 'audience' effects. External audience effects are generated by national and transnational human rights advocacy networks when they engage governments in a dialogue about norm implementation and hold them accountable for their human rights rhetoric. The publicity of a government's UPR commitments creates expectations among informed citizens and NGOs/CSOs, making it difficult for the government to contradict or deviate from the accepted commitment/recommendations. Dia in his study[134] noted how the Communist regimes' commitments under the Helsinki Accords were frequently referenced in popular struggles for freedom of association and freedom of expression.[135] Citizens over time may pressure their government to live up to their human rights rhetoric and commitments. This is referred to by O'Brien and Li as 'rightful resistance'.[136] They suggest that this grows from the space created when the state's international commitment is disconnected from local practice.[137] According to O'Brien and Li, 'so long as a gap exists between rights promised and rights delivered, there is always room for rightful resistance to emerge'.[138]

In the case of Nigeria, there is a space for civil society to hold the government accountable for its UPR commitments. A strategic and well-coordinated campaign by NGOs can contribute to meaningful human rights improvement within

130 Benjamin Gregg, 'Deploying Cognitive Sociology to Advance Human Rights' (2010) 9 *Comparative Sociology* 279, 289.

131 Ibid.

132 Ibid 304.

133 Human Rights Norms against Child Prostitution in Asia were advanced internally by means of cognitive reframing. See ibid 289.

134 Xinyuan Dai, *International Institutions and National Policies* (Cambridge University Press 2007).

135 Ibid 120.

136 Kevin J O'Brien and Li Lianjiang, *Rightful Resistance in Rural China* (Cambridge University Press 2006) 15–24; note however that the number of offences subject to the death penalty is still very high in China.

137 Relating to the situation where public conformity is disconnected from local practice; see Kevin J O'Brien and Li Lianjiang, above n 136, 64.

138 Ibid.

a state. Chapter 5 examines in greater detail how NGOs can effectively engage with the UPR and influence the state's engagement with the mechanism through the formation of a broad and representative NGO coalition and undertaking media and advocacy campaigns.

Continuous engagement of Nigeria with the UPR process has the potential to over time narrow the implementation gap. As earlier indicated, some of the UPR I recommendations to Nigeria that were not implemented during the specified time were subsequently implemented. The adoption of a UPR implementation action plan would accelerate and provide greater certainty on the implementation process. In addition, continuous engagement with the UPR process may over time influence states even on issues which it rejected in its previous review. As governments within nations change, so do their views on human rights issues in order to identify with the wider community with which they interact. This was the case with Côte d'Ivoire. During UPR I, the government of President Laurent Gbagbo rejected recommendations from the United Kingdom, Brazil and the Czech Republic to sign and ratify OP-CAT.[139] During UPR II, the government of President Alassane Ouattara accepted the same recommendations from states such as Ghana, Tunisia, the Czech Republic, Uruguay and Burkina Faso.[140] It remains to be determined whether specific recommendations on the death penalty and the rights of sexual minorities may subsequently receive a positive response from a new government in Nigeria. Acculturation in this context is seen as a continuous process which may over time produce a positive outcome.[141]

The 'spiral' effect of the fight against *Boko Haram* on Nigeria's UPR engagement

Just as terrorism has a grave impact on human rights, so too antiterrorism laws and policies can have serious implications for human rights and individual freedoms.[142] When conflicts within or between states pose a threat to the nation or citizens, governments easily justify repressive measures and human rights considerations may thereby be weakened. The role of conflict and security threats in Nigeria in hindering norm compliance is an important aspect to consider when examining its engagement with the UPR. There is always a tendency for

139 UN Human Rights Council, *Report of the Working Group on the Universal Periodic Review—Cote d'Ivoire*, 13th sess, UN Doc A/HRC/13/9 (4 January 2010) paras 101.7–101.9.

140 UN Human Rights Council, *Report of the Working Group on the Universal Periodic Review—Cote d'Ivoire*, 27th sess, UN Doc A/HRC/27/6 (7 July 2014) paras 127.3–127.4, 127.5 respectively.

141 For a description of process and outcome-based conceptions of acculturation, see John W Berry, 'Conceptual Approaches to Acculturation' in Kevin M Chung, Pamela Ball Organista and Gerardo Marin (eds), *Acculturation: Advances in Theory, Measurement and Applied Research* (American Psychology Association 2003).

142 Cephas Lumina, 'Counter Terrorism Legislation and the Protection of Human Rights: A Survey of Selected International Practice' (2007) 7(1) *African Human Rights Journal* 36.

governments to trade off human rights considerations in the name of counterterrorism measures or national security. Human rights violations mostly committed by governments under the pretext of counterterrorism measures include torture, extrajudicial executions and secret and arbitrary detention. During UPR I, Nigeria accepted a recommendation to take 'all practical measures' to end 'extra-judicial executions' and 'step up its measures to halt torture'.[143] This section considers whether the escalation of the conflict between the government and the *Boko Haram* terrorist group after UPR I had a regressive effect on Nigeria's subsequent engagement with the UPR.

There is some obscurity surrounding the origin of *Boko Haram*. Attempts at explaining the origin and leadership of the group have generated some confusion.[144] *Boko Haram*, literally translated to mean 'western education/civilization is sin', is a sect whose early recruits were indoctrinated 'to believe that their state of hopelessness was caused by government which imposed Western education on them and failed to manage the resources of the country to their benefits'.[145]

While the existence of the sect has been traced as far back as 1995,[146] it was only after Nigeria's UPR I in 2009 that the conflict between the sect and the government escalated. Two particular incidents escalated the conflict between the government and the *Boko Haram* terrorist group. These were the bombing of the Nigerian Police Headquarters in Abuja on 16 June 2011 and the bombing of the United Nations House in Abuja on 26 August 2011. Prior to these incidents, *Boko Haram* was apparently not understood as a threat to peace and to the protection of human rights in Nigeria and the region. None of the 32 recommendations during Nigeria's UPR I session on 9 February 2009 addressed the issue of terrorism. It only became a major concern during UPR II on 27 October 2013, receiving three recommendations from France, Portugal and the Republic of Korea.[147]

A major counterterrorism response by the Nigerian government immediately followed the two major incidents above. The government enacted the Terrorism (Prevention) Act 2011 (hereafter 'TPA').[148] This was amended on 21 February 2013 by the Terrorism (Prevention) (Amendment) Act 2013 (hereafter

143 *HRC UPR I Report—Nigeria,* UN Doc A/HRC/11/26 para 22.

144 See Simeon H O Alozieuwa, above n 51, 1.

145 N C Okereke, 'Implementing the Nigerian Defence Policy: Reflections on the Boko Haram Crisis' in O Mbachu and A Sokoto (eds), *Nigerian Defence and Security: Policies and Strategies* (Medusa Academic Publishers Ltd 2011) 450; for the socio-economic, political feud, vengeance, Islamic state and conspiracy theories explaining the development of *Boko Haram* sect see Simeon H O Alozieuwa, above n 51, 1.

146 Jideofo Adibe, 'Boko Haram: One Sect, Conflicting Narratives' (2012) 9(1) *African Renaissance* 50.

147 *HRC UPR II Report—Nigeria,* UN Doc A/HRC/25/6 paras 135.170, 135.171, 137.171.

148 The 41 sections of the TPA define and proscribe acts of terrorism including methods of intelligence gathering, prevention, investigation and prosecution of alleged terrorists and also mutual legal assistance.

'TPA' as Amended). While most of its provisions are human rights compliant, some are not. Some counterterrorism measures have been found to have grave impact on the enjoyment of human rights.[149] For example, Section 32(1) of TPA (as Amended), which provides that the Federal High Court 'shall have the sole jurisdiction to try an offence and impose the penalties specified in this Act',[150] is in conflict with the Child Rights Act 2003,[151] pursuant to which a child is to be tried by a Family Court.[152] This also goes against the UPR recommendations Nigeria accepted from Poland and Slovakia to '[e]nsure that neither the death penalty nor life sentence is imposed for offences committed by persons below 18 years of age'.[153]

Furthermore, subjecting the proscribed acts or omissions in the TPA[154] (including 'threats') 'to maximum of death penalty',[155] irrespective of the gravity of the offence, is open to abuse and undermines the principle of proportionality. Amnesty International notes this fact and other inconsistencies with the TPA to which it stated:

> Key provisions of the Act are incompatible with Nigeria's human rights obligations. Many of the provisions of the Act use terms and definitions that are imprecise and overbroad in scope, violating the 'legality' requirement for criminal offences, and/or unlawfully restricting a range of rights—such as freedom of thought, conscience and religion, freedom of opinion and expression, freedom of association and freedom of assembly—by failing to adhere to the requirements of demonstrable proportionality . . . some provisions relating to investigation, detention, and trial are not consistent with various provisions of human rights law.[156]

Another prominent issue during Nigeria's UPR related to the government's antiterrorism campaign was torture and extrajudicial executions. Six states, including Benin, Germany and Portugal, recommended during UPR I that Nigeria investigate and put an end to the use of torture and extrajudicial executions

149 See Edward Mogirea and Kennedy Mkutu Agade, 'Counter-terrorism in Kenya' (2011) 29(4) *Journal of Contemporary African Studies* 473; Arthur Chaskalson, 'The Widening Gyre: Counter-Terrorism, Human Rights and the Rule of Law' (2008) *The Cambridge Law Journal* 67, 69–91; Alex Conte, 'Human Rights Compliance in the Fight Against Terrorism' in Alex Conte (ed), *Human Rights in the Prevention and Punishment of Terrorism* (Springer 2010) 389.

150 *Terrorism (Prevention) Act 2011* (Nigeria), s 32 (1).

151 This is the law domesticated the Convention on the Rights of the Child.

152 Defined as a person below 18 years.

153 *HRC UPR II Report—Nigeria,* UN Doc A/HRC/25/6 paras 137.28, 137.29.

154 *Terrorism (Prevention) (Amendment) Act, 2013* s 1(2).

155 *Terrorism (Prevention) (Amendment) Act, 2013* s 2.

156 Amnesty International, 'Nigeria: Trapped in the Cycle of Violence' (2012) 47 available at <https://bit.ly/2mfhVHV> accessed 12/09/2019.

by the police.[157] These recommendations were accepted by the Nigerian government. Similarly, five states recommended during UPR II that the government of Nigeria end extrajudicial execution, investigate and prosecute perpetrators.[158]

Despite the above UPR commitment to end extrajudicial executions, there was an increase in extrajudicial executions during UPR I and II. Government security forces were implicated in numerous extrajudicial killings, torture and other serious human rights abuses.[159] The escalation of violence between *Boko Haram* and the government was prompted by an act of extrajudicial execution.[160] It was the death of Yussuf, a *Boko Haram* leader in police custody, that triggered *Boko Haram* to perpetuate the two major bombings in 2011 as acts of retaliation.[161]

During UPR II on Nigeria, Human Rights Agenda Network (HRAN) reported an increase in the number of extrajudicial executions, torture and ill treatment committed by the Joint Task Force set up by the government in the name of fighting terrorism.[162] Amnesty International also reported an increase in the number of extrajudicial executions by the government. It reported that over 950 people died in detention facilities ran by the Joint Task Force within the first six months of 2013.[163] Similarly, just one month after Nigeria's UPR I, Human Rights Watch documented 28 alleged extrajudicial executions committed by the government police between 28 July and 1 August 2009[164] and 27 extrajudicial executions carried out by the military in Maiduguri between July 2009 and May 2012.[165] The Nigerian National Human Rights Commission in its UPR II submission noted that there is no body set up to monitor and investigate extrajudicial executions in Nigeria and that the NCAT has no investigative powers.[166] During UPR II, Portugal recommended that the Nigerian government should tackle the problem of extrajudicial executions by mainstreaming human rights into counterterrorism laws and policies.[167] This can contribute to draw a clear line between law enforcement and terrorism. Besides, torture and extrajudicial executions are

157 Ibid paras 14, 22, 23.

158 *HRC UPR II Report –Nigeria*, UN Doc A/HRC/25/6 paras 135.68–135.70 and 135.170.

159 See Human Rights Watch, 'Spiraling Violence: Boko Haram Attacks and Security Force Abuses in Nigeria' (October 2012) *Human Rights Watch* 61; Human Rights Agenda Network (HRAN), above n 69.

160 Simeon H O Alozieuwa, above n 51, 1, 2.

161 Ibid.

162 See Human Rights Agenda Network (HRAN), above n 69, 4.

163 Amnesty International, 'Nigeria: Authorities Must Investigate Deaths of Boko Haram Suspects in Military Custody' Index No. AFR 44/025/2013 (16 October 2013).

164 Human Rights Watch, above n 159.

165 Ibid 64.

166 National Human Rights Commission of Nigeria, 'National Human Rights Commission Table of Commentary on 2009 UPR Recommendations and the Extent of Compliance' para 22 available at <https://bit.ly/2mbANaB> accessed 02/09/2019.

167 *HRC UPR II Report—Nigeria,* UN Doc A/HRC/25/6 para 135.171.

non-derogable rights recognised by international human rights law, and Nigeria (as of February 2017) did not officially derogate from the International Covenant on Civil and Political Rights (ICCPR) in its counterterrorism campaign.[168] Nigeria accepted all five recommendations during UPR II to end, prevent and investigate extrajudicial executions and torture by security forces and to guarantee respect for human rights in its fight against terrorism.[169] These recommendations were not implemented. In 2016, 285 cases of extrajudicial killings were reported to the Nigeria NHRC compared to 175 in 2015.

Acculturation falls within the broader socialisation theory on the ways in which human rights norms become socialised into domestic settings of states. Prominent among these theories is the five-stage spiral model developed by Risse, Ropp and Sikkink. A criticism of this theory was its failure to consider the regressive effect of serious conflicts and security threats on human rights norm implementation. This section with focus on *Boko Haram* terrorism has demonstrated that conflicts and security threats can have a regressive effect on state human rights compliance. The fight against *Boko Haram* terrorism in Nigeria has resulted in an increase by government police and militia in the perpetuation of torture and extrajudicial executions, despite its UPR commitments and other human rights obligations.

Concluding remarks

Nigeria's engagement with the UPR, in terms of its commitment to the national consultation process and the quality of its UPR delegation, indicated an effective engagement from the Nigerian government. This contrasted significantly with its engagement with the treaty bodies and the African Commission. While these bodies are non-coercive and non-adversarial in their methods of operation, they can be less cooperative, inclusive and collaborative than the UPR because of their high technical expertise and procedures. Also, the limited state involvement and control over their outcomes/findings make them less state-friendly than the UPR. The inclusive nature of Nigeria's UPR national consultation process and the quality of its UPR delegation were important indicators for an effective engagement with the UPR.

The 'soft' approach adopted by Nigeria as a reviewer strengthens the cooperative and non-confrontational nature of the UPR. The fact that such an approach generally produces more general (R4) than specific (R5) recommendations does not necessarily undermine the value and relevance of such recommendations. A major challenge for the UPR is the significant implementation gap which exists as was addressed on issues such as justice and detention, women's rights and

168 *International Covenant on Civil and Political Rights*, opened for signature 16 December 1966, 999 UNTS 14668 (entered into force 23 March 1976) arts 6 and 7. Extrajudicial execution as a non-derogable right is derived from the right to life.

169 *HRC UPR II Report—Nigeria*, UN Doc A/HRC/25/6 paras 135.68–135.70, 135.170.

torture. An important aspect that was evident in the extent of Nigeria's receptiveness to recommendations was cultural relativism. The Nigeria government was not willing to accept recommendations on sexual orientation based on culture. Approaches that employ coercion or recommend immediate normative solutions may experience negative resistance which may cause further regression. For example, calls for immediate decriminalisation or threats, such as the threat by the British government to withhold UK aid from governments that do not reform legislation banning homosexuality, were met with specific legislation further criminalising same-sex unions in countries including Nigeria and Uganda.[170] This further indicates the limits and dangers of coercive or confrontational approaches in addressing human rights issues which are perceived to be sensitive within certain cultures.

170 Same Sex Marriage Prohibition Act 2013 (Nigeria); Uganda Anti-Homosexuality Act, 2014 (Uganda).

5 Kenya and the UPR

The impact of effective NGO engagement

Introductory background

In the mid-1980s, Kenya was the subject of intensive global human rights campaigns.[1] Its record during this time was replete with gross human rights violations. Following an unsuccessful coup in August 1982, the government of President Daniel arap Moi of the ruling Kenyan African Union Congress (KANU) increased its direct control over parliament, the judiciary and CSOs.[2] To crack down on political opposition, the ensuing years witnessed civil liberties curtailed, elections rigged, political detention without trial and an increase in systemic torture.[3] The role of civil society and transnational advocacy networks in causing human rights and institutional changes in Kenya in the 1990s was invaluable[4] as it is today.

The dawn of a new millennium raised excitement and hopes especially when the KANU regime was replaced by the National Rainbow Party in 2003. Between 2003 and 2007, some improvements were made to Kenya's human rights record.[5] However, the 2007–2008 post-election violence was a major setback. Egregious human rights violations were committed in a magnitude which is yet to be fully

1 For an overview of the human rights campaigns and the struggle to bring about human rights norm socialisation in Kenya during the 1980s, see Thomas Risse, Stephen C Ropp, and Kathryn Sikkink, *The Power of Human Rights: International Norms and Domestic Change* (Cambridge University Press 1999) 39–66.

2 Makau Mutua, 'Justice Under Siege: The Rule of Law and Judicial Subservience in Kenya' (2001) 23(1) *Human Rights Quarterly* 96.

3 Korwa G Adar and Isaac M Munyae, 'Human Rights Abuses in Kenya Under President Arap Moi, 1978–2001' (2001) 5(1) *African Studies Quarterly* 1.

4 Ibid.

5 Within this period Kenya signed the African Charter on Human and Peoples' Rights on the Rights of Women in Africa; signed the International Convention on the Protection of the Rights of All Migrant Workers and Members of Their Families; acceded to Protocol to Prevent, Suppress and Punish Trafficking in Persons, especially Women and Children (supplementing the United Nations Convention against Trans-national Organised Crime) Palermo Protocol; ratified the Rome Statute of the International Criminal Court; signed the Protocol on the establishment of an African Court on Human and People's Rights; enacted the Persons with Disability Act, Act Number 14 of 2003, Laws of Kenya, adopted 2003, entered into force 16 June 2004; passed the Refugees Act (2006).

understood or resolved.[6] According to the report of the Commission of Inquiry into the Post-Election Violence, 1,133 people were killed[7] in the violence and 663, 921 people were internally displaced.[8] This formed part of the basis for the ICC's intervention in Kenya by the ICC prosecutor issuing arrest warrants on six Kenyan senior politicians and government officials. This move by the ICC prosecutor created resentment in the minds of many African leaders and increased their dislike for confrontational mechanisms of human rights enforcement.[9] Within this context, the introduction of the HRC's UPR mechanism came at a time when Kenya sought to address the 2007–2008 post-election violence issues, redeem its human rights record and find non-confrontational methods to engage with the international human rights system.

Kenya underwent its UPR I in 2010 (when it was not a HRC member) and UPR II in 2015 (by which time it was a HRC member). Kenya's UPR III is scheduled for January 2020 and is not covered in this analysis. Kenya's UPR I took place within the period when the country was undergoing a major constitutional review process. This process served as both an incentive and impediment to the realisation of many of its UPR recommendations. A distinctive feature of Kenya's engagement with the UPR mechanism is the difference which its civil society made to the state's level of engagement. The role played by NGOs in Kenya in the state's review process has been cited internationally as good practice and emulated by other states.[10] This was critical in engaging the Kenyan government in the pre-review, review and follow-up stages of the UPR.

Commitment to the pre-review process and the quality of Kenya's UPR delegation

Kenya's UPR national consultation process

HRC Resolution 5/1 requires states to undertake a broad consultation in preparing their national reports but leaves it open as to the particular approach that

6 Kenya National Commission on Human Rights, *Accounting for Human Rights Protection Under the UPR: The Difference Kenya's Stakeholders Made* (Kenya National Commission on Human Rights 2011) 3.

7 Commission of Inquiry into the Post-Election Violence (CIPEV), 'Report of the Commission of Inquiry into the Post-Election Violence' (16 October 2008) 383 (hereafter 'Waki Report').

8 Kenya National Human Rights Commission (KNCHR) and National Network for IDPs, 'Gains and Gaps: A Status Report on IDPs in Kenya, 2008–2010' (2011) 2.

9 Konstantinos D Magliveras and Gino J Naldi, 'The International Criminal Court's Involvement with Africa: Evaluation of a Fractious Relationship' (2013) 82 *Nordic Journal of International Law* 417.

10 Danish Institute for Human Rights, 'Universal Periodic Review First Cycle: Reporting Methodologies from the Position of the State, Civil Society and National Human Rights institutions' (2011) 38; OHCHR, Government of Republic of Moldova and UNDP, 'International Conference on Responding to the Recommendations of the Universal Periodic Review: Challenges, Innovation and Leadership, 4–5 November 2011' (2013) 10.

states take or what will be sufficient to amount to a broad consultation.[11] The approaches that states have adopted have not been uniform and they are sometimes inconsistent. For example, Nigeria during UPR I organised an NCF[12] but during UPR II set up an inclusive National Committee on the UPR.[13] Morocco held four meetings with ministerial departments, public agencies and institutions, and the Consultative Council on Human Rights.[14] Other states like Switzerland published its state report on their website inviting all of its citizens to make comments. Some states, like South Africa, did not meet this requirement of broad consultation because they never carried out any form of consultation with civil society during their UPR I.[15]

The preparation of the state report of Kenya during UPR I and II was coordinated by the Advisory Committee on International Human Rights Obligations (ACIHRO) that was set up by the government in 2005.[16] It is composed of 12 government officials, three CSOs and two members of the Kenyan National Commission on Human Rights (KNCHR).[17] It is mandated, among other things, to advise the government on its international human rights law obligations and to coordinate the timely preparation and submission of state reports to the various human rights monitoring bodies.[18] ACIHRO is chaired by the Attorney General of Kenya who is the head of the state law office and the principal legal advisor to the government.[19]

Both UPR reports were formulated through a broad consultation which involved the government, KNCHR and civil society stakeholders.[20] In addition to an initial consultative meeting during UPR II in November 2013, ACIHRO held another preparatory meeting in the same month in which the Office of the High Commissioner for Human Rights was an additional participant.[21] Kenya's NGO consultation was facilitated by the Kenyan Stakeholder Coalition for the UPR (KSC) which provided stakeholders like the Gay and Lesbian Coalition of

11 *Resolution 5/1*, UN Doc A/HRC/RES/5/1 para 15(a).
12 *HRC UPR I State Report—Nigeria*, UN Doc A/HRC/WG.6/NGA/1 para 2.
13 *HRC UPR II State Report—Nigeria*, UN Doc A/HRC/WG.6/NGA/1 para 4.
14 Working Group on the Universal Periodic Review, *National Report Submitted in Accordance with Paragraph 15 (a) of the Annex to Human Rights Council Resolution 5/1—Morocco,* 1st sess, UN Doc A/HRC/WG.6/1/MAR/1 (11 March 2008) para 11.
15 Lilian Chenwi, 'South Africa: State of State Reporting Under International Human Rights Law' (Research Paper Presented at the Seminar on Promoting Constitutional Rights Through International Human Rights Law: The State of South Africa's State Reporting, University of Western Cape Town, 22 September 2010) 13.
16 The Kenya Gazette, 'The Advisory/Consultative Committee on International Human Rights Obligations' (2005) Vol CVII No 9, Gazette Notice No. 489, 14.
17 Ibid.
18 The Kenya Gazette, above n 16, 14 [a] [c] and [f].
19 *The Constitution of Kenya*, art 156 (4).
20 Working Group on the Universal Periodic Review, *National Report Submitted in Accordance with Paragraph 15 (a) of the Annex to Human Rights Council Resolution 5/1—Kenya*, 15th sess, UN Doc A/HRC/15/8 (17 June 2010) para 5.
21 *HRC UPR II State Report—Kenya*, UN Doc A/HRC/WG.6/21/KEN/1 para 2.

Kenya the opportunity to be represented in the coalition.[22] The KSC comprised 97 NGOs representing nine broad human rights issues.[23] By engaging with the KSC, the government engaged with the various human rights issues they represented. A draft state report prepared by a subcommittee of the ACIHRO was endorsed by all stakeholders in a forum organised by the ACIHRO in October 2014.[24] This is an important aspect of the state's consultation process because it provides NGOs the opportunity to suggest inputs to the national report so that it is comprehensive and reflective of the actual human rights situation in the country. By considering NGO comments on the draft state report, the government can ensure that recommendations to address prevailing human rights issues are relevant and substantial.

However, many of the stakeholders' contributions were not included in the final report of the state. These included issues on the death penalty and sexual orientation.[25] Nevertheless, the pre-review consultation meetings were of mutual benefit to the state and the NGO stakeholders. It provided the NGO stakeholders with information that would enable them prioritise issues in their UPR campaign and the kind of recommendations to lobby states to make to the Kenyan UPR delegation. Also, the fact that the Kenyan government engaged various stakeholders in the preparation of its national reports can help create human rights awareness among state institutions, rights holders and various domestic stakeholders. Over time, this can help shape the logic of appropriateness[26] and create a 'symbiotic relationship'[27] between international and national human rights norms.

While ACIHRO has engaged with stakeholders and taken the UPR process seriously, its engagement with the UN human rights treaty body reporting is still to fully witness this level of commitment. Despite its establishment in 2005, Kenya before its UPR I had several overdue treaty body reports. For example, it had not submitted any report to the Committee on the Elimination of all

22 An important point to note here is that prior to the 2015 High Court judgement in the case *Eric Gitari V Non-Governmental Organisation Coordination Board and 4 Others [2015] eKLR*, Gay and Lesbian peoples' right to form an Association bearing the name gay and lesbian was not recognised in Kenya. See Section 5.6 for details on how the new constitution of Kenya impacted on this development.

23 These included Minority and Indigenous Rights Cluster; Sexual Minorities Cluster (including Gay and Lesbian Coalition of Kenya which was at this moment unregistered); Child Rights Cluster; Old Persons Cluster; Women Cluster; ESCR Cluster; Youth Cluster; Disability Cluster; and Civil and Political Rights Cluster.

24 Ibid.

25 KNCHR, 'Talking Points on the UPR' available at <https://bit.ly/2lKzhvX> accessed 13/09/2019.

26 Based on the logic of appropriateness state actions are driven by rules of appropriate or exemplary behaviour, organised into institutions. Rules are followed because they are seen to be natural, rightful, expected, and legitimate. See James G March and Johan P Olsen, 'The Logic of Appropriateness' (ARENA Working Papers No WP 04/09, Centre for European Studies University of Oslo 2004).

27 Bonita Meyersfeld, *Domestic Violence and International Law* (Hart Publishing 2010) 256–8.

Forms of Racial Discrimination. The initial report was due in October 2002, second report in October 2004 and the third and fourth reports after each subsequent two years.[28] Kenya's reporting to the treaty bodies has been described as 'inconsistent and a manifestation of lack of political will'.[29] Its initial report to the Committee against Torture which was due in 1998 was only submitted in 2007.[30] Its second report to the UN Human Rights Committee which was due in 1986 was only submitted in 2004. [31]

The UPR process has had some impact on Kenya's compliance with its UN treaty body reporting obligations. After its UPR I in 2010, the government began to meet many of its outstanding reporting obligations. While there was no specific UPR I recommendation to Kenya to this effect, Kenya had made a pledge in 2009 to continue to submit national reports to the treaty bodies when it sought membership in the HRC.[32] During UPR II, Sierra Leon recommended that Kenya '[s]ubmit overdue reports to the relevant treaty bodies'.[33] The Kenyan government took some action on these pledges and recommendation. It submitted its first, second, third and fourth reports to the Committee on the Elimination of all Forms of Racial Discrimination in 2011[34] and other outstanding reports.[35] In August 2018, Kenya submitted its third annual report to the Committee against Torture.[36] However, Kenya (as of July 2017) still has one overdue treaty body report which is more than ten years overdue.[37] Comparatively, Kenya's national report for UPR I and II were submitted in a timely manner.

From the aforementioned analysis of Kenya's pre-review consultation process, it can be concluded that the Kenyan government undertook broad consultation for its UPR process, but such broad consultation was made possible

28 P K Mbote and M Akech, *Kenya: Justice Sector and the Rule of Law* (African Minds 2011) 5.
29 See Connie Ngondi-Houghton, 'The State of Human Rights in Kenya' (A Baseline Survey Report (Main Report), Kenya National Commission of Human Rights (KNCHR) and Ministry of Justice and Constitutional Affairs (MOJCA), August 2005) 31.
30 Office of the High Commissioner for Human Rights, 'Reporting Status for Kenya' available at <https://bit.ly/2m7CDcu> accessed 13/09/2019.
31 See also Kenya's 5th and 6th reports to the Committee on the Elimination of All Forms of Discrimination against Women. They were due in 2001 but only submitted in 2006. See Ibid.
32 Human Rights Council, *Note Verbale Dated 30 January 2009 from the Permanent Mission of Kenya to the United Nations Addressed to the President of the General Assembly*, 63rd sess, Agenda Item 104 (c), UN Doc A/63/766.
33 UN Human Rights Council, *Report of the Working Group on the Universal Periodic Review—Kenya*, 29th sess, Agenda Item 6, UN Doc A/HRC/29/10 (26 March 2015) ('*HRC UPR II Report*—Kenya') 142.34.
34 See OHCHR, 'Status of Late and Non-reporting by State Parties' available at <https://bit.ly/2m7CDcu> accessed 22/09/2019.
35 CEDAW and CCPR for example; ibid.
36 Ibid.
37 Ibid.

in most part by the instrumentality of the NGO stakeholders who formed coalitions representing a broad range of human rights issues. While the government was willing to engage with many human rights issues during the consultation process, such engagement was not extended to the issues of sexual orientation and the death penalty. Nevertheless, Kenya has more actively engaged with the preparation of its UPR reports than with the treaty body reports despite the fact that the same committee (ACIHRO) is responsible for the preparation of both UPR and UN treaty body reports. This supports the argument that Kenya has more actively engaged with the UPR than with other human rights mechanisms. Moreover, as indicated earlier, the UPR has had some impact on the state's treaty body reporting obligation as Kenya began to submit many of its outstanding treaty body reports after its UPR I in 2010.

The quality of Kenya's UPR delegation

An effective engagement with the UPR process will not simply require that states send a large number of delegates for its review but rather high-level delegates. This will mean delegates with the competence to respond to questions during the interactive dialogue stage. The constitution of a state's UPR delegation and the authority that heads such a delegation will reflect the state's perspective on the UPR process. As highlighted in Chapter 4, a delegation headed by the state ministries of justice or human rights will engage more actively with the technical aspects of the human rights issues raised during the review than a delegation headed by the foreign ministries. This can help mitigate the level of politicisation. Some few states have also taken a positive approach to demonstrate gender parity and regional balance in their UPR delegation. This is in line with Resolution 5/1, which requires states to 'fully integrate a gender perspective' in the review.[38] For example, Sudan's UPR I delegation included representatives from the north and south regions of Sudan.[39] Kenya's delegation demonstrated gender parity as indicated below.

Kenya sent a delegation of 14 members during UPR I and 13 during UPR II. The number of delegates states send for the review depends on factors such as the size of the state, its financial capabilities and whether it has a permanent mission in Geneva. While large and economically powerful African states like Nigeria can send a delegation of 26 persons,[40] other smaller states like Gabon can only send a

38 *Institution Building of the United Nations Human Rights Council,* HRC Res 5/1, UN HRC OR, 5th sess, Annex [IB], UN Doc A/HRC/RES/5/1, annex (18 June 2007) ('Resolution 5/1') para 3(k).

39 International Service for Human Rights, 'International Development: Universal Periodic Review' (2011) 3 *Human Rights Monitor Quarterly* 10.

40 See *HRC UPR I Report—Nigeria,* UN Doc A/HRC/11/26, annex.

delegation comprised of six persons.[41] Kenya is one of the African states that have benefitted from the Voluntary Fund for Participation in the UPR mechanism.[42]

An examination of the composition of the Kenyan delegation indicated the government's willingness to be committed to the process rather than to simply consider it as a foreign affairs issue. The delegation for UPR I was headed by the state Minister of Justice, National Cohesion and Constitutional Affairs and UPR II by the Attorney General of the Republic.[43] More so, more than half of both delegations were comprised of legal and judicial personnel rather than diplomats. In addition, there was gender parity in both UPR delegations. Seven of the delegates during UPR I were female and eight during UPR II.[44] This is an interesting development because women are generally underrepresented in government appointments and national institutions in many states. In Kenya for example, only 10% of women were represented in parliament in 2009, placing Kenya at 112th position in the ranking of female participation in parliaments on a global scale.[45] As of February 2019, Kenya currently ranks at 90th position with 22% of women in their lower house of parliament and 31% in the senate.[46] In both UPR delegations of Kenya, there was a representative from the National Gender and Equality Commission.[47]

Kenya, therefore, had a comprehensive representation during both cycles of its UPR. The competence of its delegation and the gender balance of its composition can be an indication of the government's commitment to the UPR mechanism. However, such demonstration of gender parity in the composition of Kenya's UPR delegation should not be mistaken for the government's commitment to secure equal representation of women in government. The lower house of parliament has not met the threshold of 30% of women in parliament as required by the new Constitution.[48] This attracted many recommendations from both states and NGOs during UPR II.[49] Nevertheless, the exercise of gender parity in its

41 UN Human Rights Council, *Report of the Working Group on the Universal Periodic Review—Gabon*, 8th sess, Agenda Item 6 UN Doc A/HRC/8/35 (28 May 2008) annex.

42 See Office of the High Commissioner for Human Rights (OHCHR), *Requests for Financial Assistance Under the Voluntary Fund for Participation in the UPR Mechanism* (As of 24 February 2012) available at <https://bit.ly/2lSovng> accessed 13/09/2019.

43 *HRC UPR I—Kenya,* UN Doc A/HRC/15/8, annex; *HRC UPR II Report*—Kenya, annex.

44 Ibid.

45 Nigeria in February 2019 was ranked at 180th position with only 6% of female participation in Parliament. See Inter-Parliamentary Union, 'Women in National Parliament' (1 February 2019) available at <https://bit.ly/2lRJPcU> accessed 08/07/2019.

46 Ibid.

47 Ibid.

48 *The Constitution of Kenya*, Art. 27 (8).

49 For NGO recommendations see Civil Society Coalition on Kenya's 2nd Universal Periodic Review (CSCK-UPR), 'Report of the Civil Society Coalition on Kenya's 2nd Universal Periodic Review' (June 2014) 58–9 available at <https://bit.ly/2kMUa9Q> accessed 22/09/2019; Kenya Stakeholder's Coalition on Universal Periodic Review (KSC-UPR), 'Coalition Joint Submission' (13 June 2014) 27–8 available at <https://bit.ly/2kiAkmz>

UPR delegation may be seen as a positive step and an indication of the government's effective engagement with the UPR mechanism. Despite Nigeria's large UPR delegation (26 and 34 delegates during UPR I and II respectively), its delegation included only seven women.[50] The quality of Kenya's participation on this aspect therefore outshines that of Nigeria.

Kenya as a reviewer and as a state under review

Kenya as a reviewer

An examination of Kenya's engagement as a reviewer indicates that Kenya did not effectively engage as a reviewer in either cycle of the UPR. During UPR I (when it was not a HRC member), Kenya did not engage with the review of any state. Many states, particularly smaller states, do not participate or make recommendations to every state that comes up for review. States with limited or no permanent mission in Geneva will be very selective of the review sessions to attend. While this is not the case with Kenya and cannot explain their absence during UPR I as a reviewer, internal factors such as elections and ICC prosecution could arguably have limited their participation in the review of other states during UPR II.

During UPR II (when Kenya was a HRC member), Kenya's engagement as a reviewer improved, but the state participated selectively in the review of other states. Kenya participated in 13 of the 14 UPR II sessions and reviewed 47 states out of the total of 193 states which were reviewed during UPR II. Twenty-two of the 47 states reviewed by Kenya were African states,[51] and 14 were Asian states.[52] Kenya participated in the review of ten states from the WEOG, GRULAC and EEG groups combined. Kenya therefore tends to be more attracted to the review of its regional peers. This reinforces the theme of regionalism. During UPR II Kenya made 109 recommendations out of a total of 6,625 recommendations made by African states. This represents about 2% of the recommendations made by African states and about 0.3% of the recommendations made by all states (Kenya ranked at 108th top recommending state).[53] Figure 5.1 breaks down the recommendations made by Kenya across five regional blocs to determine the extent of its participation as a reviewer and the quality of its recommendations.

As indicated in Figure 5.1, Kenya made more recommendations to African states (49% of the overall 109 recommendations by Kenya) than to any other

accessed 13/09/2019; For state recommendations see *HRC UPR II Report*—Kenya, UN Doc A/HRC/29/10 paras 142.122, 142.130, 142.134, 142.139, 142.141, 142.144.

50 Another example is Senegal whose UPR I delegation was composed of 15 men and 5 women.

51 These are Angola, Burundi, Botswana, Comoros, Djibouti, Eritrea, Ethiopia, Nigeria, Ghana, Mauritius, Republic of Congo, and Zambia.

52 These are China, Uzbekistan, Cambodia, Yemen, United Arab Emirate and Sri Lanka.

53 UPR INFO, 'Statistics of Recommendations' available at <https://bit.ly/2kaSeYa> accessed 08/07/2019.

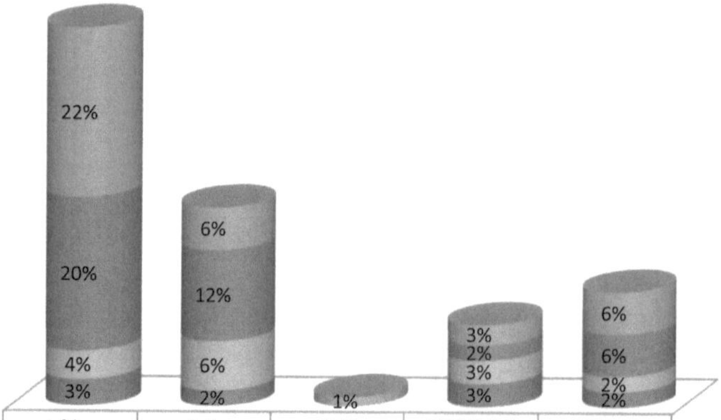

	Africa	Asia	EEG	GRULAC	WEOG
R5 - Specific Action	22%	6%	1%	3%	6%
R4 - General Action	20%	12%	0%	2%	6%
R3 - Consider Action	4%	6%	0%	3%	2%
R2 - Continue Action	3%	2%	0%	3%	2%
R1 - Minimal Action	0%	0%	0%	0%	0%

Figure 5.1 UPR II recommendations by Kenya

group of states. This is closely followed by Asian states (26% of the overall 89 recommendations). A plausible explanation for this is that both regions have adopted a softer approach to the UPR[54] and both largely share a common position on issues like the death penalty. Such commonality can be a factor that attracts mutual participation in their respective reviews. While Kenya engaged within and outside its regional group as a reviewer, it was selective in its engagement as a reviewer and engaged very little with the review of states from WEOG. With the exception of Latvia's review session, Kenya did not engage in the review of any other states from EEG. This can arguably be seen as strategic engagement given the limited resources at its disposal for the review. The principle of universality[55] has distinguished the UPR mechanism from other UN human rights monitoring mechanisms on the basis that all UN member states are subject to its review. However, the review cannot be seen as truly universal when states become selective in reviewing their peers and do not attend the review sessions of some regional groups of states. While the UPR mechanism does not prevent any state from participating in the review of its peers, the limited time allocated to each

54 Edward McMahon, 'The Universal Periodic Review: A Work in Progress, an Evaluation of the First Cycle of the New UPR Mechanism of the United Nations Human Rights Council' (2012) *Friedrich Ebert Stiftung* 1, 3.

55 *Resolution 5/1,* UN Doc A/HRC/RES/5/1 para 3(a).

state and for the interactive dialogue session may discourage the participation of some states in the review of their peers.[56]

States were very receptive to the recommendations made by Kenya. About 81% of the recommendations made by Kenya were accepted by its peers. However, the majority of the accepted recommendations (86%) were non-specific recommendations. These recommendations touched on general issues (R4) or required the state under review to 'consider' undertaking a particular action (R3). As such, the recommendations were not critical enough to trigger specific action on the part of the state under review.

A combined 37% of the total 109 recommendations made by Kenya during UPR II required a specific action (R5) from the states under review. Thirty-nine per cent of the recommendations required a general action (R4), such as the recommendation for Eritrea to '[e]nhance its cooperation with the mechanisms of the Human Rights Council and OHCHR'.[57] Such general recommendations can be frustrating to both the state under review and other UPR stakeholders. This is because they are vague in terms of the means of implementation and measuring outcomes. Also, it has been observed that general recommendations (R4) tend to be more attractive to states because they are more easily 'implemented' as a result of the fact that their implementation is open to interpretation.[58] Abebe has even argued that African states largely make general recommendations (R4) which are at times too general to be implemented.[59] However, African states have in some cases not hesitated to make specific recommendations (R5), even to their African peers. Twenty-two per cent of the total 109 UPR II recommendations made by Kenya to its African peers required specific action (R5). As indicated in Figure 5.1, Kenya made more specific recommendations to its African peers than to any other group of states. Kenya, for example, recommended during UPR II that Angola '[c]omplete, without delay, the ratification of the Convention against Torture and Other Cruel, Inhuman or Degrading Treatment or Punishment'.[60] It also recommended that Mozambique '[r]atify the International Covenant on Economic, Social and Cultural Rights'.[61] Both recommendations were accepted.

56 Ibid paras 21–24.

57 See Human Rights Council, *Report of the Working Group on the Universal Periodic Review—Eritrea*, 26th sess, Agenda Item 6, UN Doc A/HRC/26/13 (7 April 2014) para 122.79.

58 UPR Info, 'Beyond Promise: The Impact of UPR on the Ground' (2014) 24 available at <https://bit.ly/1JyZVMZ> accessed 13/09/2019.

59 Allehone M Abebe, 'Of Shaming and Bargaining: African States and the Universal Periodic Review of the United Nations Human Rights Council' (2009) *Human Rights Law Review* 1, 16; The pacific approach adopted by most African states to the UPR largely prompts them to make general recommendations.

60 Human Rights Council, *Report of the Working Group on the Universal Periodic Review—Angola*, 28th sess, Agenda Item 6, UN Doc A/HRC/28/11 (5 December 2014) para 134.21.

61 Human Rights Council, *Report of the Working Group on the Universal Periodic Review—Italy*, 28th sess, Agenda Item 6, UN Doc A/HRC/28/4 (10 December 2014) para 145.163.

In addition, the fact that the recommendations states make may be general does not necessarily imply that they are not valuable.

It has also been suggested that African states mostly make recommendations which require minimal action (R1).[62] Such recommendations call upon the state under review to seek technical and financial assistance in the implementation of human rights. Twenty per cent of the recommendations made by Nigeria to African states during UPR I fell in this category. All the recommendations made by Nigeria to Chad during UPR I required Chad to seek technical and financial assistance in the implementation of human rights.[63] Interestingly, Kenya made no recommendation under this category as indicated in Figure 5.1. This would suggest that there is no particular preference for R1 recommendations among African states.

Kenya has not actively engaged as a reviewer compared to Nigeria. Nigeria, as indicated in the Chapter 4, participated in 12 sessions during UPR I and made a total of 108 recommendations to 60 states. During UPR II, Nigeria participated in 11 of the 14 sessions and made a total of 102 recommendations to 64 states across the five different regional groups with recommendations across the five action categories. In the case of Kenya, it did not participate in the review of any state during UPR I, but during UPR II there was limited improvement in the nature of its engagement as a reviewer. Also, both Nigeria and Kenya have displayed a double standard in their engagement. Kenya, just like Nigeria,[64] refused to accept a similar recommendation it made to its peer. Kenya recommended that the United Arab Emirates should consider ratifying the migrant workers' convention among other instruments[65] but did not accept similar recommendations

62 Edward McMahon and Marta Asherio, 'A Step Ahead in Promoting Human Rights? The Universal Periodic Review of the Human Rights Council' (2012) 18(2) *Global Governance* 231, 235.

63 Human Rights Council, *Report of the Working Group on the Universal Periodic Review—Chad*, 12th sess, Agenda Item 6, UN Doc A/HRC/12/5 (5 October 2009) para 74; The African group has the majority of states that have applied and benefitted under the Voluntary Fund for participation in the UPR and the UPR Voluntary Fund for Financial and Technical Assistance. See Out of the 67 states that have applied to this fund, 27 are from Africa including Kenya. See Office of the High Commissioner for Human Rights (OHCHR), above n 42, 21 African states have requested assistance from this fund compared to 13 states from Americas, 11 states from Asia and Pacific, 12 states from Europe and Central Asia and two states from Middle East.

64 Nigeria recommended during UPR I that Argentina 'Ratify the Second Optional Protocol to the International Covenant on Civil and Political Rights already signed by Argentina, aiming at the abolition of the death penalty'. Argentina accepted this recommendation. When the same recommendation was made by Brazil and Montenegro to Nigeria during UPR II, Nigeria did not accept the recommendation. See *HRC UPR I Report—Nigeria*, UN Doc A/HRC/11/ para 137.5.

65 See Human Rights Council, *Report of the Working Group on the Universal Periodic Review—United Arab Emirates*, 23rd sess, Agenda Item 6, UN Doc A/HRC/23/13 (21 March 2013) para 128.12.

from Sierra Leone, Madagascar and the Philippines.[66] Nevertheless, the nature of Kenya's engagement as a reviewer was reflective of the theme of regionalism as it made more recommendations to African states and participated more in the review of states within the African regional group during UPR II than states in the EEG or WEOG regional groups. The disparity between Kenya's engagement with the UPR when it was a member of the HRC (UPR II) and when it was not (UPR I) underscores the potential for membership in the HRC to have some influence on state engagement with the UPR. Kenya engaged more as a reviewer during UPR II when it was a HRC member compared to its non-engagement during UPR I when it was not a HRC member, although there may be other reasons contributing to this result.

Kenya as a state under review

Kenya was reviewed by the HRC in May 2010 and January 2013 for UPR I and II respectively. During UPR 1, 50 states made recommendations to Kenya, 14 of which were African states. A total of 150 recommendations were made and Kenya accepted 128.[67] It rejected seven of the recommendations and postponed its response to 15 of the recommendations.[68] However, during the 15th session of the HRC, the Kenyan delegation accepted two recommendations on the rights of Indigenous people that were previously rejected.[69] Furthermore, the government responded to recommendations to abolish the death penalty by stating that 'any attempt to abolish it would not enjoy parliamentary approval at the present time'.[70] In addition, the government 'rejected in full' the recommendations on the decriminalisation of same-sex unions.[71] This reinforces the cultural relativist approach of African states highlighted in Chapter 4.[72]

During UPR II, there was an increase in the number of recommendations made to Kenya as well as an increase in the number of recommending states. Ninety-one states made 253 recommendations to Kenya. Kenya accepted 192 and rejected 61 of the recommendations.[73] African states engaged with the review of Kenya at a similar rate to their engagement with Nigeria. During UPR I, 13 African states made recommendations to Nigeria and 14 to Kenya. During UPR II, 26 African states made recommendations to Nigeria and 27 to Kenya. The

66 *HRC UPR II Report—Kenya*, UN Doc A/HRC/29/10 paras 142.1–143.61.
67 *HRC UPR I—Kenya*, UN Doc A/HRC/15/8 paras 101.1–103.7.
68 Ibid paras 102.1–102.15.
69 UN Human Rights Council, *Report of the Human Rights Council on Its Fifteenth Session*, 15th sess, Agenda Item 1, UN Doc A/HRC/15/60 (31 October 2011) ('*Report of the HRC on Its 15th* Session') para 419.
70 Ibid para 417.
71 Ibid para 420.
72 Nigeria for example rejected all the recommendations on same sex marriage during UPR I and subsequently strengthened its position through the enactment of the Same Sex Marriage Prohibition Act in 2010, officially criminalising same sex relations.
73 *HRC UPR II Report—Kenya*, UN Doc A/HRC/29/10.

majority of recommendations to Kenya during UPR II related to issues such as women and children's rights; ratification of international human rights instruments; socio-economic rights; the rights of civil society and human rights defenders; and the death penalty. Recommendations on issues relating to cooperation with international mechanisms and the rights of women, children and persons with disabilities represented about 72% of the total rejected recommendations. Figures 5.2 and 5.3 provide an overview of Kenya's responses to UPR I and II recommendations. They provide a general overview and compare Kenya's responses to the recommendations made by its regional peers and those made by other groups of states.

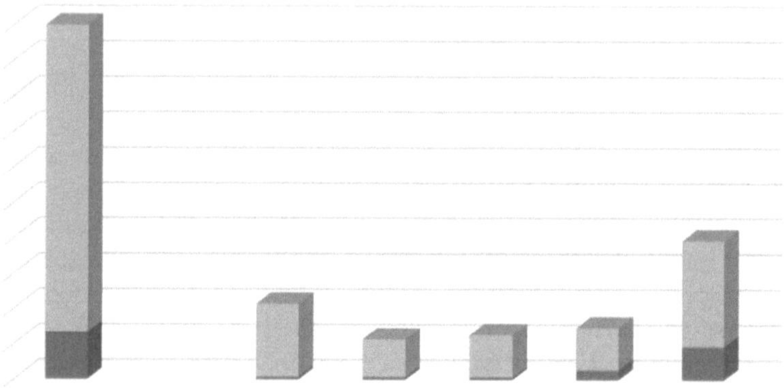

	Total Rec.	Africa	Asia	EEG	GRULAC	WEOG
Accepted	86.7%	20.7%	10.7%	12%	12%	30%
Rejected	13.3%	0.7%	0.7%	0.7%	2.7%	9.3%

Figure 5.2 Kenya UPR I percentage of recommendations accepted

	Total Rec.	Africa	Asia	EEG	GRULAC	WEOG
Accepted	76%	19%	12%	12%	11%	20%
Rejected	24%	4%	2%	8%	3%	7.5%

Figure 5.3 Kenya UPR II percentage of recommendations accepted

Figures 5.2 and 5.3 indicate that Kenya actively engaged with the recommendations from both its regional group and all other groups of states. While Kenya was more inclined to accept recommendations from its regional peers during UPR I (Figure 5.2), it also accepted most of the recommendations from states outside its regional group. None of the recommendations during its UPR I (Figure 5.2) was rejected outright except for the one which required the state to decriminalise same-sex relations and provide protection and equal treatment to LGBT persons.[74]

During UPR II (Figure 5.3), there was a significant increase in the percentage of rejected recommendations (from 13% to 24%). The increase in the number of rejected recommendations can be explained by the rise in the number of recommendations calling for the ratification of international instruments, abolition of the death penalty and the decriminalisation of same-sex relationships. For example, during UPR I, 22 recommendations required Kenya to take an action on certain international treaties, the majority of which were accepted by the state. During UPR II, 35 recommendations were made on this issue, the majority of which were rejected by the state and most of which required the state to ratify optional protocols to various human rights treaties. This indicates that the Kenyan delegation was not willing to allow for greater scrutiny of its human rights record as these optional protocols either establish a communication procedure or an inquiry procedure or both.[75]

The right for states to reject recommendations has been a major criticism of the UPR.[76] However, the fact that states reject recommendations does not necessary imply it creates no effect. The social and cognitive pressures generated by the process of acculturation can over time influence a state to alter its position and act on the rejected recommendations. The UPR Info study on mid-term implementation of UPR I recommendations also revealed that 15% of the rejected recommendations had nevertheless triggered an implementation action.[77]

Kenya's overall high acceptance level during UPR I (about 87%) and UPR II (76%) and its high intra-regional acceptance level may demonstrate the state's general receptiveness to UPR recommendations. This supports two earlier general findings made on UPR I. First, African states accepted more recommendations from their regional group than did any other state from their respective

74 *HRC UPR I—Kenya,* UN Doc A/HRC/15/8 para 101.8.

75 The communication procedure permits individuals to petition the state about human rights violations before a competent treaty body. The inquiry procedure allows for an inquiry into systematic and serious human rights abuses in states that are parties to the relevant optional protocol.

76 Heather Collister, 'Rituals and Implementation in the Universal Periodic Review' in Hilary Charlesworth and Emma Larking (eds), ***Human Rights and the Universal Periodic Review: Rituals and Ritualism*** (Cambridge University Press 2015) 116–19.

77 UPR Info, 'Universal Periodic Review: On the Road to Implementation' (2012) 63 available at <https://bit.ly/2mepWwI> accessed 13/09/2019; UPR Info, 'Mid-term Implementation Assessment on China' (13 February 2012) 13.

regional groups.[78] This aspect of identification is an important micro element which can facilitate the process of acculturation by causing recommendations made by states within a regional block, which otherwise may not have been accepted, to be accepted by members of that regional block. Second, African states accepted a higher percentage of recommendations during UPR I than any other group of states.[79] However, such a superficial analysis may cloud other potential aspects of a state's receptiveness to the UPR recommendations. A clearer picture of this level of receptiveness can be seen when the acceptance level is broken down into the various categories of recommendations. Figure 5.4 examines this aspect to determine whether Kenya was receptive to the various categories of recommendations made by its peers during its reviews. The rank under which a recommendation falls equally plays a crucial role in the state's implementation. This is because states generally are keener to accept recommendations that are general (R4) because it gives the implementing state greater autonomy to define how such a recommendation is to be implemented and a comfortable margin of appreciation as to the meaning of implementation. However, the more general a recommendation, the harder it is to measure implementation.

UPR I (Figure 5.4) shows that the state's acceptance level reasonably spreads across the various categories of recommendations from those requiring a minimal action (R1) to those requiring a specific action (R5). Similar findings are made in Figure 5.5 in relation to UPR II. As earlier indicated, the Kenyan government accepted all its UPR I recommendations except for that which required the state

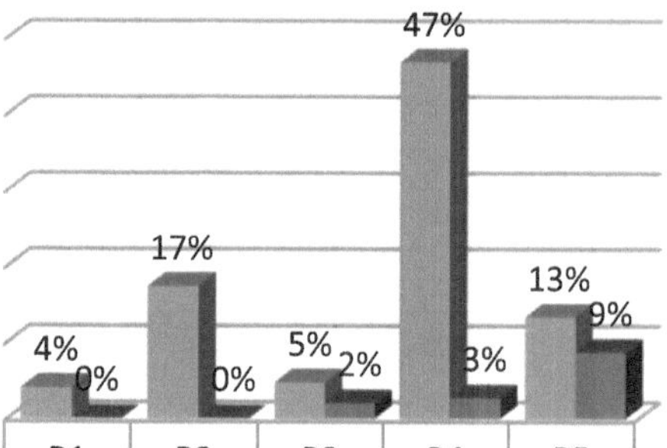

	R1	R2	R3	R4	R5
Accepted	4%	17%	5%	47%	13%
Rejected	0%	0%	2%	3%	9%

Figure 5.4 Kenya UPR I acceptance level by category

78 African states accepted 94% of the recommendations from African states, Asian states accepted 92% from Asian states and WEOG states 62% from WEOG states. See Edward McMahon, above n 54, 19.

79 Ibid.

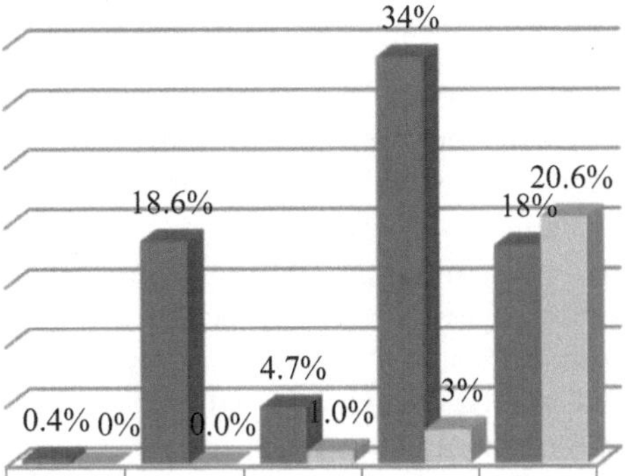

	R1	R2	R3	R4	R5
Accepted	0.4%	18.6%	4.7%	34%	18%
Rejected	0%	0.0%	1.0%	3%	20.6%

Figure 5.5 UPR II acceptance level by category

to take concrete steps to provide for protection and equal treatment of LGBT persons, classified as a general recommendation (R4). However, the percentage of specific recommendations (R5) that were rejected by Kenya increased from 9% to 21% across UPR I and II (see Figure 5.5). More than half of the total specific recommendations made to Kenya were rejected, and this constituted 19% of the overall UPR recommendations to Kenya. This aspect of the state's receptiveness could be clouded by the overall high percentage of accepted recommendations and indicates a significant resistance to the acceptance of specific recommendations.

Specificity of recommendations and a 'softer approach'

An interesting development in the review of Kenya is that it was engaged by its regional peers in some sensitive issues within the region like the death penalty and in some specific recommendations (R5) such as to '[a]dopt the bill on persons deprived of liberty'.[80] Kenya tends to be more inclined to accept a sensitive recommendation if it requires a continuing action (R2) or to consider an action (R3) rather than one requiring a specific action (R5). In other words, the state would easily accept recommendations which required 'softer' actions than those calling for 'tougher' actions. For example, during UPR II, it accepted R2 recommendations (to continue action) from Angola and Rwanda to '[c]ontinue its efforts towards the abolition of the death penalty'[81] but rejected R5 recommendations

80 See *HRC UPR II Report—Kenya*, UN Doc A/HRC/29/10 paras 143.32, 142.34, 142.47, 142.15; *HRC UPR I—Kenya*, UN Doc A/HRC/15/8 para 101.

81 See *HRC UPR II Report—Kenya*, UN Doc A/HRC/29/10 paras 142.63, 142.87.

(specific action) from France and Poland to '[a]bolish the death penalty'.[82] Similarly, during UPR II, it accepted a 'softer' recommendation from Albania to '[r]aise public awareness on the abolition of the death penalty . . .'[83] but rejected a 'tougher' recommendation from Australia to 'formalize its moratorium on the death penalty'.[84] This indicated the unwillingness of the state to engage with specific recommendations which accounted for 85% of the overall 61 rejected recommendations and 19% of the overall 150 recommendations to Kenya.

While Abebe observed during UPR I that African states largely made general recommendations,[85] UPR II has witnessed greater specificity in the recommendations from African states. About 31% of recommendations made by African states during UPR II to Kenya required a specific action. Some have stepped out of the regional dynamics to make specific recommendations on issues like the death penalty. Gabon during Kenya's UPR II recommended that Kenya '[c]omplete the process of abolition of the death penalty'.[86] Madagascar recommended that Kenya '[a]ccede to all human rights instruments that it is not yet a party'.[87] While Kenya rejected this recommendation, it accepted a 'softer' one from Lesotho and Nicaragua to consider or pursue efforts to adopt international instruments which it is not yet a party to.[88] This further reflects the inclination of Kenya to accept only 'softer' recommendations. All rank 2 recommendations (to continue action) were accepted by Kenya during UPR II. This is because the majority of the recommendations required the state to continue the implementation of certain actions which were triggered by the transitional justice processes within the state and the new Constitution. Some of these actions included police and judicial reforms,[89] socio-economic rights[90] and cooperation with international mechanisms such as the ICC[91] and had been recommended by states during UPR I. The Kenyan delegation therefore had no difficulty accepting recommendations which required it to continue implementation on these issues. A similar 'soft' approach to the UPR was demonstrated in the engagement of Nigeria with the UPR and generally reflects the approach of African states in the review of their regional peers.

However, while the 'soft' approach tends to be attractive to states, a more critical perspective is that they sometimes produce general recommendations which are vague and consequently it is very difficult to assess their implementation outcome. For example, Azerbaijan recommended that Kenya should

82 Ibid paras 143.39, 143.44.
83 Ibid 142.61.
84 Ibid 143.38.
85 Allehone M Abebe, above n 59, 1, 16.
86 *HRC UPR II Report—Kenya*, UN Doc A/HRC/29/10 para 143.140.
87 Ibid para 143.23.
88 Ibid paras 142.1, 142.2.
89 *HRC UPR II Report—Kenya*, UN Doc A/HRC/29/10 paras 142.118, 142.120.
90 Ibid para 142.98.
91 Ibid para 142.112.

'[f]urther promote good governance'.[92] The KNCHR when commenting on the implementation of this recommendation noted that it was difficult to assess.[93] General recommendations (R4) tend to be vague and pose a difficulty in assessing implementation. However, this criticism is not unique to the UPR mechanism as the recommendations and concluding observations of treaty bodies have been criticised for their lack of 'clarity, degree of detail, level of accuracy and lack of specificity'.[94] Nevertheless, recommendations which are phrased in general terms (R4) may at times subsequently translate to specific action (R5) at the implementation stage. For example, the general recommendation (R4) by the Netherlands that Kenya '[p]rovide adequate protection for witnesses of human rights violations'[95] was implemented through a specific action, the enactment of the Witness Protection Amendment Act 2010 which established a Witness Protection Agency.

To an extent, Kenya engaged effectively with different categories of recommendations as a state under review and accepted a high percentage of recommendations. Nevertheless, it can be argued that Kenya has not always been consistent with its position between UPR I and II as there is a potential finding of double standards in its engagement. During UPR I, it accepted a recommendation from Burkina Faso to ratify ICRMW.[96] During UPR II, it refused to accept the same recommendation from Sierra Leone,[97] while at the same time recommending that the United Arab Emirates should consider ratifying ICRMW among other instruments.[98] Charlesworth and Larking have observed the tendency of the UPR to degenerate to this aspect of ritualism where a state criticises another state for rights failures but itself does not provide adequate protection for the right in question.[99]

The role of the KNCHR and domestic NGOs in Kenya's UPR process

As highlighted in Chapter 1, the inclusion of NGOs as participants in the UPR process was a compromise which limited the extent of their participation in the

92 See section 5.6 for other examples and the implementation outcome.

93 *See Kenya National Commission on Human Rights, 'Kenya Recommendations—Session 21—UPR Info' available at <https://bit.ly/2kWx5Bv> accessed 22/09/2019.*

94 Secretary General, *Effective Functioning of Bodies Established Pursuant to United Nations Human Rights Instruments*, UN Doc. E/CN.4/1997/74 (27 March 1997) Annex para 109.

95 *HRC UPR I—Kenya*, UN Doc A/HRC/15/8 para 101.66.

96 *International Convention on the Protection of the Rights of All Migrant Workers and Members of Their Families*, opened for signature 18 December 1990, A/RES/45/158 (entered into force 1 July 2003).

97 *HRC UPR II Report—Kenya*, UN Doc A/HRC/29/10 paras 143.1–143.1.

98 See Human Rights Council, above n 65 para 128.12.

99 Hilary Charlesworth and Emma Larking (eds), *Human Rights and the Universal Periodic Review: Rituals and Ritualism* (Cambridge University Press 2015) 15.

UPR process. Their formal participation is generally limited to the pre-review national consultation process. While they can attend the adoption of state outcome reports at the plenary session of the HRC, they cannot make statements or pose questions during the interactive dialogue session. According to Schokman and Lynch, there are three obstacles to effective NGO engagement with the UPR process.[100] These are the political nature of the process, limited formal opportunities for NGOs and the lack of knowledge about the UPR.[101] However, Schokman and Lynch in their analysis did not consider the domestic operational environment and constraints. In addition to the limitations to direct NGO participation in the UPR process, domestic NGOs within many African states are further constrained by the domestic NGO operational environment which tends to be hostile or distrustful of NGO activities. Many African states have either restricted the establishment or activities of NGOs or limit, by legislation, their ability to secure foreign financial aid.[102]

Despite the limitations to NGO participation in the UPR process, Schokman and Lynch have provided pragmatic suggestions on how NGOs can effectively engage in the UPR process. These include the formation of NGO coalitions, effective media engagement and a focused advocacy strategy.[103] While these three suggestions by Schokman and Lynch are practical ways for effective NGO engagement, they are yet to be tested on specific state engagement. This section builds on these practical suggestions and empirically tests them in the case of Kenya to determine their impact on Kenya's UPR process. This section examines the formation and composition of the Kenya Stakeholder Coalition (KSC) for the UPR, its media and advocacy campaigns, and the impact on Kenya's UPR process. It also considers whether the NGO domestic operational environment in Kenya and other factors may have hampered their effective engagement with the UPR process.

100 Ben Schokman and Phil Lynch, 'Effective NGO Engagement with the Universal Periodic Review' in Hilary Charlesworth and Emma Larking (eds), *Human Rights and the Universal Periodic Review: Rituals and Ritualism* (Cambridge University Press 2015) 132–44.

101 Ibid.

102 In Angola, domestic legislation prohibits NGOs from taking part in 'all activities of state organs; electoral processes.' See *Law of Association 1991* (Angola), 14/91 of 11 May 1991, Art. 8; In Eritrea, UN and bilateral agencies have been restricted by the Eritrean government from directly funding domestic NGOs. See *Administration Proclamation No. 145/2005* (Eritrea); In 2009, Nigeria characterised the allegations in some International NGOs reports for the UPR as 'preposterous', 'patently false' and 'unhelpful to the UPR process'. See *HRC UPR I Report—Nigeria,* UN Doc A/HRC/11/26 para 8; In March 2016, Sudan obstructed the participation of the representatives of four civil society organisations in the UPR of Sudan by confiscating their passports. See The Worldwide Human Rights Movement (FIDH), 'Sudan blocks civil society participation in the UN-led human rights review' (2016).

103 Ben Schokman and Phil Lynch, above n 100, 132–44.

The formation and composition of the KSC

The KNCHR was very instrumental in the formation of the KSC.[104] The KNCHR introduced the UPR process to NGOs in Kenya in a four-day conference in October 2008. It convened another meeting on 10 March 2009, attended by 22 people from 17 CSOs.[105] It was during this second meeting that the Kenya Stakeholders' Coalition (KSC) for the UPR was established. Schokman and Lynch have identified three key benefits in forming NGO coalitions. These are the provision of expert input on the scope and nature of recommendations; the creation of validity and credibility; and ensuring a long-term focus on implementation.[106] First, a strong domestic NGO coalition can help provide expert input and guidance in identifying and prioritising the major relevant human rights issues. This is because of their on-the-ground experience and their understanding of the national legal, political, social and economic context.[107] Second, given the distrust and hostility by African governments towards NGOs, as noted previously, the formation of NGO coalitions can empower NGOs and enhance their credibility and capacity to influence state engagement at various phases of the UPR. NGO coalitions can have more influence on the UPR process than individual NGOs, especially by influencing state UPR recommendations through their advocacy strategies. As Schokman and Lynch observe, 'representing a large NGO coalition opens the door to many Geneva-based missions, which means that greater effort can be made to ensure that the recommendations ultimately made to the state are as relevant and practical as possible'.[108]

Notwithstanding, for any UPR NGO coalition to effectively engage in the UPR process, it is important that such a coalition is stable and broadly representative. If the membership of the coalition does not broadly represent all relevant NGOs, then some particular issues may be overlooked. Equally, if the membership is not stable, then arguably certain issues may not be appropriately represented at certain times. The membership of the KSC after its formation grew to more than 97 NGOs, broadly representing nine clusters.[109] However, a weakness of this coalition is that its membership has not been stable and has fluctuated at

104 The Kenya National Commission on Human Rights (KNCHR) is an autonomous national human rights institution accredited with an 'A' status in accordance with the Paris Principles. See Global Alliance of National Human Rights Institutions (GANHRI), 'Chart of the Status of National Institutions Accredited by the Global Alliance of National Human Rights Institutions (Accreditation status as of 5 August 2016)' (GANHRI 2016) available at <https://bit.ly/2kksSHC> accessed 13/09/2019.

105 Kenya National Commission on Human Rights, above n 6, 15.

106 Ben Schokman and Phil Lynch, above n 100, 133–5.

107 Ibid 133.

108 Ibid 134–5.

109 These are minority and Indigenous rights; sexual minorities rights; child rights; the rights of the elderly; women's rights; ESCR; youth rights; disability rights; and civil and political rights. See Kenya Stakeholder's Coalition on Universal Periodic Review (KSC-UPR),

different stages of the review when some coalition members leave the coalition. According to the KNCHR, some NGOs that initially were members of the KSC stopped attending meetings of the coalition.[110] It is unclear whether they left due to financial constraints or disagreements about the agenda of the KSC, but this in some ways has limited the effectiveness of the coalition.

After its formation, the KSC agreed on a common approach to the UPR. While it was debated whether the KSC should prepare a single or multiple report, the coalition ultimately submitted a joint UPR stakeholders' report for Kenya under the nine human rights thematic clusters mentioned earlier.[111] The single report had more credibility than the disjointed content issues which multiple reports could raise.[112] This report was comprehensive and included findings and recommendations from at least 97 Kenyan NGOs working on different human rights issues. However, there is a limitation on the length of such reports. The word limit for reports prepared by NGOs is 10,700, while the OHCHR summary of stakeholders' information is limited to 8,500 words. Therefore, NGO reports cannot detail every human rights issue in Kenya due to the limitation set out. Moreover, the summary of NGO reports prepared by the OHCHR potentially diminishes and dilutes the substance of NGO reports.[113] This makes it vital for NGOs to highlight and prioritise the most critical issues. An NGO coalition is essential in the prioritisation process and needs to be broadly representative.

Despite these weaknesses identified, the KSC represents an example of a strong African NGO coalition for the UPR. This can be contrasted with the NGOs in other African states in which there were no NGO coalitions for the UPR or where there was one but it lacked a broad and representative mandate. For example, in South Africa, while there were a few joint submissions, there were no NGO coalitions during UPR I and II. In Nigeria, the CSO Coalition for the UPR in 2013 was neither broad nor representative as its membership was composed of only 13 NGOs and their report failed to address key issues such as socio-economic rights and the death penalty.[114] Therefore, a broad, stable and representative NGO coalition can enhance NGO engagement in the UPR process.

'Coalition Joint Submission' (13 June 2014) Annexure 2 available at <https://bit.ly/2kKUc1R> accessed 13/09/2019; Ibid 18–19.

110 Kenya National Commission on Human Rights, above n 105, 19.

111 Kenya Stakeholder's Coalition on Universal Periodic Review (KSC-UPR), above n 109.

112 Ibid 19.

113 The summary of stakeholders' information prepared by the OHCHR is one of the three documents used to review each state in the UPR process. NGOs would therefore like to see their concerns reflected in the summary prepared by the OHCHR. See Julie Billaud, 'Keepers of the Truth: 'transparent' documents for the Universal Periodic Review' in Charlesworth and Larking (eds), Human Rights and the Universal Periodic Review: Rituals and Ritualism (Cambridge University Press 2015) 76–7.

114 See Coalition of Nigerian Human rights CSOs on UPR, 'Report on the Human Rights Situation in Nigeria Submitted to the Office of the UN Human Rights Council' (2013) 10 available at <https://bit.ly/2kfCfbo> accessed 13/09/2019.

The advocacy campaign

After the KSC was established, the KNCHR carried out a capacity-building training workshop to empower the KSC members with the skills they would require to effectively participate in the UPR process. A workshop organised by the KNCHR on 19–20 May 2009 equipped the KSC members with a detailed understanding of the principles, technical and practical aspects of the UPR for them to effectively engage in Kenya's review.[115] As highlighted previously, Schokman and Lynch have identified the lack of knowledge about the UPR as a major obstacle to effective NGO engagement. The KNCHR therefore played a key role in providing NGOs with the knowledge and technical skills and in building their capacity to effectively engage with the UPR process. After the KNCHR workshop, the KSC engaged in three important campaigns on Kenya's UPR. These were an awareness-raising campaign, an advocacy campaign and a media campaign. The purpose of the awareness-raising campaign was to sensitise the public and domestic human rights organisations about the new UPR mechanism. It was designed to raise awareness in the grassroots communities and to ensure that the end report of the KSC is a comprehensive picture of the human rights situation in the country.[116]

The advocacy campaign was designed to engage the government, international NGOs and foreign diplomats in Kenya on Kenya's UPR process. The KSC established an Advocacy Charter for this purpose.[117] The Charter highlighted the key human rights concerns in Kenya for the purpose of Kenya's UPR review. It was intended to influence the government's approach to the UPR. The KSC presented its list of 15 issues to the government, which committed to address 13 of them excluding the death penalty and sexual orientation.[118] This selection further reinforced the cultural relativist approach adopted by Kenya in its UPR engagement. The aim of the Advocacy Charter developed by the KSC was to get foreign diplomats to make similar recommendations to Kenya and assist regional and international NGOs to leverage their networks to influence diplomats during Kenya's review.

The pre-review side events for NGOs which are organised by UPR Info before each UPR session in Geneva provide further opportunity for NGO advocacy. There are many factors, including high financial costs and lack of familiarity with procedure, which may prevent domestic NGOs from participating in the review

115 Kenya Stakeholder's Coalition on Universal Periodic Review (KSC-UPR), above n 109, 15.

116 Ibid 22.

117 The Kenyan Stakeholder Coalition for the UPR, 'UN Human Rights Council—Universal Periodic Review Kenya's Human Rights Balance Sheet: The Advocacy Charter of KSC-UPR' (2010) available at <>www.upr-info.org/sites/default/files/general-document/pdf/knchr_accounting_for_human_rights_protection_under_the_upr_2011.pdf>.

118 KNCHR, 'Talking Points on the UPR' above n 25.

process in Geneva.[119] However, in the case of Pacific Island states, Natalie Baird argues that

> it is possible to envisage a system whereby an international NGO offers a service to national NGOs to appear at side events on its behalf, undertake one-on-one lobbying of individual missions and make a statement at the HRC plenary session.[120]

According to Baird, the pre-review side events can facilitate collaboration and networking between national and international NGOs which can help provide legitimacy to international NGOs as well as increase the capacity of domestic NGOs for effective lobbying and advocacy.[121] The inclusion of international NGOs in the membership of national NGO coalitions for the UPR can promote this collaboration and networking between national and international NGOs. The advocacy campaign by the KSC potentially contributed to influence the recommendations made by states to Kenya during its reviews.

The advocacy campaign by the KSC contributed to proactively engage the Kenyan government in its UPR process. While HRC Resolution 5/1 requires that states prepare their state report for the UPR 'through a broad consultation with all relevant stakeholders at the national level',[122] an advocacy plan by an NGO coalition can enable them to proactively engage a reluctant government. An advocacy campaign which focuses on the national UPR consultation process, lobbies state UPR delegates to make key recommendations in Geneva and has a follow-up strategy, can contribute to the effectiveness of NGO engagement with the UPR process. Nevertheless, while effective NGO engagement in this regard can contribute to the effectiveness of the UPR process, it is important to be wary of NGOs that are in reality 'government mouth pieces' or those that prioritise the agenda of their donors which may not necessarily be the priority of the people they claim to serve.[123]

The media campaign

The interactive dialogue phase of the UPR in Geneva is webcast. This provides an excellent opportunity for sensitisation about the UPR and awareness-raising of a state's human rights record. A 2015 study by Sarah Joseph revealed that media

119 Lucia Nader, 'The Role of NGOs in the UN Human Rights Council' (2007) 7 *International Journal on Human Rights* 7, 10.

120 Natalie Baird, 'The Role of International Non-governmental Organisations in the Universal Periodic Review of Pacific Island States: Can 'doing good' be done better?' (2015) 16(2) *Melbourne Journal of International Law* 1, 35.

121 Ibid 34–5.

122 *HRC Decision 6/102.*

123 See Makau Mutua, *Human Rights NGOs in East Africa* (University of Pennsylvania Press 2008) 47.

coverage of the UPR is generally insignificant.[124] She argues that where coverage exists, it only highlights 'a "contest" between antagonistic states rather than focusing on its potential to help provide for better human rights outcomes'.[125] However, an important finding in her study is that the few instances of UPR media coverage in developing states were sophisticated and tended to be supportive of the UPR process.[126] This provides an opportunity for NGOs to use the media as a vehicle for sensitisation and to mobilise wider public engagement with the UPR process.

During Kenya's UPR review, the KSC undertook a media campaign that mobilised international media to attend Kenya's review in Geneva, engaged the public with Kenya's UPR process and disseminated information on Kenya's UPR.[127] In particular, Media 21[128] assisted the KSC in getting international coverage by mobilising Kenyan journalists and the international media to attend the stakeholders' press briefings in Geneva.[129] Media 21 mobilised the international media to attend KSC's press briefings in Geneva and arranged for a meeting between the KSC team and Kenyan journalists attending a UPR training activity in Geneva.[130] In addition, the KSC held a national press briefing on 13 April 2010, attended by seven media organisations.[131] Although this did not result in a significant media coverage of Kenya's UPR process, it was a step towards engaging the media in the UPR process. However, to promote and mobilise wider national public engagement with the UPR, the KSC and other NGOs within Africa can effectively engage with the domestic media. The KSC did not achieve any significant domestic coverage of Kenya's UPR process despite a few attempts to engage the domestic media through press briefing and talk-shows.[132] The KSC could engage in a more elaborate media campaign so as to promote and mobilise wider public engagement which can help counter state ritualism in the UPR. However, it may be difficult to overcome the general lack of interest by the media in the UPR process.

Resolution 5/1 requires states to engage stakeholders in the preparation of their UPR national reports. Notwithstanding, the KNCHR and the KSC took a proactive approach in engaging the state at different stages of the review. The approach adopted by the KSC to Kenya's review process has been referenced in many international forums as an inspiring example of good practice in the UPR

124 See Sarah Joseph, 'Global Media Coverage of the Universal Periodic Review Process' in Hilary Charlesworth and Emma Larking (eds), *Human Rights and the Universal Periodic Review: Rituals and Ritualism* (Cambridge University Press 2015) 147–66.

125 Ibid 148.

126 Ibid 163–6.

127 Kenya Stakeholder's Coalition on Universal Periodic Review (KSC-UPR), above n 109, 26–7.

128 Media 21 is a leading provider of audio-visual technology registered in Trinidad and Tobago. See Media 21 available at <www.media21ltd.com/> accessed 13/09/2019.

129 Ibid.

130 Ibid 26.

131 Ibid 26–7.

132 Kenya National Commission on Human Rights, above n 6, 26–7.

mechanism because of the dynamic ways in which it sought to engage the state in its review process.[133] However, the KSC could have secured the participation of grassroots organisations in Kenya whose involvement thus far has been limited by budgetary constraints. The fact that KSC's meetings and workshops were mostly held in the capital city limited the participation of grass roots organisations. The KSC could have secured their participation in subsequent review cycles by holding these meetings and training workshops across the country.

NGO operational environment in Kenya

While NGOs have found ways to bypass the limitations to their direct participation in the UPR as examined previously, the domestic NGO operational environment, financial constraints, and the lack of transparency and accountability are factors which can hamper their effective engagement with the UPR process. I focus my analysis on the first two issues because the problem of lack of transparency and accountability among many NGOs in Africa has been adequately addressed by several scholars.[134]

The Kenyan government has made attempts to improve the legal environment for NGOs. However, according to Frank Holmquist, it was not until 1992 when multi-party democracy compelled the state to permit independent citizen activity.[135] The specific legislation which directly regulated NGOs in Kenya was the NGO Coordination Act 1990.[136] The Act established an NGO Coordination

133 Danish Institute for Human Rights, above n 10, 38; OHCHR, Government of Republic of Moldova and UNDP, above n 10, 10.

134 Burger Owens found high incidence of corruption in the NGO sector in Uganda. See Burger R Owens, *Promoting Transparency in the NGO Sector: Examining the Availability and Reliability of Self-reported Data* (Centre for Research in Economic Development and International Trade, University of Nottingham 2011) available at <https://bit.ly/2mfJKQl> accessed 13/09/2019; Assad and Goddard, and Daniel Smith made similar findings about NGOs in Tanzania and Nigeria respectively. See Assad M and A Goddard, 'Stakeholder Salience and Accounting Practices in Tanzanian NGOs' (2010) 23(3) *International Journal of Public Sector Management* 276; Daniel J Smith, 'Corruption, NGOs, and development in Nigeria' (2010) 31(2) *Third World Quarterly* 243; Douglas Kimemia, Hassan Abdulkadir, Transparency International, and the Institute for the Study of African Realities et al., have all provided evidence of corrupt practices among domestic NGOs in Kenya. See Douglas Kimemia, 'Non-governmental Organizations and Corruption: The Case of Kenya' in Gedeon M Mudacumura and Göktuğ-Morçöl (eds), *Challenges to Democratic Governance in Developing Countries* (Springer 2014) 161; Hassan Sheba Abdulkadir, 'Challenges of Implementing Internal Control Systems in Non-Governmental Organizations (NGO) in Kenya: A case of Faith-Based Organizations (FBO) in Coast Region' (2014) 16(3) *IOSR Journal of Business and Management* (IOSR-JBM) 57; Transparency International-Kernya, 'The Kenya Bribery Index 2008' (2008) available at <https://bit.ly/2lSdL8s> accessed 13/09/2019; Institute for the Study of African Realities and others, 'Corruption and Its Consequences in Kenya' (2013) available at <https://bit.ly/2kKkAc1> accessed 13/09/2019.

135 Frank Holmquist, 'Kenya's Antipolitics' (2005) 209 *Current History: A Journal of Contemporary World Affairs* 104, 682.

136 *Non-Governmental Organizations Co-Ordination Act 2012* (Kenya); The Act only went operational in 1992 and it is still the Law until the Public Benefits Organisation Act 2013 goes operational.

Board which previously governed NGOs and their operations.[137] Between 1997 and 2005, there was a proliferation of NGOs in Kenya. In 1997 there were 836 NGOs in Kenya, most of which were located in the capital, Nairobi. By 2005, there were 4,099 NGOs in Kenya.[138] In 2013, this number had doubled to 8,260 and contributed a total of *KES* 80 billion (about USD 1 billion) to the national economy. [139] NGOs therefore play a vital role in Kenya.

However, the NGO Coordination Act 1990 was criticised by many as gravely flawed.[140] Patricia Kameri-Mbote, Founding Director of the International Environmental Law Research Centre, has criticised the wide discretion and sweeping powers the Act grants the NGO Coordination Board and the Minister in sections 12, 14, 19 and 32 of the Act.[141] These wide discretionary powers granted to the NGO Coordination Board were exercised in 2014 when the government deregistered 510 NGOs in an antiterror crackdown, including 15 NGOs accused of having links with terrorism.[142] The UPR tries to promote cooperation and understanding between civil society and governments through the requirement of broad consultation in the preparation of national reports. However, the barriers erected by an atmosphere of suspicion, especially in the face of terrorism, have not been dismantled. There was also a definitional problem in the 1990 Act as the definition of 'NGO' in the Act was limited and failed to encompass other CSOs that are for public benefit such as trusts.[143] An additional flaw of the Act was the absence of a complaint and dispute resolution mechanism for CSOs.

Attempts were made to improve the civil society space in Kenya through the enactment of the Public Benefit Organisations (PBO) Act 2013 by parliament, which replaced the 1990 NGO Coordination Act.[144] The PBO Act resolved the

137 Ibid s 3.

138 Karuti Kanyinga, Winnie Mitullah, and Sebastian Njagi, *The Non-profit Sector in Kenya: Size Scope and Financing* (The Institute for Development Studies, University of Nairobi 2007) 16.

139 Yves Niyira Gira, 'Current Challenges Facing the Civil Society in Kenya' *Rosa Luxemburg Foundation*, 4 available at <https://bit.ly/2D8vo90> accessed 13/09/2019.

140 Odundo Carolyne Achieng, 'Determinants of Non-Governmental Organizations' Accountability to the Community in Kisumu East District, Kenya' (MA Thesis, The University of Nairobi 2014) 5; for details of the problems the NGO Coordination Act 1990 posed to NGOs see P K Mbote and M Akech, above n 28.

141 Ibid 17.

142 This occurred after a number of terrorist incidents earlier in 2014. These included the armed attacks on 15 June 2014 in the village of Mpeketoni in Lamu County left at least 48 people dead; a bus hijacking in November in Mandera County in Northeast Kenya which left 28 people dead; and an armed attack on December 2 at a quarry in Mandera County that killed 36 workers. See United States Department of State, 'Country Reports on Terrorism 2014' (2015) 27 available at <www.hsdl.org/?view&did=767094> accessed 13/09/2019; BBC News, 'Kenya "deregisters" NGOs in anti-terror clampdown' (16 December 2014) available at <www.bbc.com/news/world-africa-30494259> accessed 13/09/2019; Samuel Karanja, '15 NGOs Deregistered Over Terrorism Funding Claims' *Daily Nation* (Online) (16 December 2014) available at <https://bit.ly/2keODbB> accessed 13/09/2019.

143 Rebecca B Vernon, 'Restrictions on Foreign Funding of Civil Society' (2009) *The International Journal of Not-for-Profit Law* 1, 48.

144 *The Public Benefit Organisations Act 2013*, Law No. 18 of 2013 (Kenya).

definitional problem and established a complaint and redress mechanism for NGOs. It also established an Independent Registration and Regulatory Agency which would eliminate the wide discretion and sweeping powers exercised by the NGO Coordination Board and the Minister under the 1990 Law.

However, after parliament enacted the PBO Act into law in 2013, the Kenyan government made many attempts to amend the law before making it operational. The first attempt to amend the PBO Act was through the Statute Law (Miscellaneous Amendments) Bill, 2013. It sought, among many other things, to limit the amount of external funding NGOs can receive to 15%[145] and to prevent NGOs from receiving funding directly from foreign donors.[146] This was defeated in parliament during its second reading and withdrawn from the Bill.[147] The second attempt by the government in 2014 intended to give the PBO Regulatory Agency wide discretionary powers, cut down the number of NGO representatives on the PBO Regulatory Agency Board and give the government greater powers in appointing members to the Board.[148] The last attempt was at the end of 2014 with 54 proposed amendments to the PBO Act. These amendments modified, but largely maintained, the issues in the previous attempts.[149] After more than 1,000 days since the PBO Act was signed into law the government has delayed its entry into operation. On 31 October 2016, the High Court of Kenya ordered the government to operationalise the law within 14 days, describing the delay as an abuse of 'discretion' and 'unconstitutional'.[150] However, the government has reportedly refused to comply with the court order.[151]

While the government has been unsuccessful in containing civil society through its proposed amendments, it has been very successful in intimidation, harassment and ill treatment of civil society representations.[152] There was an increase in the

145 There are no special rules in Kenya governing the receipt of foreign funds by NGOs and under section 65 of the PBOs Act, NGOs may engage in lawful economic activities provided income is sued solely to the NGOs registered purposes.

146 *Statute Law (Miscellaneous Amendments) Bill 2013* (Kenya), Kenya Gazette Supplement No. 146 (Bills No. 32) s 27A para 1, 2.

147 The International Federation for Human Rights (FIDH), 'Kenya: Parliament Decides to Withdraw Controversial Amendments Targeting Public Benefit Organisations (PBO)' (2013) available at <https://bit.ly/2lUirdZ> accessed 13/09/2019.

148 The International Centre for Not-for-Profit Law, 'NGO Law Monitor: Kenya' (2015) available at <www.icnl.org/research/monitor/kenya.html> accessed 13/09/2019.

149 The provisions the government sought to remove included that which required it to provide financial assistance to NGOs and to compel every state organ to ensure that its policies are carried out in a manner that supports a favourable environment for NGOs. See ibid.

150 See *Trusted Society of Human Rights Alliance v Cabinet Secretary Devolution and Planning & 3 others* (2016) eKLR, 59; See also Kenya National Human Rights Commission, 'Open Letter on Amendments to the PBO Act' (11 November 2013) available at <https://bit.ly/2lOBR42> accessed 13/09/2019.

151 International Federation for Human Rights, 'KENYA: Last Warning from the Court to Implement the PBO Act 2013 Within 30 Days' (18 May 2017) available at <https://bit.ly/2lSfyKI> accessed 13/09/2019.

152 For example, in 2009, Oscar Kamau Kingara and John Paul Oulu of the Oscar Foundation, a legal aid organisation, were murdered reportedly by Police agents in Nairobi after they had briefed UN Special Rapporteur Philip Alston on summary executions by the

number of UPR recommendations by states and NGOs across UPR I and II for the Kenyan government to repeal any laws that would constrain NGOs or restrict their access to foreign funding. During Kenya's UPR II, Australia and the Netherlands expressed concerns about the intimidation and ill treatment of civil society representatives and the restrictive legislation that constrains them.[153] The United States, Canada and Ireland recommended that Kenya implement the PBO Act, repeal any laws that may constrain CSOs and create a safe environment for CSOs which is free from hindrance and insecurity.[154] Germany's recommendation to Kenya during UPR II targeted one of the proposed amendments to the PBO by recommending that Kenya repeals restrictions on NGO access to foreign funding.[155] Kenya accepted all these recommendations. The impact of the new Kenyan Constitution (2010) in further protecting NGOs is highlighted in the section Kenya's implementation of UPR recommendations.

Financial constraints

Limited financial resources constitute another major problem for NGOs in Kenya, most of which depend largely on foreign donations to sustain their activities. This large dependence on foreign donors poses a problem as to whether they are accountable to their foreign donors or to the people they serve and whose agenda they represent. Makau Mutua criticises the dependence of Kenya's CSOs on foreign donors for their sustainability and agrees with Mahmood Mamdami's argument that it results in retrogression of civil society.[156] This is because the agenda of the domestic NGOs arguably is owned by the donors.[157] As such, NGOs in Kenya sometimes design programmes which suit donor agendas but which may have little connection with domestic priorities. As noted earlier, the government of Kenya attempted to limit NGO access to foreign funding at 15% of their budget and to prevent them from directly receiving such funds. However, this could potentially cripple the important work of many NGOs and affect their ability to participate effectively in the UPR process. Due to limited financial resources it is difficult for many NGOs, especially from developing countries, to participate during the plenary sessions of the UPR. For example, despite Nigeria's large state representation during UPR I, none of the domestic NGOs was able to attend and make oral submissions during its plenary session. Similarly, despite the strategic and fruitful engagement of the KSC during the first review of Kenya, financial constraints hampered the participation of many KSC members in

police. See Kenneth Roth, 'The Abusers' Reaction: Intensifying Attacks on Human Rights Defenders, Organizations, and Institutions' (2010) *Human Rights Watch World Report* 4 available at <https://bit.ly/2kHOvBL> accessed 13/09/2019.

153 *HRC UPR II Report—Kenya*, UN Doc A/HRC/29/10 paras 62, 142.140.

154 Ibid paras 142.128, 142.133, 142.137.

155 Ibid para 143.53; See a similar recommendation by Canada and Netherlands, ibid paras 142.133, 142.140 respectively.

156 Makau Mutua, above n 123, 46.

157 Ibid.

the review process in Geneva.[158] Apart from the KNCHR, none of the 97 members of the KSC made oral submissions during Kenya's UPR I plenary session of the HRC.[159] More so, while the participation of states in the UPR mechanism is supported by the Voluntary Fund for Participation in the UPR Mechanism, NGO participation is not supported by this fund.

Overall, the KSC strategically engaged in the review of Kenya through its awareness raising, advocacy and media campaigns. This was a positive approach to engaging the state, especially at a time when other domestic NGOs in Africa are still struggling to understand and learn the dynamics of the UPR mechanism and the role they can play. Nevertheless, the KSC needs to ensure stability in its membership, reach out to grassroots organisations and intensify its local media campaigns. Engaging the state in its advocacy campaign demonstrated two things. First, the state has been consistent in its culturally relative approach to the UPR in its engagement with both NGOs and states. It was not willing to accept recommendations on issues of sexual orientation from its peers during the review and when addressing the 15 issues raised in the Advocacy Charter of the KSC. Second, the advocacy campaign demonstrated the potential for NGOs to influence state recommendations to Kenya through the advocacy charter. However, this section argued that the ability of the KSC and other domestic NGOs to effectively engage in the UPR is threatened by the NGO operational environment. Many of the proposed amendments to the PBO Act could further constrain the NGO environment and impact on their ability to effectively engage in the UPR process. While the government was unsuccessful in achieving the proposed amendments, it has made the environment for NGOs less secure through threats, intimidation and harassment. These, as indicated previously, have been reflected in Kenya's UPR which has shown a rise in state recommendations targeting these NGO issues.

Kenya's implementation of UPR recommendations

This section engages with an analysis of the aggregate percentage of recommendations that were fully, partially and not implemented by Kenya. The analysis is limited to the UPR I and II implementation period for Kenya.[160]

158 Another reason is that most of the members of the KSC had not been accredited by the Economic and Social Council (ECOSOC). Only accredited NGOs can participate in the Geneva-based sessions. See Kenya National Commission on Human Rights, above n 6, 59.

159 Apart from the KNCHR, a total of 8 NGOs (all international) made oral submissions during Kenya's UPR I plenary session. These included Action Canada for Population and Development, Conectas Direitos Humanos, FIDH, Franciscans International, RADDHO and World Organization against Torture.

160 The UPR I implementation period for Kenya ran from May 2010 when the UPR Working Group adopted Kenya's UPR I report to November 2014 when it submitted its UPR II report. UPR II implementation period covered is January 2015 to July 2018.

At the end of Kenya's UPR I cycle, more than 50% of the accepted recommendations had triggered an action on the part of the Kenyan government. Out of the 149 recommendations that were accepted, about 16% were fully implemented (FI), 43% were partially implemented (PI), and 37% were not implemented (NI).[161] A higher level of implementation was observed during UPR II where 26% of 253 recommendations were fully implemented and 32% partially implemented.[162] In terms of the FI recommendations during UPR I, Kenya fully implemented the specific recommendation (R5) to '[e]stablish an independent, credible and authoritative Police Oversight Authority, with sufficient powers and resources' and to '[a]dopt legislation and a coherent national policy criminalizing female genital mutilation'. The state, NGOs and the UN Country Team for Kenya,[163] all agreed that these recommendations were fully implemented.[164] The aforementioned recommendations were implemented through the establishment of an Independent Police Oversight Authority and through the enactment of the *Prohibition against Female Genital Mutilation Act*, 2011.[165] UPR II recommendations that were fully implemented include to '[c]ontinue its efforts to establish an institutional and legislative framework for the provision of affordable legal aid and awareness services for all'; '[f]ully implement the Kenya National Water Master Plan'; and '[a]dopt the human rights action plan'.[166]

However, some recommendations such as the recommendation (R4) to '[f]urther promote good governance'[167] were quite difficult to assess implementation because of their vagueness. Little action on the part of the state could result in a full or partial implementation. The KNCHR stated that the recommendation to '[f]urther promote good governance' was 'difficult to assess' implementation.[168] Notwithstanding, the fact that Kenya fully implemented some of the

161 About 4% of the recommendations were not assessed because stakeholders did not provide any commentary on implementation.

162 See The Kenya UPR Stakeholders' Coalition, *Kenya's 2nd Cycle Universal Periodic Review Mid Term Report* (UPR INFO 2018) 3 available at <https://bit.ly/2kMqxpa> accessed 22/09/2019.

163 Article 19 is a NGO working on the right to freedom of expression and has branches in many parts of the world including Bangladesh, Brazil, Kenya, Mexico, Senegal, Tunisia and the USA.

164 See Republic of Kenya, 'Universal Periodic Review of the United Nations Human Rights Council: National Mid Term Report' (2012) 8, 31–2 available <https://bit.ly/2kxboI4> accessed 22/09/2019; Kenya UPR Stakeholder Coalition (KSC), *An Assessment by Stakeholders of Government's Performance in Implementation of UPR Recommendations—Annual Progress Report* (Nairobi 2012) viii and 3 available at <https://bit.ly/2kMSopc> accessed 22/09/2019; United Nations Country Team—Kenya, 'Universal Periodic Review Report—2nd Cycle January 2015' (2014) para 10.

165 See *Prohibition of Female Genital Mutilation 2011*, Law No. 32 of 2011 (Kenya).

166 The Kenya UPR Stakeholders' Coalition, above n 162, 38, 50, 16.

167 See *HRC UPR I—Kenya,* UN Doc A/HRC/15/8 paras101.28.

168 UPR Info, 'Mid-Term Implementation Assessment—Kenya' (2013) 49 available at <https://bit.ly/2m1B7Zu> accessed 22/09/2019.

specific recommendations underscores the government's commitment and the impact of stakeholder advocacy at the follow-up stage of the review. Arguably, the transitional justice processes that were taking place in Kenya during this period facilitated the full and partial implementation of many of Kenya's UPR recommendations. The enactment of a new Constitution in 2010 provided the basis for the full realisation of many of the state's UPR commitments.[169]

The recommendations which were partially implemented by Kenya targeted several key issues, including institutional failure identified as a major factor which made Kenya predisposed to violence following the 2007 presidential elections.[170] The judiciary was weak, lacked independence and police brutality and a culture of impunity went unabated. Most of the recommendations partially implemented by Kenya during UPR I were on police and judicial reform, a process which in some respects is still unfinished.[171] The government carried out major judicial reforms, including the vetting of judges, but was slow on police reforms. Other prominent UPR recommendations which were partially implemented targeted issues included poverty and socio-economic recovery, violence to women and children, and internally displaced persons.[172]

About 37% and 29% of the recommendations accepted by Kenya during UPR I and II respectively were not implemented. None of the 12 UPR I recommendations which required Kenya to sign or ratify international human rights treaties was implemented. According to various stakeholders, the implementation of any of these recommendations was hindered by the delay in the enactment and operationalisation of the Treaty Making and Ratification Act.[173] This law gives effect to Article 2 (6) of the Kenya Constitution, defines the procedure for the making and ratification of treaties, and entrusts the general responsibility for the initiation, negotiation and ratification of treaties to the executive arm of government.[174] While the constitutional reform process may have impeded the realisation of these recommendations within the implementation period, the Treaty Making and Ratification Act was passed in 2012 and many of the recommendations on treaty ratification during UPR I and II were yet to be implemented.[175]

It can be observed from the earlier analysis that the Kenyan government engaged with the implementation of specific and general recommendations which have contributed to positive human rights changes in Kenya by their

169 See for example the recommendations by Zimbabwe, Niger, UK and Republic of Korea for Kenya to support the enactment of a new constitution, *HRC UPR I—Kenya,* UN Doc A/HRC/15/8 para 101.6–101.9.

170 Susanne D Mueller, 'Dying to Win: Elections, Political Violence, and Institutional Decay in Kenya' (2011) 29(1) *Journal of Contemporary African Studies* 99, 104; Commission of Inquiry into the Post-Election Violence (CIPEV), above n 7, 355–460.

171 An example is the vetting of police officers see *HRC UPR II State Report—Kenya*, UN Doc A/HRC/WG.6/21/KEN/1 para 77.

172 See Kenya UPR Stakeholder Coalition (KSC), above n 164.

173 See Treaty Making and Ratification Act 2012, Law No. 45 of 2012 (Kenya).

174 Ibid.

175 The Kenya UPR Stakeholders' Coalition, above n 162, 13.

full or partial implementation. Cooperative mechanisms have traditionally been overlooked as a model for human rights implementation in favour of a compliance-centred paradigm which leans more on coercive mechanisms. The potential impact of the UPR mechanism should not be dismissed or it cannot be labelled as 'weak and inefficient'. It can contribute to improve the human rights situation on the ground as evident in the case of Kenya where more than 50% of the recommendations have either been fully or partially implemented during UPR I and II.

However, while the state has made progress on the implementation of some recommendations to improve the human rights situation on the ground, a significant percentage of the recommendations were not implemented during UPR I (37%) and II (29%). Continuous effective NGO engagement is invaluable and can play a significant role to pressure the government to live up to its UPR commitments. The development of a four-year UPR II implementation plan by the Kenyan government through an inclusive UPR consultation plan with government ministries, domestic NGOs and the KNCHR was an indication of the government's particular commitment to implementing the UPR II recommendations.[176] The plan outlined individual UPR recommendations, the specific priority action areas and the indicators to measure progress in realising their implementation.[177] This was particularly useful in measuring UPR II implementation and monitoring mid-term implementation progress by the Kenyan government.

The impact of the new constitution of Kenya in the implementation of UPR recommendations

Kenya undertook its UPR I within the context of addressing the legacies of the post 2007–2008 election violence. The enactment of a new Constitution in 2010 was a major development immediately after Kenya's UPR I. The struggle towards a new Constitution started as early as 1963 with numerous constitutional amendments.[178] The role of civil society in the struggle was significant and contributed to ensure that the new Constitution enshrines a wide range of human rights.[179]

176 Office of the Attorney General and Department of Justice (Kenya), 'Universal Periodic Review Second Cycle Implementation Matrix 2015–2019' (2015) available at <https://bit.ly/2moD2aB> accessed 22/09/2019.

177 Ibid.

178 There were 38 amendments to the old constitution see *Njoya and 6 Others v Attorney General & 3 others* (2004) 1 *Kenya Law Reports* 298–9; For details on the journey to a new constitution see P L O Lumumba, 'A Journey Through Time in Search of a New Constitution' in M K Mbondenyi, P L O Lumumba Steve and O Odero (eds), *The Constitution of Kenya: Contemporary Readings* (LawAfrica Publishing Ltd 2011) 23–44.

179 See P L O Lumumba, above n 178, 37–43; Grace Maingi, 'The Kenyan Constitutional Reform Process: A Case Study on the work of FIDA Kenya in Securing Women's Rights' (2011) 15 *Feminist Africa* 63.

While the UPR did not directly impact on the provisions of the Constitution,[180] it contributed to speed up the process of adoption of the Constitution, and some of the UPR recommendations were reflected in the new Constitution. As an example, it was recommended that the Kenyan government '[u]nite behind a new Constitution through a fair referendum, and fully implement the result' and equally '[e]nsure that the new Constitution of the country takes greater account of the dimension of human rights protection and promotion, as well as of democracy'.[181] The new Constitution contributed to the realisation of many of the rights that were the subject of UPR I recommendations to Kenya. This section examines the extent to which the new Constitution impacted on socio-economic rights and strengthened NGOs in Kenya. It focuses on these two issues because they represented the priorities of NGOs during Kenya's UPR I and II.

The Kenyan constitution 2010 and the implementation of socio-economic rights from the UPR

The realisation of socio-economic rights in Kenya has been enhanced through the new constitutional machinery which incorporates a Bill of Rights. Article 43 of the new Constitution enshrines socio-economic rights which are enforceable through the courts under Article 23 of the Constitution. The socio-economic rights dealt with under Article 43 include health, housing and sanitation, food, social security and education.[182] Examples of the UPR I recommendations to Kenya targeting these issues include develop education policies that ensure quality education, particularly for the poor, marginalised and vulnerable segments of its population; ensure the equitable distribution of water and food to the entire population, especially during times of drought; and continue to develop programmes and measures aimed at ensuring quality and free education and health services for its population.[183] The government made little effort to fully implement many of these UPR recommendations and to ensure the realisation of these constitutional rights. However, the Constitution gives the courts a primary role in the enforcement of these rights. In the 2013 case of *Mutemi v Permanent Secretary, Ministry of Education*,[184] the High Court of Kenya emphasised its readiness to enforce the socio-economic rights enshrined in the Constitution and cautioned the government stating:

> Let this judgment therefore be a wakeup call to the Respondents that Article 43 of the Constitution does not sit there like a [defeated] football player who

180 The time between the adoption of Kenya's UPR I report at the HRC (May 2010) and the adoption of the constitution (August 2010) was just about 3 months.
181 *HRC UPR I—Kenya*, UN Doc A/HRC/15/8 para 101.7.
182 *The Constitution of Kenya*, art 43 (1).
183 *HRC UPR II Report—Kenya*, UN Doc A/HRC/29/10 paras 101.110, 101.93, 101.113.
184 *Michael Mutinda Mutemi v Permanent Secretary, Ministry of Education and Others* (2013) eKLR Petition No. 133 of 2013.

> has lost a match. It is indeed alive and has started the run towards full realisation as opposed to a slow shuffle in the name of progressive realisation.[185]

The first case in which the courts enforced socio-economic rights under Article 43 of the 2010 Constitution of Kenya was *Kariuki v Town Clerk*, relating to the right to housing.[186] The case concerned the demolition of the homes of the applicants by the Nairobi City Council which threatened their eviction on grounds that the houses were built on road reserves.[187] The High Court had to decide whether or not the respondents owed the applicants a duty to respect, protect and fulfil their socio-economic rights under the Constitution. The High Court relied on jurisprudence from the UN Committee on Economic Social and Cultural Rights, to determine that the respondents had violated the rights of the applicants to housing under the Constitution.[188] In addition to awarding damages and ordering restitution, the High Court ordered the respondents to expeditiously put in place the required legislative, policy and programmatic framework so as to sufficiently cater for the housing needs of everyone especially the most vulnerable and marginalised.[189] This case set an important precedent on the enforcement of socio-economic rights under the Constitution and the Court's willingness to give life to these constitutional rights.

In *Consumer Confederation of Kenya (COFEK) v Attorney General*,[190] the High Court acknowledged its competence to adjudicate on the right to adequate food under the Kenyan Constitution. The relevant government authorities failed to stabilise the rise in fuel prices which resulted in high cost of subsistence goods and services. As a result, the petitioner claimed that their right to be free from hunger and the right to adequate food under Article 43 of the Constitution had been violated.[191] While the High Court was willing to adjudicate and develop the content of this right, it was rendered helpless by the fact that the petitioner failed to link the acts or omissions of the state respondents to the violation of the relevant socio-economic rights.[192] One of the recommendations during Kenya's UPR I on the right to food required the government to '[e]nsure the equitable distribution of water and food to the entire population, especially during times of drought'.[193]

185 The High Court is a premier court in interpreting the Constitution in Kenya. Matters from the High Court can be appealed to the Court of Appeal and finally to the Supreme Court of Kenya. Ibid para 21.

186 *Susan Waithera Kariuki and 4 Others v Town Clerk, Nairobi City Council and 2 others* (2011) HCC 66/2010.

187 Ibid 8–9.

188 Ibid 5.

189 Ibid 16–17.

190 *Consumer Confederation of Kenya (COFEK) v Attorney General & 4 Others* (2011) High Court Petition No. 88 of 2011, 1–3.

191 Ibid.

192 Ibid 4–5.

193 *HRC UPR I—Kenya*, UN Doc A/HRC/15/8 para 101.93.

While the new Constitution has served as a door for the implementation of some UPR recommendations, it has equally served as a facade to cover up the government's non-implementation of other UPR recommendations. For example, it was recommended during UPR I that the government '[f]urther strengthen relations with the Indigenous communities with a view to promoting and protecting their rights and assisting them in their development initiatives' and to 'devote attention to the recommendations made by the Special Rapporteur on the situation of human rights and fundamental freedoms of Indigenous peoples, after her visit to the country'.[194] In responding to their implementation outcome, the government stated that 'Kenya's new Constitution provides several avenues for the protection and strengthening of Indigenous peoples' personal and collective rights'.[195] However, the KSC noted that the Endorois decision of the African Commission,[196] which found the government to have violated the land rights of Indigenous peoples and recommended recognition, restitution and compensation of the Endorois people for ownership over their lands,[197] had not been implemented.[198] The Committee on Economic, Social and Cultural Rights and the Committee on the Elimination of all forms of Racial Discrimination expressed concern on the Kenyan government's non-implementation of the decision by the African Commission in the Endorois case.[199] The KSC also submitted that the implementation of similar recommendations made to Kenya has been assumed and overlooked.[200] Moreover, the UPR I recommendation on the right to food mentioned earlier was only partially implemented. While the government relied on the provisions of the new Constitution to justify its implementation,[201] NGO stakeholders submitted that the government's action 'falls short of an express commitment to tackle food distribution during times of drought'.[202]

194 Ibid paras 103.6, 103.7.

195 Ibid para 25.

196 African Commission for Human Rights, *Centre for Minority Rights Development (Kenya) and Minority Rights Group International on Behalf of the Endorois Welfare Council v The Republic of Kenya* (4 February 2010) Communication No. 276/2003 available at <www.escr-net.org/sites/default/files/Endorois_Decision.pdf> accessed 22/09/2019.

197 Ibid paras 71–298.

198 See Civil Society Coalition on Kenya's 2nd Universal Periodic Review (CSCK-UPR), above n 49 para 29.

199 UN Committee on Economic, Social and Cultural Rights, 'Concluding Observations on the Combined Second to Fifth Periodic Reports of Kenya' UN Doc E/C.12/KEN/CO/2–5 (6 April 2016) paras 15–16.

200 See Ogiek People Development Programme (OPDP), 'Indigenous & Minorities—UPR Info' available at <https://bit.ly/2kXxsf8> accesses 22/09/2019.

201 *HRC UPR II State Report—Kenya*, UN Doc A/HRC/WG.6/21/KEN/1 para 57.

202 Franciscans International (FI), Edmund Rice International (ERI) and Foundation for Marist Solidarity International (FMSI), 'UPR Mid-Term Assessment Kenya' (2012) 1 available at <https://bit.ly/2m08DPZ> accessed 22/09/2019; Kenya National Commission on Human Rights, above n 93.

The Kenyan 2010 constitution and the protection of NGOs and CSOs

The 2010 Kenyan Constitution has strengthened the protection of NGOs in Kenya who now have the potential to influence the government's cultural relativist position on some human rights issues. Articles 196 and 118 (1) (b) of the Constitution which require public involvement in the legislative and other business of its county assemblies and in the national parliament have increased the role NGOs play within the state. Examples of UPR recommendations in this area required the government to '[e]ngage in a participatory and inclusive process with civil society in the implementation of universal periodic review recommendations' and to '[i]nvestigate harassment and attacks against journalists and human rights defenders in order to bring those liable to justice';[203] '[e]nsure that non-governmental organizations and human rights defenders can freely conduct their activities' and '[c]reate and maintain, in law and in practice, a safe an enabling environment, in which human rights defenders and civil society can operate. . . .'[204]

The Kenyan courts have in a few cases enforced the provisions of the new Constitution with the effect of strengthening NGOs/CSOs in Kenya with particular focus on the constitutional right to public participation and freedom of association. In *Gakuru v Governor Kiambu County*,[205] the High Court had to determine whether the Kiambu Finance Act 2013 was passed with sufficient public participation as required by Article 196 of the Constitution of Kenya, among other things.[206] The Court found that although newspaper advertisements had been published and a number of persons had been consulted, the effort was insufficient to amount to public participation in the language of Article 196 (1) (b).[207] Odunga J stated:

> In my view public participation ought to be real and not illusory and ought not to be treated as a mere formality for the purposes of fulfilment of the Constitutional dictates. It is my view that it behoves the County Assemblies in enacting legislation to ensure that the spirit of public participation is attained both quantitatively and qualitatively.[208]

203 *HRC UPR I—Kenya,* UN Doc A/HRC/15/8 paras 101.119, 101.89.

204 *HRC UPR II Report—Kenya*, UN Doc A/HRC/29/10 paras 142.136, 14.137.

205 *Robert W Gakuru and Others v The Governor Kiambu County and 3 others* (2014) eKLR Petition No. 532 of 2013 (Consolidated with) Petition Nos. 12, 35, 36, 42, 74 of 2014.

206 Ibid para 40.

207 Ibid para 84, Judge Richard Mwongo subsequently relied on this judgment in the case of *Andrew Ireri Njeru and 34 Others v County Assembly of Embu and 3 Others* [2014] eKLR to find that there was no adequate public participation in respect of the removal of the Governor and that the Petitioners' rights were violated. See *Andrew Ireri Njeru and 34 Others v County Assembly of Embu and 3 Others* [2014] eKLR para 57.

208 Ibid para 75.

This echoes the importance of a broad and representative consultation with NGOs and civil society necessary for the state's effective engagement at the consultation phase of the UPR when the state report is being drafted. Rather than relying on stakeholders to facilitate the broad and representative representation, the state needs to be more proactive at its consultation phase and engage the various public stakeholders in the preparation of its UPR report in a broad and representative way.

A more recent case invoking constitutional provisions was *Gitari v Non- Governmental Organisations Co-ordination Board*.[209] This was a landmark ruling and represents a step towards a change in the attitude of the state towards LGBT rights in Kenya. As reinforced earlier on in this chapter, the theme of cultural relativism especially on gay rights runs through the engagement of African states with the UPR. They have neither made nor accepted recommendations advocating for these rights. Examples of such recommendations which Kenya rejected required that Kenya '[t]ake concrete steps to provide for the protection and equal treatment of lesbian, gay, bisexual and transgender persons'[210] and '[d]ecriminalise consensual same sex conduct between adults'.[211]

The *Gitari* case related to the right to freedom of association under Article 36 of the Kenyan Constitution. The petitioner sought three times to register an Association with the names 'Gay and Lesbian Human Rights Council'; 'Gay and Lesbian Human Rights Observancy'; and 'Gay and Lesbian Human Rights Organization'.[212] His application to register the Association was rejected by the NGO Coordination Board on the basis that the names were inappropriate and contravened sections 162, 163 and 165 of the Penal Code which criminalises same-sex relations.[213] Regulation 8(3)(b) of the NGO Regulations empowers the Director of the NGO Coordination Board to reject an application to register an Association if it has a name which is 'in the opinion of the director repugnant to or inconsistent with any law or is otherwise undesirable'.[214] The High Court had to determine whether LGBT people had the right to form associations, and whether the decision of the Board to reject the petitioner's application because of the names violated the petitioner's constitutional rights under Articles 36 and 27 of the Constitution, relating to freedom of association, equality and non-discrimination. After examining international and comparative jurisprudence on these issues, the Court found that rejecting the petitioner's application was unjustified and contravened the provisions of Articles 36 and 27 of the Constitution

209 *Eric Gitari v Non- Governmental Organisations Co-ordination Board & 4 others* [2015] eKLR.

210 *HRC UPR I—Kenya*, UN Doc A/HRC/15/8 para 103.5.

211 *HRC UPR II Report—Kenya*, UN Doc A/HRC/29/10 para 143.48.

212 *Gitari v Non- Governmental Organisations Co-ordination Board* [2015] eKLR para 10.

213 Article 165 criminalises homosexuality with 5 years' imprisonment. See *Penal Code 2012* (Kenya), Chapter 63, s 165.

214 Non-Governmental Organizations Co-Ordination Regulations, 1992 (Kenya), 8 (3) (b) (ii).

in 'failing to accord just and fair treatment to gay and lesbian persons living in Kenya seeking registration of an association of their choice'.[215] The Court issued an order of *mandamus* for the registration of the Association with the intended names.[216] While the Kenyan government rejected all the UPR recommendations on the above issue, this case marks a step towards a change of culture within Kenya.

In summary, the adoption of the new Constitution was a factor that facilitated some of this implementation but equally impeded and disguised the non-implementation of some of the UPR I recommendations. While the High Court's adjudication of socio-economic rights in the Constitution impacted on the implementation of related UPR recommendations, its approach has not been consistent. A consistent and strong interpretive approach that favours the enforcement of these rights is needed. Nevertheless, the constitutional requirement of public participation and the court's landmark ruling in the case of *Gitari* further strengthens NGOs/CSOs. It pierces the veil of cultural relativism behind which the government conceals its attitude towards sexual minorities. This could be a potential stepping stone for a change in the government's attitude towards related recommendations in subsequent reviews.

Concluding Remarks

This chapter highlighted the benefits of NGOs forming coalitions such as the prioritisation of human rights concerns and the need for stability and broad representation in such coalitions. Charlesworth and Larking have argued that the ability of the UPR to move beyond ritualism and act as an effective regulatory mechanism depends profoundly on effective NGO engagement.[217] Effective NGO engagement can improve a state's UPR engagement and potentially contribute to narrow the UPR implementation gap. Because NGOs can be credible voices on the human rights situation on the ground, their recommendations can enrich the UPR process and strengthen its ability to improve the human rights situation on the ground. By influencing state recommendations to their peers, NGOs can indirectly gain a voice in the UPR process and ensure that states make recommendations which are relevant and have the capacity to promote meaningful and measurable human rights change on the ground.

State engagement will not be meaningful if it does not contribute to some degree to improve the human rights situation on the ground by implementation. The social and cognitive pressures generated by the UPR process can over time influence changes within states as was evident in some of the UPR

215 *Eric Gitari v Non- Governmental Organisations Co-ordination Board & 4 others* [2015] eKLR para 148(ii).

216 Ibid para 148(iv).

217 Charlesworth and Larking, 'Introduction: The Regulatory Power of the Universal Periodic Review' in Hilary Charlesworth and Emma Larking (eds), *Human Rights and the Universal Periodic Review: Rituals and Ritualism* (Cambridge University Press 2015) 16.

recommendations to Kenya that were not implemented within the implementation time frame but were subsequently implemented by the state. While implementation of UPR recommendations continues to remain a major issue across UPR I and II, the positive attitude by Kenya and other African states towards the UPR process could have long-term positive implications for the nature of their implementation of UPR recommendations and similar recommendations by other domestic, regional and UN mechanisms.

6 NGOs versus state recommendations and the relationship between the UPR and other human rights mechanisms

The case of Kenya

Introduction

The question has been asked whether civil society recommendations really matter.[1] This question is justified given that NGOs are not peers, and the UPR does not require states to respond directly to NGO recommendations but only recommendations from peers. Resolution 5/1 which lays down the modalities for the UPR permits NGOs to attend the interactive dialogue session in the UPR Working Group in Geneva, but they cannot make any statements or pose questions to states.[2] However, they are allowed to participate in the adoption of the outcome of the review during the plenary session of the HRC and can make statements then.[3] Even though states are not obliged to respond directly to NGO statements, many do so in their concluding remarks. But how important are NGO recommendations in the UPR process? Effective NGO engagement with the UPR can influence state recommendations. Moreover, NGOs help to keep the UPR reporting process honest by providing relevant information for a state's review[4] and can be credible voices on the human rights situation on the ground.[5] By effectively participating in the UPR process, NGOs can contribute to ensuring that state recommendations are relevant and target the major human rights concerns within states. There is also the question of whether the UPR complements other human rights mechanisms or rather duplicates and undermines their

1 During UPR I McMahon found that recommendations by CSOs matter because they largely influenced the recommendations of states. See Edward McMahon, 'The Universal Periodic Review. Do Civil Society Organisation-Suggested Recommendations Matter?' (2013) *International Policy Analysis* 1–14.

2 *Resolution 5/1*, UN Doc A/HRC/RES/5/1 para 18(c).

3 Ibid para 31.

4 Gudmundur Afredsson, 'Concluding Remarks: More Law and Less Politics' in Gudmundur Afredsson and others (eds), *International Human Rights Monitoring Mechanisms: Essays in Honour of Jakob Th Möller*, 1st edn (Martinus Nijihoff 2001) 925.

5 Ben Schokman and Phil Lynch, 'Effective NGO Engagement with the Universal Periodic Review' in Hilary Charlesworth and Emma Larking (eds), *Human Rights and the Universal Periodic Review: Rituals and Ritualism* (Cambridge University Press 2015) 146.

work.[6] This chapter examines whether there is a correlation between state and NGO recommendations to Kenya during UPR I and II and considers whether there is a synergy between UPR recommendations and those of other national and international human rights mechanisms.

The relationship between NGOs and state recommendations to Kenya

The existence of a correlation between both classes of recommendations could indicate that NGO participation in the UPR process is productive and that state recommendations are relevant and address similar issues identified in NGOs reports on how to improve the human rights situation on the ground. In addition, this could contribute to determining whether Kenya indirectly avoided or engaged with NGO recommendations when it engaged with the recommendations of other states. In the analysis in Tables 6.1 and 6.2, the various human rights issues raised by NGOs during Kenya's UPR I and II are grouped into 19 categories to facilitate analysis and presentation of data. To arrive at these broad clusters/categories, the analysis considered how frequently each category was mentioned,[7] the logic and structure of national reports, the categorisation adopted by the OHCHR in the summary of stakeholders' submissions[8] and those of other studies.[9] Most domestic NGOs in Kenya made written submissions for the UPR as a coalition. For example, apart from the KSC, which comprised at least 97 NGOs, there were four other joint submissions during Kenya's UPR I. In the analysis that follows, a reference to a particular human rights issue by the

6 Nadia Bernaz, 'Reforming the UN Human Rights Protection Procedures: A Legal Perspective on the Establishment of the Universal Periodic Review' in Kevin Boyle (ed), *New Institutions for Human Rights Protection* (Oxford University Press 2009); Sir Nigel S Rodley, 'UN Treaty Bodies and the Human Rights Council' in Helen Keller and Geir Ulfstein (eds), *UN Human Rights Treaty Bodies: Law and Legitimacy* (Cambridge University Press 2012) 320, 327; Olivier de Frouville, 'Building a Universal System for the Protection of Human Rights: The Way Forward' in M Cherif Bassiouni and William A Schabas (eds), *New Challenges for the UN Human Rights Machinery* (Intersentia 2011) 251; Heather Collister, 'Rituals and Implementation in the Universal Periodic Review' in Hilary Charlesworth and Emma Larking (eds), *Human Rights and the Universal Periodic Review: Rituals and Ritualism* (Cambridge University Press 2015) 116–19.

7 For example, the death penalty, internally displaced persons and sexual orientation were each separately categorised because they were mentioned several times by state recommendations and stakeholders' reports.

8 The categorisation considered included minorities and Indigenous peoples, internally displaced persons and human rights and counterterrorism; see Working group on the Universal Periodic Review, *Summary Prepared by the Office of the United Nations High Commissioner for Human Rights in Accordance with Paragraph 15 (c) of the Annex to Human Rights Council Resolution 5/1 and Paragraph 5 of the Annex to Council Resolution 16/21-Kenya*, 21st sess, UN Doc A/HRC/WG.6/21/KEN/3 (27 October 2014) 3–10.

9 See Fateh Azzam, 'Arab States and the Universal Period Review' (Report of the United Nations Development Program, Regional Centre in Cairo, November 2012) 27; Takhmina Karimova, *UPR in the CIS Countries: Regional Trends* (Analytical Report, United Nations Development Programme in Ukraine 2013) 11–30; see also the classification by UPR INFO available at <https://bit.ly/2lNcnUK> accessed 13/09/2019.

KSC is counted as '1', rather than '97'.[10] Nineteen UPR I and 24 UPR II stakeholders' reports were analysed.[11] The reports of both domestic and international NGOs are included in this analysis.

With the above in mind, Tables 6.1 and 6.2 provide a panoramic view of all the human rights issues raised by NGO submissions during Kenya's UPR I and II and compare them with recommendations made by states.

The comparative tables (Tables 6.1 and 6.2) indicate that ESC rights figured prominently among NGO recommendations during Kenya's UPR I. This is most likely explained by the fact that socio-economic grievances were important underlying causes of the 2007–2008 post-election violence in Kenya. Scholars and commentators agree on this especially as widespread poverty, corruption and radical inequality, particularly on land policies, were precarious issues predating the 2007 elections.[12] NGOs therefore focused more on socio-economic rights, which, just like justice, truth and reconciliation, made significant gains into the new Kenyan Constitution and the transitional justice process in general after its UPR I.[13] The little attention given to ESC rights by states reflected the priorities of various regional groups during Kenya's review. The European regional groups (EEG and WEOG) and GRULAC made the majority of the recommendations to Kenya. Their priorities were police and judicial reform, death penalty, women and children's rights and the ratification of international instruments. African and Asian states, which made fewer recommendations, prioritised socio-economic recovery, development, poverty and health. The low level of attention to ESC rights therefore only reflects the priorities of the European and GRULAC groups which made the majority of the recommendations to Kenya.[14]

10 It is important to note that while counting issues raised by the KSC as '1' rather than '97' may diminish the weight of issues supported by more than one member of the coalition, counting the issues raised as '97' may skew the analysis as each recommendation made by the coalition was only reflective of the position taken by one of the 9 clusters that worked on particular issues. In addition, counting the issues as '1' would prevent duplication from individual NGOs in the KSC who submitted separate reports on behalf of their individual organisations.

11 This number includes the report of the Kenyan National Human Rights Commission.

12 See generally, Kenya National Commission on Human Rights, 'On the Brink of the Precipice: A Human Rights Account of Kenya's Post-2007 Election Violence' (2008) 32–9; Human Rights Watch (HRW), 'Ballots to Bullets: Organised Political Violence and Kenya's Crisis of Governance' (2008); Kenya Land Alliance, 'National Land Policy in Kenya: Addressing Historical Injustices' (Issues Paper No.2/2004); Republic of Kenya, 'Presidential Commission of Inquiry into Illegal and/or Irregular Allocation of Public Land' (2004).

13 For the significant gains made by ESC rights into the new Kenyan Constitution see N W Orago, 'Limitation of Socio-Economic Rights in the 2010 Kenyan Constitution: A Proposal for the Adoption of a Proportionality Approach in the Judicial Adjudication of Socio-Economic Rights Disputes' (2013) 16 *The Potchefstroom Electronic Law Journal* 169. See also Mugambi Laibuta, 'Socio-economic Rights in Kenya's New Constitution: Conference Paper' (2010) 11(3) *ESR Review* 20.

14 In 2016, the Special Rapporteur on extreme poverty and human rights, Philip Alston, criticised the limited attention given to socio-economic rights by states in their UPR recommendations. See Human Rights Council, *Report of the Special Rapporteur on Extreme Poverty and Human Rights*, 32nd sess, Agenda Item 3, UN Doc A/HRC/32/31 (28 April 2016) 16–17.

UPR I: Comparative Table 6.1—NGO versus state recommendations

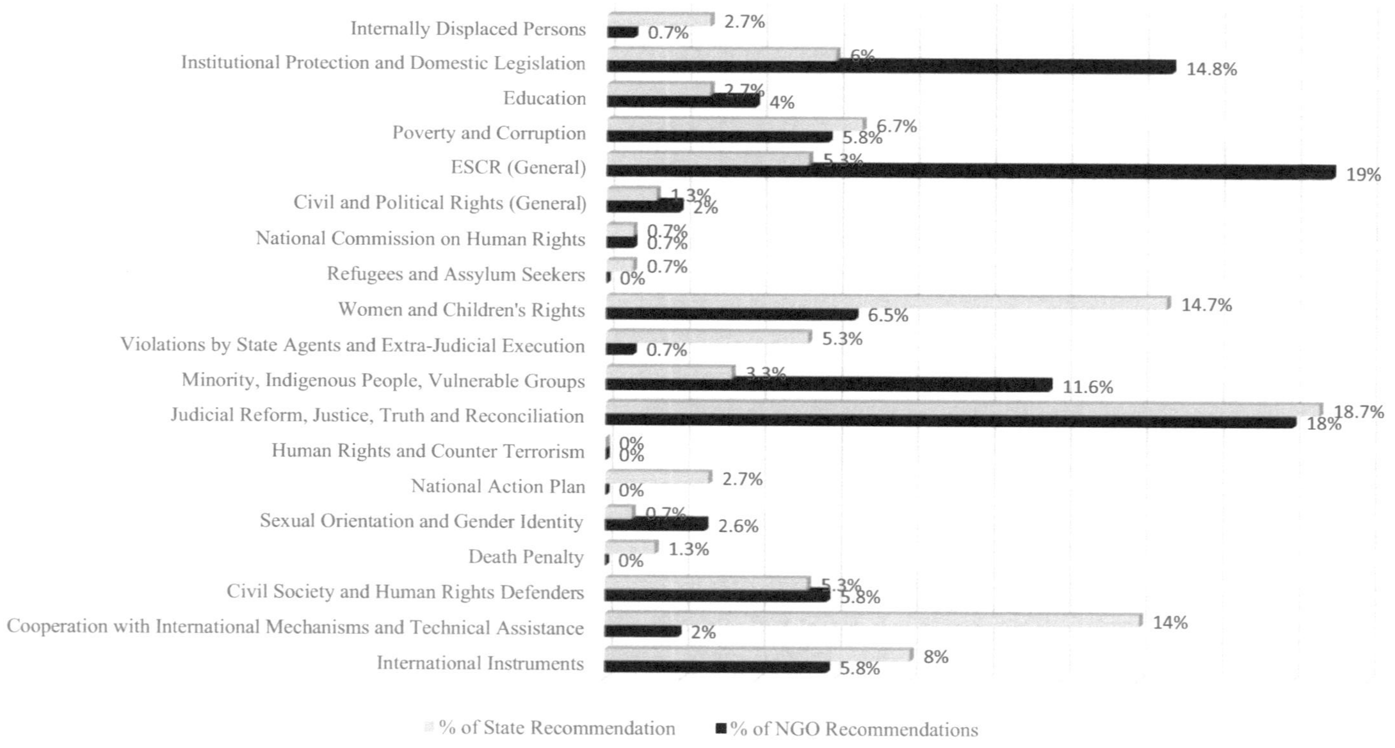

UPR II: Comparative Table 6.2—NGO versus state recommendations

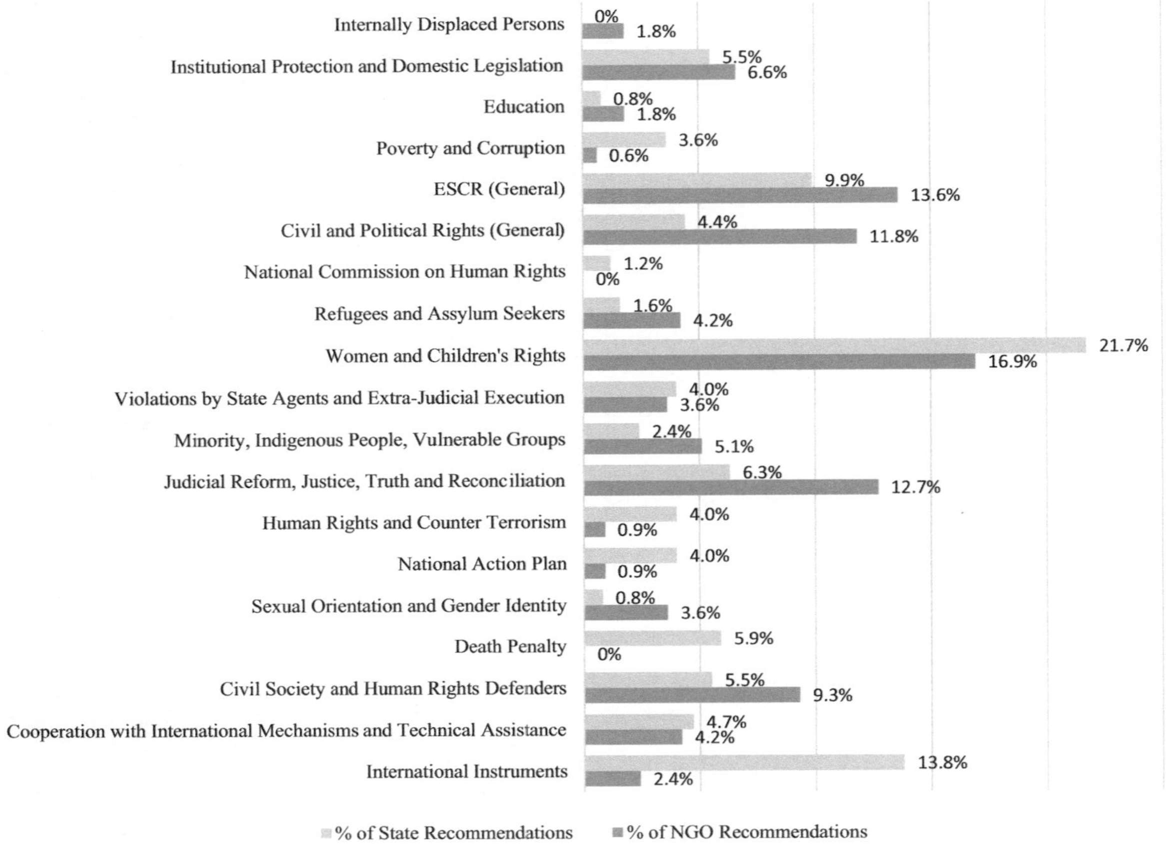

During UPR II, recommendations on ESC rights and truth, justice and reconciliation remained a major issue. However, among NGO recommendations, recommendations on women and children's rights were prominent as well as an increasing focus on civil and political rights. This was largely as a result of the commitment to address the post-election violence issues in Kenya. The new Constitution of Kenya, which was part of the post-conflict resolution process, incorporated a Bill of Rights. This resulted in more demands for civil and political rights resulting in the rise of such recommendations from both states and NGOs (from about 1% to 4% and from about 2% to 12% respectively). Examples of state recommendations reflecting these demands include recommendations to amend 'the security bill in the spirit of the new Constitution'; 'promote and fulfil all the rights and fundamental freedoms as stipulated in the bill of rights'; '[a]dopt the bill on persons deprived of liberty'; and '[e]nact without delay the 2013 Access to Information Bill and Data Protection Bill'.[15] Similar recommendations from NGOs included recommendations to enact 'the Access to Information Bill, 2012 and the Data Protection Bill 2012'[16] and '[g]uarantee the rights to freedom of expression as enshrined by the Constitution'.[17]

Overall, NGO recommendations appeared to largely correlate with state recommendations on many human rights issues raised, but there were also some differences. While ESC rights and the rights of minorities/Indigenous/vulnerable groups were of great concern to NGOs, they received far less attention from states.[18] This suggests that NGO recommendations did not impact much on the substance of state recommendations in these areas. Progress was apparently made during UPR II where the percentage of state recommendations on ESC rights doubled (from about 5% to 10%). Conversely, human rights issues such as extrajudicial execution, cooperation with international mechanisms/technical assistance and the death penalty received over three times more attention by states compared to NGOs during UPR I. NGOs made no specific recommendations on extrajudicial executions and only two recommendations on cooperation with international mechanisms.[19] However, during UPR II there was a relative balance

15 *HRC UPR II Report—Kenya*, UN Doc A/HRC/29/10 paras 142.5, 142.18, 142.82.

16 Kenya Stakeholder's Coalition on Universal Periodic Review (KSC-UPR), 'Coalition Joint Submission' (13 June 2014) 4 available at <https://bit.ly/2kiAkmz> accessed 13/09/2019.

17 Commonwealth Human Rights Initiative (CHRI), 'Stakeholder Submission of the Commonwealth Human Rights Initiative (CHRI) for the 2nd Universal Periodic Review of Kenya Initiative (CHRI)' (2014) 4 available at <https://bit.ly/2kiFdfp> accessed 13/09/2019.

18 This contrasts with an earlier finding on Ukraine where states made more recommendations on ESC rights than NGOs see; Takhmina Karimova, above n 9, 28–30.

19 Only Joint Submission 3 Report made the two recommendations see Mainyoito Pastoralist Integrated Development Organization (MPIDO), Endorois Welfare Council Pastoralist Integrated Support Programme, Ogiek People Development Programme Maa Civil Society Forum, Ndugu Zangu Charitable Trust, Ilchamus Development Consortium Trust, The Pastoralists' and Hunter Gatherers' Ethnic Minorities Network, Centre for Minority Rights Development and International Work Group for Indigenous Affairs (IWGIA), 'Joint NGO Submission to the Human Rights Council Universal Periodic Review Mechanism UPR 8th

between state and NGO recommendations on these issues. Human rights and counterterrorism was a non-issue to both states and NGOs during Kenya's UPR I as no recommendation was made in this regard. However, 4% of state recommendations in UPR II addressed this issue. This arguably is as a result of the terrorism crackdown efforts by the Kenyan government.

Analysis of UPR II recommendations from states and NGOs also points towards a strong relationship: both made more recommendations on the women/children/disability than on any other issue. Other areas where NGO recommendations matched state recommendations included recommendations on violations by state agents/extrajudicial executions, institutional protection/domestic legislation, cooperation with international mechanisms and civil society/human rights defenders. NGOs focused more on justice, truth and reconciliation than states did. Conversely, adherence to international instruments was an issue of greater interest to states but an issue of relatively less interest to NGOs.

In addition, an examination of the statistical correlation coefficient between state and NGO UPR recommendations reinforced the strong relationship between both groups of recommendations. The linear correlation coefficient (r) measures the strength and direction of a linear relationship between two variables. The correlation analysis of the relationship between state and NGO UPR recommendations finds a moderate positive relationship of 0.5 for UPR I and a strong positive relationship of 0.6 for UPR II.

It is also important to comment on the death penalty and sexual orientation/gender identity, which attracted the most recommendations rejected by many African states. During UPR I and II, NGOs and states made recommendations on sexual orientation/gender identity with an observable increase across both cycles of the UPR, but NGOs made more recommendations on this issue than states. The percentage of NGO recommendations increased from 2.6% to 3.6% across UPR I and II respectively while the percentage of state recommendations on the issue of sexual orientation increased insignificantly from 0.7% to 0.8% respectively. On the death penalty, there was a significant difference on the issue between NGOs and states. While it was a 'non-issue'[20] for NGOs during UPR I and II, there was a significant rise in the percentage of state recommendations on the death penalty across UPR I and II (from about 1% to 6% respectively). The scant attention given to the issue of the death penalty by Kenyan NGOs is arguably a result of existing public support for the death penalty, and it reinforces

Session, 10–21 May 2010-Review of Kenya' (2009) available at <https://bit.ly/2kKAXFt> accessed 13/09/2019.

20 This language has repeatedly been used by the Kenya President when addressing the issue of gay rights in Kenya. For a recent press conference between the Presidents of US and Kenya on Gay rights in Kenya see 'Obama and Kenyan President Spar Over Gay Rights in Joint Speech' available at <www.youtube.com/watch?v=ZQs4M-VAlq0> accessed 13/09/2019. Also, important to note is the discrepancy between the issues raised by the KSC in the Advocacy Charter which included the death penalty and the issues raised in the KSC's UPR Submission which did not include the death penalty.

the government's position during UPR II that 'any attempt to abolish it would not enjoy parliamentary approval at the present time'.[21]

Amplification and synergy between the UPR and other national and international mechanisms

When the UPR was established a major concern was that it would undermine the work of other human rights mechanisms, especially the treaty bodies.[22] It was therefore included as one of the essential base of the review that it shall complement and not duplicate the work of the treaty bodies.[23] Nadia Bernaz contends that the UPR duplicates the work of the UN human rights treaty bodies because of an overlap in their respective functions.[24] Sir Nigel Rodley and Olivier de Frouville argued that the UPR weakens and overshadows treaty body recommendations and facilitates the evasion by states of their obligation to implement recommendations by treaty bodies.[25] However, Helen Quane has argued that the UPR enhances state engagement with the UN treaty bodies.[26] She demonstrated in the case of ASEAN states that the UPR has contributed to greater and more constructive engagement between many ASEAN states and the UN human rights treaty bodies by facilitating the submission of overdue treaty body reports and the ratification of specific human rights treaties.[27] This research made similar findings in the case of Nigeria (Chapter 4) and Kenya (Chapter 5), where the UPR has facilitated the submission of overdue treaty body reports.

The analysis in this section takes a different approach to the relationship between the UN human rights treaty bodies and the UPR. The UPR, arguably, can potentially create a synergy with other national, regional and international human rights mechanisms. It can facilitate the amplification of issues highlighted in various human rights mechanisms and equally amplify the concerns of NGOs/CSOs. Rather than duplicate their function, the various human rights mechanisms can generally reinforce and complement each other.

In Kenya, the UPR has been a very important mechanism to support and strengthen the transition and development process. The UPR recommendations can play a role at the national level by promoting the inclusion of international human rights standards in constitutional or legislative drafting and

21 *Report of the HRC on Its 15th* Session, UN Doc A/HRC/15/60 para 417.

22 The sentiments of Australia and the African Group on this issue during the negotiations on the modalities for the UPR are highlighted in Chapter two. See Felice D Gaer, 'A Voice Not an Echo: Universal Periodic Review and the UN Treaty Body System' (2007) 7(1) *Human Rights Law Review* 109, 122.

23 *Resolution 5/1,* UN Doc A/HRC/RES/5/1 para 3(f).

24 Nadia Bernaz, above n 6.

25 Sir Nigel S Rodley, above n 6, 320, 327; Olivier de Frouville, above n 6, 251; Heather Collister, above n 6, 116–19.

26 Helen Quane, 'The Significance of an Evolving Relationship: Asian States and the Global Human Rights Mechanisms' (2015) 15 *Human Rights Law Review* 283.

27 Ibid.

by strengthening mechanisms that will improve access to justice, especially for vulnerable and marginalised groups. This can be very valuable to transitional societies undergoing institutional reforms. In Kenya, for example, the UPR occurred at a time of increased local calls for transitional justice, police and judicial reforms, constitutional change, demand for socio-economic rights and to address the plight of internally displaced persons. Many of the recommendations during Kenya's UPR I re-emphasised and reinforced transitional justice processes that were taking place within Kenya. For example, in 2008, Kenya's Commission of Inquiry on Post-Election Violence (CIPEV) made a number of recommendations regarding police reforms.[28] In particular, CIPEV recommended the establishment of an Independent Policing Oversight Authority. This and similar recommendations were re-emphasised in the 2009 report of the National Task Force on Police Reforms.[29] These were subsequently amplified by many states in their recommendations to Kenya. The United Kingdom recommended that Kenya 'establish an independent, credible and authoritative Police Oversight Authority, with sufficient powers and resources'.[30] This was subsequently implemented. Another state recommendation called Kenya to 'fully implement the proposals made by the National Task Force on Police Reforms'.[31] Also, CIPEV in 2008 had recommended that the Freedom of Information Bill be enacted forthwith.[32] Norway reinforced this recommendation during UPR I by recommending that Kenya 'Enact as a matter of urgency the Freedom of Information Bill'.[33] While this was not implemented within the UPR I implementation time frame, it was subsequently implemented on 31 August 2016 when the Access to Information Act was signed into Law.[34] During UPR II, nine states buttressed the recommendations of the Kenyan Truth and Reconciliation Commission's report by each recommending that the state should implement the recommendations in the Commission's report.[35] Kenya accepted these recommendations.

Similarly, Kenya's reviews were also used by states to reinforce recommendations made by other regional and international human rights mechanisms regarding the human rights situation in Kenya. During Kenya's UPR I, Denmark recommended that the government implement the recommendations of both the UN Special Rapporteur on extrajudicial killing and that of the UN

28 Set up by the Kenyan government to investigate the facts and circumstances surrounding the 2007/2008 post-election violence. See Commission of Inquiry into the Post-Election Violence (CIPEV), 'Report of the Commission of Inquiry into the Post-Election Violence' (16 October 2008) 383 (hereafter 'Waki Report').

29 Republic Of Kenya, 'Report of the National Task Force on Police Reforms: Abridged Version' ICC-01/09-02/11-91-Anx3 (December 2009) 13.

30 *HRC UPR I—Kenya,* UN Doc A/HRC/15/8 para 101.15.

31 Ibid 101.20.

32 See Waki Report, above n 28, 476.

33 *HRC UPR I—Kenya,* UN Doc A/HRC/15/8 para 101.10.

34 See *Freedom of Information Act, 2016,* Law No. 31 of 2016 (Kenya).

35 *HRC UPR II Report—Kenya,* UN Doc A/HRC/29/10 paras 142.91, 142.96, 142.101, 142.102, 142.104, 142.107, 142.107, 142.108, 142.116, 142.117.

Special Rapporteur on the rights of Indigenous peoples following the latter's visit to Kenya in 2007.[36] Kenya did not accept Denmark's recommendation and has remained in denial of many of the findings in the report of the UN Special Rapporteur on Extrajudicial, Summary or Arbitrary Executions.[37] However, it accepted another recommendation to '[i]mplement the recommendations and decisions of its own judicial institutions and of the African Commission on Human and Peoples' Rights, particularly those relating to the rights of Indigenous peoples'[38] but did not implement the recommendation.[39]

With regard to the treaty bodies, the UPR has equally reinforced their recommendations. The UPR reinforced many of the previous recommendations to Kenya by the UN Committee on Economic Social and Cultural Rights. The Committee had recommended in 2008 that Kenya criminalise domestic violence and FGM and allocate sufficient resources for the fight against poverty.[40] The UPR strengthened and amplified the importance of these recommendations during Kenya's UPR I in 2010. States made more than 20 recommendations addressing these issues, many of which were specific.[41] For example, it was recommended that Kenya '[i]mplement measures to prevent, punish and eradicate all forms of violence against women . . . and also completely eradicate the practice of female genital mutilation'[42] and to '[u]rgently adopt legislation criminalizing female genital mutilation'[43] Kenya accepted all these recommendations. According to the KNCHR and the KSC, the recommendations to adopt legislation that would criminalise and eradicate the practice of FGM were fully implemented as the government enacted the Prohibition of Female Genital Mutilation Act in 2011 and an anti-FGM policy was developed.[44]

36 *HRC UPR I—Kenya*, UN Doc A/HRC/15/8 paras 102.5, 103.4.

37 The Government of the Republic of Kenya, 'Response to the Report of the Special Rapporteur on Extra-judicial, Arbitrary or Summary Executions, Professor Philip Alston, on His Mission to Kenya from 16–25 February, 2009' (Nairobi, 22 May 2009) available at <>www.nation.co.ke/blob/view/-/604192/data/80408/-/7rjry0z/-/gava>.

38 Ibid 101.114.

39 See Civil Society Coalition on Kenya's 2nd Universal Periodic Review (CSCK-UPR), 'Report of the Civil Society Coalition on Kenya's 2nd Universal Periodic Review' (June 2014) para 29 available at <www.upr-info.org/sites/default/files/document/kenya/session_21_-_january_2015/js4_-_joint_submission_4.pdf> accessed 19/09/2019.

40 Committee on Economic Social and Cultural Rights, *Report on the Fortieth and Forty-First Sessions*, UN Doc E/C.12/2008/3 (2008) paras 375–380.

41 Ibid paras 101.48–101.57, 101.97–101.108.

42 Ibid para 101.51.

43 Ibid para 101.56.

44 See *Prohibition of Female Genital Mutilation 2011*, Law No. 32 of 2011 (Kenya); UPR Info, 'Kenya Mid-Term Implementation Assessment' (2013) <>www.upr-info.org/sites/default/files/document/kenya/session_08_-_may_2010/mia-kenya.pdf>; The Kenya Stakeholders Coalition for the UPR (KSC-UPR), 'An Assessment by Stakeholders of Government's Performance in Implementation of UPR Recommendations' (2012) 31 available at <www.knchr.org/Portals/0/InternationalObligationsReports/Universal%20Periodic%20Review%202012.pdf?ver=2013-02-21-150138-333> accessed 19/09/2019.

Concluding remarks

A major finding of this chapter is the significant extent to which states' UPR recommendations do in fact correlate with NGO recommendations.[45] While this finding does not assert a direct causal link between NGO and state recommendations, it is credible to infer that NGO recommendations do have an impact on state recommendations. As indicated in the comparative Tables 6.1 and 6.2, state recommendations correlate with NGO recommendations to a significant extent. This is reinforced by a positive correlation finding of 0.5 and 0.6 during UPR I and II respectively. It indicates that NGOs do have some influence on the recommendation states make to their peers and that by engaging with the recommendations of its peers, the state may be indirectly engaging with NGO recommendations. This would give a voice to NGOs that they do not formally enjoy in the UPR process. State recommendations, as seen in the case of Kenya, largely reflect the perspectives and inputs from NGOs. The dynamic ways in which the Kenyan NGOs engaged the state and its peers played a significant role in influencing the recommendations of states to Kenya. This highlights the potential for NGOs to have their voices heard in the UPR, enrich the UPR process and strengthen its ability to improve human rights situation on the ground.

This chapter also considered the ability of the UPR to reinforce and amplify the concerns of domestic, regional and international human rights mechanisms. Despite the worries about the potential for the UPR to weaken and facilitate the evasion by states of treaty body recommendations, it is important to acknowledge that the 'soft' approach of the UPR is reflective of its very nature as a cooperative mechanism. More so, the rejection of a UPR recommendation or failure to implement it cannot invalidate a state's legal obligation under the relevant treaties or under customary international law. The ability of the UPR to strengthen and reinforce human rights concerns raised by other human rights mechanisms is seen to serve as a model that has inspired proposals on human rights and the post-2015 development agenda, which advocates for a web of global effective monitoring that complements and reinforces efforts at the domestic and regional levels.[46] In the case of Kenya, the UPR has been used as a platform to strengthen and support judicial and police reform, and the truth and reconciliation processes, among other human rights issues challenging the state.

45 This finding corresponds with the finding of Karimova on Ukraine. Takhmina Karimova, above n 9; See Edward McMahon, above n 1, 1–14.

46 Centre for Economic and Social Rights, *Who Will Be Accountable? Human Rights and the Post-2015 Development Agenda* (New York and Geneva 2013); OHCHR, 'President of the General Assembly: Interactive Dialogue "Elements for a Monitoring and Accountability Framework for the Post-2015 Development Agenda"' (New York, 1 May 2014); Centre for Reproductive Rights and others, 'Accountability for the Post-2015 Agenda: A Proposal For A Robust Global Review Mechanism' available at <www.cesr.org/downloads/post-2015_accountability_proposal.pdf> accessed 19/09/2019.

7 The effectiveness of South Africa's engagement with the UPR

Potential for ritualism?*

Background to South Africa's UPR

In 1994, South Africa underwent a democratic transition after 45 years of apartheid rule. Having experienced gross human rights violations under the apartheid regime, there were domestic and international expectations that in the future South Africa would serve as a beacon of hope in the advancement of human rights.[1] There was reason to be optimistic. Commitment to democracy and respect for human rights were the essence—if not the totality—of President Mandela's foreign policy.[2] In 1996, South Africa enacted a highly progressive Constitution that incorporated a Bill of Rights.[3] The six core international human rights treaties that existed at the time of drafting greatly inspired the language and content of the Bill of Rights.[4] In 2006, South Africa became the first African country to legalise same-sex unions.[5] Furthermore, Article 9 (3) of the 1996 Constitution of South Africa prohibits discrimination on grounds of sexual orientation.[6] As mentioned earlier, cultural relativism with regard to sexual orientation is an issue that limits the engagement of African states with the UPR mechanism. This chapter therefore considers whether the South African government is committed to protecting the rights of sexual minorities in its engagement with the UPR mechanism.

The optimism ushered by the immediate post-apartheid period in relation to the advancement of human rights may have been premature. South Africa's post-apartheid human rights policy has been fraught with significant inconsistencies. These include the 'quiet diplomacy' in response to repression and abrogation of

* First published in the *South African Journal on Human Rights* (2017) 33(2) 258–285.

1 Tristan Anne Borer and Kurt Mills, 'Explaining Post-apartheid South African Human Rights Foreign Policy: Unsettled Identity and Unclear Interests' (2011) 10 *Journal of Human Rights* 76.

2 Laurie Nathan, 'Consistency and inconsistencies in South Africa's Foreign Policy' (2005) 81(2) *International Affairs* 364.

3 Constitution of the Republic of South Africa Act 1996 (South Africa).

4 The Constitution has been described by Heyns and Viljoen as 'Highly "International human rights law friendly"'. See Christof Heyns and Frans Viljoen, *The Impact of the United Nations Human Rights Treaties on the Domestic Level* (Martinus Nijhoff Publishers 2002) 542, 552.

5 See Civil Union Act 2006 (South Africa).

6 Constitution of the Republic of South Africa Act 1996 (South Africa), Art. 9 (3).

the rule of law in Zimbabwe;[7] the denialist position of President Thabo Mbeki on HIV/AIDS; South Africa's controversial arms procurement programme; domestic xenophobia; and threatened withdrawal from the ICC.[8] On domestic xenophobia in particular, NGOs have criticised the South African government for failing to combat the 2008 xenophobic attacks and to prevent their recurrence in 2015 and 2019.[9]

Furthermore, the institutions set up by the Constitution to monitor and scrutinise rights enforcement have been criticised, even by UPR stakeholders, for failing to make use of their powers and for lack of governmental support.[10] Many commentators have lauded the South African Constitutional Court for its active engagement in the enforcement of socio-economic rights.[11] Yet, despite the brilliance with which the Constitutional Court has articulated decisions on socio-economic rights, the government has been reluctant to implement them. A point of reference is the case of *South Africa v Grootboom*.[12] Despite successful litigation, the decision did very 'little to change the social conditions of the complainants'.[13] In addition, violence and discrimination based on sexual orientation are reportedly on the rise, despite the legal recognition of same-sex unions in 2006.[14]

7 A detailed analysis of this was carried out by Schoeman and Alden. See Maxi Schoeman and Chris Alden, 'The Hegemon That Wasn't: South Africa's Foreign Policy Towards Zimbabwe' (2003) 25 *Strategic Review for Southern Africa* 1.

8 See Laurie Nathan, above n 2, 361–72; 'South Africa—ICC: Withdrawal Plan' (13 November 2015) 52(10) *African Research Bulletin* 20766C–20767C.

9 See University of Pretoria. Centre for Human Rights, *The Nature of South Africa's Legal Obligations to Combat Xenophobia* (Centre for Human Rights, Faculty of Law, University of Pretoria 2009) 1–117. The government failed to address recommendations in this study resulting in further xenophobic attacks in 2015 and 2019. See South African Litigation Centre, 'Open Letter to the African Commission Regarding the Xenophobic Attacks in South Africa' (2015) available at <https://bit.ly/2mf4GqH> accessed 12/09/2019; Tom Head, *Confirmed: Three South Africans Killed During Xenophobic Attacks* (The South African, 4 September 2019) available at <https://bit.ly/2ke1Gdv> accessed 04/09/2019.

10 Human Rights Institute of South Africa et al., 'Republic of South Africa: Joint Submission to the UN Universal Periodic Review (UPR) 13th Session of the UPR Working Group' (2011) 2 available at <https://bit.ly/2kGbM6Y> accessed 12/09/2019; Thomas Keil, 'Supporting Constitutional Democracy in South Africa: A Study in the Effectiveness of Three Chapter 9 Institutions' (Twente Centre for Studies in Technology and Sustainable Development, 28 December 2010) 9.

11 Danie Brand and Christof Heyns, *Socio-Economic Rights in South Africa* (PULP 2005); Christopher Mbazira, *Litigating Socio-Economic Rights in South Africa: A Choice Between Corrective and Distributive Justice* (PULP 2009); Malcolm Langford et al., *Socio-Economic Rights in South Africa: Symbols or Substance* (Cambridge University Press 2013).

12 *Government of the Republic of South Africa and Others v Grootboom and Others* (2001) 1 SA 46 (Yacoob J) (Appellate Division).

13 Christopher Mbazira, above n 11, 3–4; Malcolm Langford et al. (eds), above n 11; Mariette Brennan, 'To Adjudicate and Enforce Socio-Economic Rights: South Africa Proves That Domestic Courts Are a Viable Option' (2009) 9 *Queensland University of Technology Law and Justice Journal* 79.

14 Human Rights Council, *Report of the Special Rapporteur on Violence Against Women, Its Causes and Consequences on Her Mission to South Africa*, UN Doc A/HRC/32/42/Add.2 (14 June 2016) para 33.

Human rights scholars have viewed South Africa's human rights commitment from three different broad perspectives. The first perspective assumes that South Africa is still strongly committed to the human rights cause.[15] In 2009, Alison Brysk placed South Africa in the group of Sweden and Canada as a model international citizen that promotes human rights.[16] The second perspective sees South Africa as no more or less committed to human rights than other democracies.[17] From this perspective, South Africa is committed to human rights whenever it serves its national interest. This may explain why South Africa, despite its significant role in the creation of the ICC, would spearhead a movement to prevent the ICC from issuing an arrest warrant on Sudanese President Omar al-Bashir and subsequently fail to arrest him.[18] Since its re-election to the HRC in 2014, South Africa has consistently abstained from all country-specific resolutions except those on Israel and the Occupied Territories.[19] However, Nigeria and Kenya have exhibited similar voting patterns in the HRC. In 2011, Human Rights Watch criticised Nigeria for having the worst voting record among African states in the HRC because it either voted against or abstained on all country-specific resolutions.[20]

The third perspective to South Africa's human rights commitment takes a different stand. Eduard Jordaan has argued that South Africa has scaled back in its human rights commitments, shielded regimes with odious human rights records and obstructed the international human rights cause.[21] Jordaan's argument is based on his 2014 analysis of South Africa's actions in the HRC. He criticised South Africa for opposing the singling out of specific countries through HRC country mandates and for voting against UN Security Council resolutions that targeted the human rights situation in specific countries.[22] According to Jordaan,

15 See Alison Brysk, *Global Good Samaritans: Human Rights as Foreign Policy* (Oxford University Press 2009) 171.

16 Ibid.

17 David Black, 'South Africa, Multilateral Institutions and the Promotion of Human Rights' in Philip Nel et al. (eds), *South Africa's Multilateral Diplomacy and Global Change: The Limits of Reformism* (Ashgate 2001) 76.

18 President Omar al-Bashir is Sudan's long-serving ruler who has been accused of war crimes by the prosecutor of the International Criminal Court. See Erika de Wet, 'The Implications of President Al-Bashir's Visit to South Africa for International and Domestic Law' (2015) 13(4) *Journal of International Criminal Justice* 1–23.

19 South Africa has abstained from HRC resolutions targeting Syria, Iran, Belarus, Democratic People's Republic of Korea, Eritrea, but has voted in favour of resolutions targeting Israeli settlements in the Occupied Palestinian Territory, including East Jerusalem, the occupied Syrian Golan and the right of the Palestinian people to self-determination.

20 Human Rights Watch, '"Keeping the Momentum": One Year in the Life of the UN Human Rights Council' (September 2011) available at <www.hrw.org/node/101646/section/6> accessed 12/09/2019.

21 Edoard Jordaan, 'South Africa and the United Nations Human Rights Council' (2014) 36(1) *Human Rights Quarterly* 90–122.

22 Ibid 100–9; for voting patterns within the HRC and their political implications, see Simon Hug, 'Dealing with Human Rights in International Organisations' (2016) 15(1) *Journal of Human Rights* 21.

South Africa appeared to 'believe that international pressure and "naming and shaming" are counterproductive . . . and at best, it is naïve'.[23] However, as earlier mentioned, Nigeria and Kenya, two key players in the African continent, took a similar position to South Africa in their opposition to country-specific resolutions in the HRC. This reinforces the argument against the 'naming and shaming' approach. As argued in Chapter 2, the 'naming and shaming' approach is limited and the benefits of an inclusive and cooperative approach to human rights implementation need to be considered. The opposition of many African states to 'naming and shaming' through country-specific resolutions is not just because they breed selectivity and double standards but also partly as a result of their belief that it is a neo-colonial tool.

Like other African states, South Africa is inclined to support the UPR mechanism because of its inclusive, cooperative and collaborative approach to human rights implementation. However, the extent to which the South African government engages with the UPR, the factors undermining its engagement and the perspective which best describes this engagement are some of the issues that this chapter seeks to address. South Africa undertook its UPR I in 2008 (when it was a HRC member) and UPR II in 2012 (when it was not a HRC member).

Commitment to the national consultation process and the quality of South Africa's UPR delegation

South Africa's UPR national consultation process

The UPR pre-review process is marked by a national consultation that culminates with the preparation and submission of the UPR state report, as well as reports by other UPR stakeholders. An effective engagement at this stage of the review would require that states undertake a broad and representative consultation with all relevant stakeholders. The extent of consultation carried out by states has not been identical. While Nigeria during its first two reviews did not engage all relevant stakeholders, it engaged with all relevant human rights issues during its consultation meetings.[24] The Kenyan government carried out a broad and representative consultation through the instrumentality of NGOs that formed coalitions and proactively engaged the state in the UPR process.

In the case of South Africa, the government did not effectively engage with the UPR national consultation process. During South Africa's UPR I when it was a member of the HRC, it did not undertake any consultation in the preparation of its UPR state report. Some NGOs in their UPR I submissions stated that no consultation was undertaken and that it was unknown whether a state

23 Ibid 100–3.

24 Including sensitive issues like the death penalty and same-sex relations. However, the national consultation process was not representative because the state did not include gay rights organisations in the process.

report was being prepared.[25] In fact, South Africa is reported to be the only UN member state that did not submit a written report in advance of its UPR I.[26] State reports for the UPR are generally due six weeks prior to the review.[27] South Africa's report that was due in January 2008 was only submitted on 15 April 2008, the same day South Africa was reviewed in Geneva. In addition, the late report submitted by the state during the interactive dialogue did not follow some other guidelines for the state report.[28] The guidelines for the preparation of state reports require that states provide in their UPR reports a 'description of the methodology and the broad consultation process' followed in the preparation of their state reports.[29] South Africa's late UPR I report did not comply with this guideline, presumably because there was no such consultation.[30] The South African Human Rights Commission (SAHRC) criticised the government for its lack of commitment to the reporting process.[31]

The South African government made improvements during South Africa's UPR II and III. It submitted the state report in time and complied with the structural guidelines of the UPR state report. This provides evidence of an ongoing process of acculturation through the microprocess of identification. The need for South Africa to identify itself with the UPR practice of its regional and international peers generates social pressures to subsequently conform to the practice of timely submission of its UPR report. However, while the state UPR II and III report provided information on the nature of the national consultation process, the process did not satisfy the requirement for a broad and representative UPR consultation. On this issue, the government stated in its UPR II report that it undertook an 'extensive national consultative process across government' in

25 Commonwealth Human Rights Initiative, 'Submission of the Commonwealth Human Rights Initiative for the Universal Periodic Review' (2007) 3 available at <https://bit.ly/2kxXMwj> accessed 12/09/2019; Children Now, 'Submission by Children Now, an Alliance Of South African NGOs Brought Together to Prepare the Alternate Report to the UN Committee on the Rights of the Child' (2007) 1 available at <https://bit.ly/2lKtJBM> accessed 12/09/2019.

26 Lilian Chenwi, *South Africa: State of State Reporting Under International Human Rights Law* (Community Law Centre 2010) 64; See also Parliamentary Monitoring Group, 'Strategic Planning Workshop: Human Rights Commission, Commission on Gender Equality, Child Rights Institute, Human Sciences Research Council, University of Stellenbosch, Disability Alliance presentations' (2009) available at <https://bit.ly/2mdiamO> accessed 12/09/2019.

27 *Resolution 5/1,* UN Doc A/HRC/RES/5/1 para 17.

28 Lilian Chenwi, above n 26.

29 Human Rights Council, *Follow-up to the Human Rights Council Resolution 16/21 with Regard to the Universal Periodic Review*, 17th sess, Agenda Item 1, UN Doc A/HRC/DEC/17/119 (19 July 2011).

30 See also criticisms by the CAT on the Initial Report of South Africa to CAT that was not in conformity with the guidelines. Committee Against Torture, *Conclusions and Recommendations of the Committee Against Torture, South Africa*, 37th sess, UN doc CAT/C/ZAF/CO/1 (7 December 2006) para 3.

31 See Parliamentary Monitoring Group, above n 26.

the preparation of its state report.[32] This implicitly suggests that there was no meaningful national consultation with NGO stakeholders as the consultation was solely across government institutions. Lawyers for Human Rights and the Consortium for Refugees and Migrants in South Africa, in their UPR II submission, criticised the failure of the South African government to consult NGO stakeholders in a timely and meaningful manner during UPR II.[33] During UPR III, a joint stakeholder submission recommended that the South African government consult with CSOs during the preparation of the UPR national report and the implementation phase of the UPR process.[34]

Comparatively, the African Peer Review Mechanism (APRM), a self-monitoring initiative established by the African Union to promote freedom and human rights among other values, has had a higher level of engagement from South Africa than the UPR.[35] For example, in the preparation of its 2014 country report to the APRM, the South African government organised consultations across various provinces with various stakeholders, including NGOs, faith-based organisations and the business sector.[36] In addition, this report was discussed and adopted in parliament.[37] While the level of consultation in the preparation of the state report for the APRM has been criticised as insufficient,[38] that mechanism has witnessed greater involvement of parliament, CSOs and individuals than the UPR.

However, the UPR is comparatively a more recent mechanism than the APRM, and there is potential for this aspect of state engagement to improve in

32 Working Group on the Universal Periodic Review, *National Report Submitted in Accordance with Paragraph 15 (a) of the Annex to Human Rights Council Resolution 5/1—South Africa*, 13th sess, UN Doc A/HRC/WG.6/13/ZAF/1 (7 March 2012) ('*UPR II National Report—South Africa*') para 1.

33 Lawyers for Human Rights and the Consortium for Refugees and Migrants in South Africa, 'Submission from Lawyers for Human Rights and the Consortium for Refugees and Migrants in South Africa to the Second Cycle of the South African Universal Periodic Review 2012' (2012) 11 available at <https://bit.ly/2m6WM2n> accessed 12/09/2019.

34 CIVICUS: World Alliance for Citizen Participation and Human Rights Institute of South Africa (HURISA), 'Republic of South Africa: Joint Submission to the UN Universal Periodic Review 27th Session of the UPR Working Group' (2016) 11 available at <https://bit.ly/2kITNNc> accessed 12/07/2019.

35 In 2003, the African Union established the APRM as a self-monitoring initiative to promote good governance in Africa. APRM is designed to promote three fundamental values of the African Union: Freedom and Human Rights, Participatory Development, and Accountability and share a similar cooperative framework to the UPR. See Edward McMahon et al., 'Comparing Peer Reviews: The Universal Periodic Review of the UN Human Rights Council and the African Peer Review Mechanism' (2013) 12 *African and Asian Studies* 266–89.

36 Yarik Turiansky, 'South Africa's Implementation of the APRM: Making a Difference or Going Through the Motions' (2014) *South African Institute of International Affairs* 1–4 <https://bit.ly/2kGcWzm> accessed 20/09/2019.

37 Parliamentary Monitoring Group, 'African Peer Review Mechanism: Department of Public Service & Administration Briefing' (2014) available at <https://pmg.org.za/committee-meeting/16800/> accessed 12/09/2019.

38 Ross Herbert and Steven Gruzd, *The African Peer Review Mechanism: Lessons from the Pioneers* (The South African Institute of International Affairs 2008) 267, 271.

subsequent reviews. Notwithstanding the greater level of consultation by South Africa with the APRM compared to the UPR, the general enthusiasm and level of engagement by African states with the UPR can be contrasted with their engagement with the APRM. According to McMahon, Busia and Asherio, despite the progress made by the APRM, it faces major challenges among African states because of the 'lack of political will and capacity . . . and the number of acceded countries "sitting on the fence" with no serious signals to kick-start the review process could dilute the initial enthusiasm and effectiveness of the mechanism overall'.[39] Nineteen African states have not yet signed up to the review, and of the 35 African states that have signed up to the APRM, more than half of them are yet to undertake their self-assessment process.[40] The fact that all African states participated in both cycles of the UPR and engaged in the UPR reporting and interactive dialogue processes is an indication of a greater enthusiasm and level of engagement for the UPR.

Furthermore, the UPR may have had some impact on South Africa's human rights treaty body reporting obligations across South Africa's UPR I, II and III. At the time of South Africa's UPR I in 2008, South Africa, as many UN member states, had a backlog of overdue reports before the various human rights treaty bodies.[41] After UPR II in 2012, the South African government has made a concerted effort to comply with its reporting obligations. On 26 November 2014, it submitted to the various UN human rights committees 12 of its 14 outstanding treaty body reports. These include the initial report to the Human Rights Committee (due in 2000); II–IV reports to the Committee on the Elimination of all forms of Discrimination against Women (due in 2009); IV–VIII reports to the Committee on the Elimination of Racial Discrimination (CERD; due in 2002); and the initial report to the Committee on the Rights of Persons with Disabilities.[42] A similar observation was made in Chapter 5 in relation to the positive impact of Kenya's UPR engagement on the state's compliance with its treaty body reporting obligations. While it may be uncertain to draw a causal relationship between engagement with the UPR and compliance with treaty body reporting obligations, it is plausible that the former has an impact on the latter, given that about 828 of the total UPR I recommendations by all states (about 4% of the total recommendations) were on state engagement with the treaty bodies.[43]

39 See Edward McMahon et al., above n 35, 266, 276.

40 The African Peer Review Mechanism, '13th Anniversary of the African Peer Review Mechanism' (2016) available at <www.aprm-au.org/viewNews?newsId=101> accessed 12/09/2019.

41 In 2010, South Africa had 14 overdue reports to the UN human rights treaty bodies. See Lilian Chenwi, above n 26, 28–50.

42 South Africa (as of May 2019) only has one overdue reports. The Department of Justice and Constitutional Development in South Africa is also responsible for the preparation of various treaty body and UPR reports of South Africa. See OHCHR, 'Status of Late and Non- reporting by state Parties' available at <http://tbinternet.ohchr.org/_layouts/TreatyBodyExternal/LateReporting.aspx> accessed 12/09/2019.

43 There were 621 UPR II recommendations on treaty bodies (about 2% of the total UPR recommendations to states). See UPR Info <www.upr-info.org/database/statistics/index.php?cycle=1> accessed 12/09/2019.

Notwithstanding the potential impact of the UPR process on the treaty body reporting obligations, it is important for the state to engage with domestic NGO stakeholders through the national consultation process. In addition, as I argued in Chapter 5, NGOs have found ways to bypass the limitations to their direct participation in the UPR process and effectively engage the state. Unlike Nigeria and Kenya, there was no NGO coalition in the case of South Africa during UPR I and II.[44] The absence of such a coalition limited the ability of NGOs in South Africa to engage effectively with the government in the review process. Through the formation of a broad and representative NGO coalition, NGOs in South Africa can potentially undertake media and advocacy campaigns on the UPR that would proactively engage the government. This would strengthen their capacity to impact and influence South Africa's subsequent UPR process, considering the reluctance of the South African government to engage NGOs during the UPR national consultation process as highlighted previously.

The quality of South Africa's UPR delegation

There are no stated guidelines on the composition of a state's UPR delegation.[45] However, for a state to participate effectively in the interactive dialogue, the delegates should have the competence to respond to questions and have up-to-date information on the efforts taken by their state to comply with its human rights obligations. An analysis of the composition of South Africa's UPR I delegation clearly indicates that the government took the UPR process more as a foreign affair rather than a process for the examination and improvement of human rights. The delegation was composed of seven delegates. The South African Ambassador and Permanent Representative to the UN Office at Geneva headed the delegation, and all the delegates were from her Department of Home and Foreign Affairs.[46] Judith Cohen, Head of Parliamentary and International Affairs Programme of the SAHRC, criticised the government for sending an exclusively Geneva-based delegation for its review.[47] She expressed disappointment at the inability of the delegation to provide sufficient responses and up-to-date information to questions asked during the review.[48]

During UPR II and III, the government made improvements to the quality of its UPR delegation and included representatives from the Justice and Human Rights Departments.[49] The UPR II and III delegation were both headed by the

44 While there has been an increase in the number of joint submissions by NGOs in South Africa, an NGO Coalition for the UPR was not established at the conclusion of UPR II.

45 HRC Resolution 5/1 provides that 'Each member State will decide on the composition of its delegation'. See *Resolution 5/1*, UN Doc A/HRC/RES/5/1, 18(a).

46 UN Human Rights Council, *Report of the Working Group on the Universal Periodic Review—South Africa*, 8th sess, Agenda Item 6, UN Doc A/HRC/8/32 (23 May 2008) ('*HRC UPR I Report—South Africa*') annex.

47 See Parliamentary Monitoring Group, above n 26.

48 Ibid.

49 *HRC UPR II Report—South* Africa, UN Doc A/HRC/21/16, annex.

Deputy Minister of Justice and Constitutional Development.[50] In addition, the South African government fully integrated gender balance in its UPR delegation, as was the case with the composition of the Kenyan UPR delegations.[51] During UPR I, South Africa's delegation was headed by Ms Glaudine Mtshali, Ambassador, Permanent Representative of South Africa to the United Nations Office at Geneva, and four of the seven delegates were female. During UPR II, seven of the 13 delegates were female. Women constituted eight of the 17 delegates during UPR III. However, the future composition of the South African UPR delegation could be strengthened by including representatives from parliament, as was earlier seen in the composition of the Nigerian UPR delegation.[52] It is important to note that parliament has an important role to play in the UPR process. Parliament could ensure that government complies with its UPR reporting obligations. Moreover, including parliamentary representatives in the UPR delegation can facilitate collaboration between government and parliament, regarding the implementation of UPR recommendations that require parliamentary approval, such as treaty ratification by the executive branch of government.

The quality of the UPR I South Africa delegation may have indicated that the state was less committed to the process by viewing it simply as a foreign affairs exercise. However, the improvement that was evident in the UPR II and III delegation in the case of Nigeria, Kenya and South Africa by incorporating legal and judicial personnel, as well as instituting a gender balance in their respective delegations, signals an increasing commitment to the UPR mechanism. The lesser commitment of South Africa to this aspect of the review during UPR I when it was a HRC member compared to the improved commitment during UPR II and III when it was not a HRC member suggests that membership in the HRC may not necessarily have a direct influence on state engagement with the UPR.

South Africa as a reviewer and as a state under review

South Africa as a reviewer

To engage effectively as a reviewer, it is important that states make quality recommendations in a non-selective manner. This would fall in line with the UPR principles of universality and non-selectivity. An examination of South Africa's engagement as a reviewer reinforces the universality and non-selectivity of the UPR mechanism. During UPR I, South Africa participated in 11 of the 12 UPR sessions and reviewed states in all five regional groups of states. It participated and made recommendations to 32 African states, 16 Asian states, three states

50 Ibid.

51 Slovenia during UPR I recommended that South Africa should continuously integrate a gender perspective in its UPR process. See *HRC UPR I Report—South Africa*, UN Doc A/HRC/8/32 para 67(3).

52 This can equally be contrasted with its engagement with the APRM which has had parliamentary involvement. See Economic Commission for Africa, 'The Role of Parliament in the APRM' (2011) 12–23 available at <https://bit.ly/2kJ0C1h> accessed 12/09/2019.

from the EEG,[53] 11 states from GRULAC and 10 states from WEOG.[54] It participated in a similar manner during UPR II.[55] South Africa is among the top six African states that have made the highest number of recommendations during the first two cycles of the UPR.[56]

However, only the quality—not the quantity of recommendations—has the capacity to improve the human rights situation on the ground. As argued in Chapter 5, a good recommendation should be relevant and have the capacity to promote meaningful and measurable human rights changes on the ground. This falls in line with what Roland Chauville describes as SMART recommendations, those that are specific, measurable, achievable, relevant and time-bound.[57] Figures 7.1, 7.2 and 7.3 provide further analysis of South Africa's participation as a reviewer to determine the extent of its participation and the quality of its recommendations.

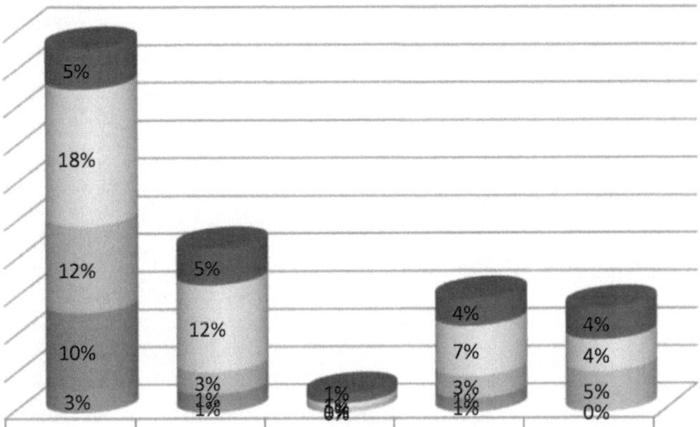

	Africa	Asia	EEG	GRULAC	WEOG
R5 - Specific Action	5%	5%	1%	4%	4%
R4 - General Action	18%	12%	1%	7%	4%
R3 - Consider Action	12%	3%	1%	3%	5%
R2 - Continue Action	10%	1%	0%	1%	0%
R1 - Minimal Action	3%	1%	0%	1%	0%

Figure 7.1 UPR I recommendations by South Africa

53 This included Russia, Slovakia and Azerbaijan.

54 This included Australia, France, Belgium, Germany, Denmark, the Netherlands and New Zealand.

55 During UPR II South Africa made recommendations to 42 African states, 15 Asian states, three states from the EEG, 13 states from GRULAC and 11 states from WEOG.

56 The others are Algeria, Egypt, Ghana, Morocco and Sierra Leone. See UPR Info, 'Statistics of Recommendations' available at <www.upr-info.org/database/statistics/index.php> accessed 12/09/2019.

57 UPR Info, 'Seminar on the Role of "Recommending States" at the UPR' (2014) available at <https://bit.ly/2kbU8ry> accessed 12/09/2019.

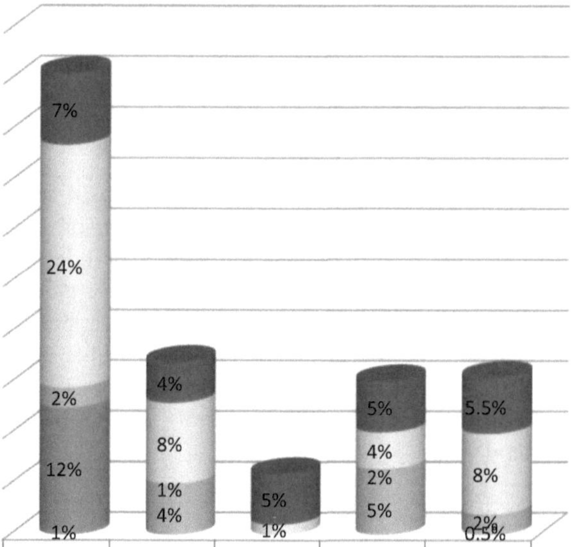

	Africa	Asia	EEG	GRULAC	WEOG
R5 - Specific Action	7%	4%	5%	5%	5.5%
R4 - General Action	24%	8%	1%	4%	8%
R3 - Consider Action	2%	1%	0%	2%	2%
R2 - Continue Action	12%	4%	0%	5%	0.5%
R1 - Minimal Action	1%	0%	0%	0%	0%

Figure 7.2 UPR II recommendations by South Africa

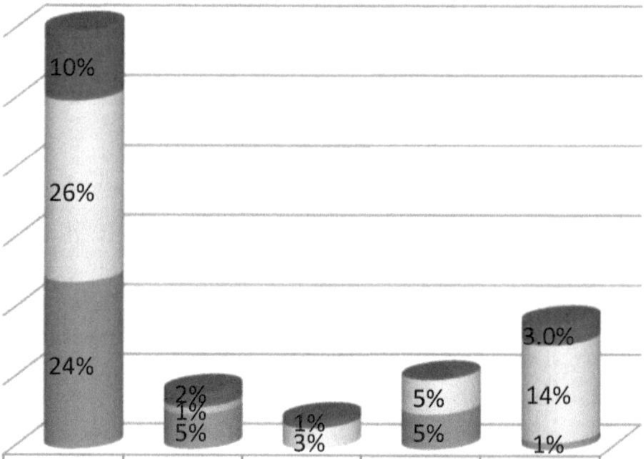

	Africa	Asia	EEG	GRULA C	WEOG
R5 - Specific Action	10%	2%	1%	0%	3.0%
R4 - General Action	26%	0%	3%	5%	14%
R3 - Consider Action	0%	1%	0%	0%	0%
R2 - Continue Action	24%	5%	0%	5%	1%
R1 - Minimal Action	0%	0%	0%	0%	0%

Figure 7.3 UPR III recommendations by South Africa

Figures 7.1, 7.2 and 7.3 indicate South Africa reviewed states across all the regional groups, with some variation. The fact that it participated and made more recommendations to states within the African Group indicates that its first loyalty is to the African Group. About 48% and 46% of the total South African recommendations made during UPR I and II respectively were to African states.[58] Sixty per cent of the recommendations made during UPR III (May 2017–May 2019) were to African states. In terms of the specificity of the recommendations made (R5 recommendations), South Africa engaged the various groups of states with specific recommendations across the first two cycles of the UPR. The African Group, in particular, has experienced an increase in the percentage of specific recommendations made by South Africa across the three cycles of the review from 5% to 7% and 10%. This might be explained by the commitment undertaken after UPR I by the African Group (including South Africa) and 89 other states to make specific recommendations during subsequent cycles of the review.[59] There was a general improvement in the specificity of UPR recommendations across UPR I and II. For example, Nigeria's percentage of specific recommendations (R5) to its African regional peers increased from 1% to 4% across UPR I and II, as well as its percentage of specific recommendations to WEOG increased from 2% to 3%.[60] This is in line with the commitment entered into in 2013 jointly by the African Group (including South Africa) together with other states to make UPR recommendations that are 'precise, practical, constructive, forward-looking and implementable'.[61]

The engagement of South Africa as a reviewer also helped to amplify human rights concerns and recommendations made by other human rights mechanisms. About 8% of the total 166 recommendations made by South Africa during UPR 1 required states to implement recommendations from the treaty bodies. For example, South Africa recommended that Mauritius '[i]mplement the recommendations of the Committee on the Rights of the Child'[62] and that Germany should '[i]mplement the recommendations of the CERD'.[63]

The tendency for states to emulate good practice from their peers by improving on the quality of their UPR recommendations provides evidence of acculturation through the microprocess of mimicry. This underscores the potential for the

58 This is calculated from 166 recommendations made by South Africa during UPR I and 138 during UPR II.

59 See 'Joint Statement on the Universal Periodic Review' (2013) Item 6 General Debate HRC22-15 March 2013 available at <https://bit.ly/2kGdqFG> accessed 12/09/2019.

60 As mentioned earlier, Kenya did not make any recommendations during UPR I. Sixteen per cent of the total 89 UPR II recommendations made by Kenya required specific action (R5) from its African peers compared to only 1% of its recommendations to EEG and 1% to GRULAC states. However, it is important to note that Kenya was very selective in its participation as a reviewer and reviewed only one state from the EEG.

61 See 'Joint Statement on the Universal Periodic Review' above n 59.

62 UN Human Rights Council, *Report of the Working Group on the Universal Periodic Review—Mauritius*, UN Doc A/HRC/11/28 (3 March 2009) para 58.

63 UN Human Rights Council, *Report of the Working Group on the Universal Periodic Review—Germany*, UN Doc A/HRC/11/15 (4 March 2009) para 60.

UPR to evolve over time in relation to the nature of UPR recommendations and to address early criticism with regard to their general lack of specificity.

An examination of the substance or relevance of the recommendations made by South Africa tends to support the perspective that South Africa, like many other states, is committed to human rights whenever it serves its foreign policy interest. The 'quiet diplomacy' in the review of Zimbabwe undermines the objectivity of South Africa's participation as a reviewer. During UPR I, South Africa made comments about the obstacles impeding the human rights efforts of the Zimbabwean government[64] but ignored the government's repression and failed economic policies which impact on rights enjoyment. In addition, most of South Africa's recommendations to African states were on socio-economic and development rights issues. However, no recommendation on these issues were made to Zimbabwe in spite of the fact that South Africa has experienced an unprecedented influx of Zimbabweans, largely attributed to failed economic policies and a governance crisis.[65] South Africa equally failed to be critical of Sudan despite its appalling human rights situation by making just one general recommendation with no particular focus.[66] This recommendation lacking specificity required Sudan to '[g]ive priority to the promotion and protection of human rights in all policies developed by the government'.[67]

Further analysis of South Africa's participation as a reviewer raises questions on its commitment to human rights, especially to protecting the rights of sexual minorities. Amidst criticism from the African Group, South Africa tabled a draft resolution before the HRC titled 'Human Rights, sexual orientation and gender identity', which expressed concern at violence and discrimination against sexual minorities.[68] However, South Africa's participation as a reviewer during the UPR process does not reflect its support for the rights of sexual minorities, at least within the African region. African states received the highest number of recommendations on the decriminalisation of same-sex relations.[69]

64 *South Africa Referred Specifically to Economic Sanctions: See UN Human Rights Council, Report of the Working Group on the Universal Periodic Review—Zimbabwe*, UN Doc A/HRC/19/14 (19 December 2011) para 28.

65 Nicola de Jager and Catherine Musuva, 'The Influx of Zimbabweans into South Africa: A Crisis of Governance That Spills Over' available at <https://bit.ly/2ku4rHP> accessed 12/09/2019.

66 This contrasts with the recommendations made by most Western states specifically targeting issues such as treaty ratification, torture, enforced disappearance, justice, freedom of the press, public security and the death penalty. See UN Human Rights Council, *Report of the Working Group on the Universal Periodic Review—Sudan*, UN Doc A/HRC/18/16 (11 July 2011).

67 Ibid para 83.48.

68 Human Rights Council, *Human Rights, Sexual Orientation and Gender Identity*, UN Doc A/HRC/RES/17/19 (14 July 2011); Also, South Africa voted in favour of a follow-up resolution in 2014. See Human Rights Council, *Human Rights, Sexual Orientation and Gender Identity*, UN Doc A/HRC/RES/27/32 (2 October 2014).

69 This constituted 27% of the total recommendations made during UPR I and II. See UPR Info, available at <www.upr-info.org/database/statistics/index_issues.php?fk_issue=47&cycle=> accessed 12/09/2019.

Despite this fact, South Africa made no recommendation on the issue to an African state, ignoring the specific legislation criminalising same-sex relations within Africa. It made recommendations on sexual orientation to many states, including the United States, Denmark and Cuba, except to states within Africa and Asia where criminalisation is predominant.[70] While this undermines South Africa's commitment to protecting the rights of sexual minorities, it, however, reinforces the theme of regionalism in the engagement of African states with the UPR mechanism by underscoring the inability for South Africa to break away from the general position of the African Group in its intra-African UPR engagement.

Overall, South Africa, unlike Kenya, effectively engaged as a reviewer in a non-selective manner across the various regional groups. It demonstrated the universality of the UPR while at the same time consolidating regionalism by reviewing more states in the African Group than any other group of states. However, while South Africa engaged various groups of states with specific recommendations, the substance of its recommendations to some African states avoided human rights issues that were of serious concern within those states. The little criticism of its regional peers like Zimbabwe and Sudan and avoidance of the issue of sexual orientation when reviewing its African peers raise questions about South Africa's international commitment to protecting the rights of sexual minorities. It equally reinforces the perspective that South Africa, like many other states, is committed to human rights whenever it serves its national interests. Nonetheless, the increasing relevance and specificity of UPR recommendations and the ability for the UPR to reinforce treaty body recommendations underscore the potential for the UPR mechanism to evolve into an effective cooperative mechanism for monitoring human rights implementation.

South Africa as a state under review

South Africa undertook its UPR I in April 2008, UPR II in May 2012 and UPR III in May 2017. Eighteen states made 22 recommendations to South Africa during UPR I.[71] South Africa did not directly respond or clarify its position on any of the 22 recommendations at the adoption of its UPR I outcome report, contrary to the norm.[72] This may be explained by the fact that South Africa was the second state reviewed under the UPR mechanism and the practice for states to clearly communicate their responses to UPR recommendations had not fully developed. Responses to UPR recommendations are crucial because the modalities for the UPR provide that '[t]he second and subsequent cycles of the review should focus

70 UN Human Rights Council, *Report of the Working Group on the Universal Periodic Review—Cuba*, UN Doc A/HRC/24/16 (8 July 2013) para 170.132.

71 *HRC UPR I Report—South Africa*, UN Doc A/HRC/8/32 para 67.

72 *Report of the HRC on Its 8th Session*, UN Doc A/HRC/8/52 paras 562–592; because South Africa did not clearly communicate acceptance of any of the UPR I recommendations, the data on the figures below are limited only to UPR II and III recommendations, most of which received a clear response from South Africa.

on, inter alia, the implementation of the accepted recommendations'.[73] In 2011, a review of the work and functioning of the HRC resulted in the adoption of a resolution requiring states under review to 'clearly communicate to the Council, in a written format preferably . . . its positions on all received recommendations'.[74]

During UPR II, there was an improvement in South Africa's responses to recommendations from its peers. Sixty-seven states made 151 recommendations to South Africa. South Africa directly responded to about 90% of the recommendations but still failed to declare its position on about 10% of the recommendations. From the 151 recommendations, South Africa declared 80% as 'acceptable', about 9% 'not acceptable' and less than 1% were 'rejected'.[75] The only recommendation explicitly rejected concerned allegations of sexual exploitation and abuse by South African peacekeepers.[76] The South African delegation stated that '[i]n view of the political gravity of this exaggerated allegation, the South African government has decided to reject this allegation and take the matter up bilaterally with the Canadian government at a political level'.[77] South Africa did not provide a clear response to about 10% of the recommendations. These included recommendations such as to '[a]ccede to the Agreement on Privileges and Immunities of the ICC' and to establish without delay an independent national monitoring mechanism on the Rights of Persons with Disabilities. During UPR III, South Africa received 243 recommendations and accepted 77% of the total recommendations. Figures 7.4 and 7.5 break down the recommendations made to South Africa during UPR II and III and the responses to the various categories of recommendations.

Figures 7.4 and 7.5 indicate that South Africa engaged with various categories of recommendations. The majority of the recommendations accepted by South Africa during UPR II and III were general recommendations (37% and 40% respectively). However, it accepted some specific recommendations (20% in UPR II and 14% in UPR III). Another observation is that South Africa rejected more specific (R5) recommendations (9% in UPR II and 15% in UPR III) when compared to the percentage of recommendations rejected from the other categories.[78] The majority of recommendations made by African states to South Africa during UPR II and III (74% and 69% respectively) required a 'general' or

73 See *Resolution 16/21* para 6; it therefore becomes difficult to assess implementation when a state under review does not directly communicate its position on the recommendations made.

74 Ibid para 16.

75 UN Human Rights Council, *Report of the Working Group on the Universal Periodic Review—South Africa—Addendum*, 21st sess, Agenda Item 6, UN Doc A/HRC/21/16/Add.1 (12 July 2012) ('*HRC UPR II Report—South Africa—Addendum*') annex B; The justification provided by South Africa was that the recommendations were under national consultation and as a result inappropriate to anticipate the outcome of the consultative process.

76 Canada made this recommendation. See ibid para 124.96.

77 Ibid.

78 This included the recommendations South Africa considered unacceptable and those it failed to provide a direct response to.

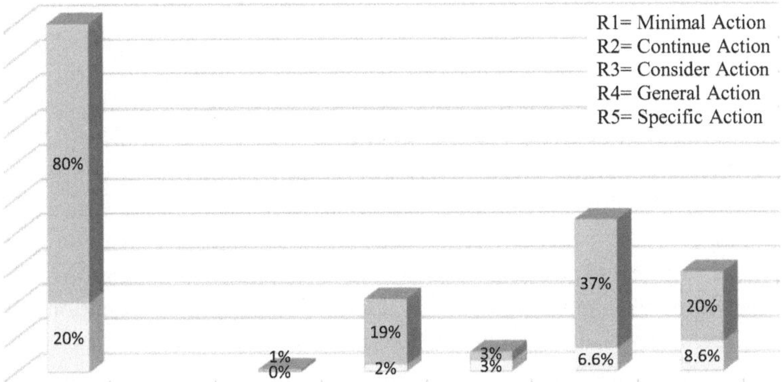

	Total Rec.		R1	R2	R3	R4	R5
Accepted	80%		1%	19%	3%	37%	20%
Rejected	20%		0%	2%	3%	6.6%	8.6%

Figure 7.4 South Africa—UPR II percentage of recommendations accepted by category

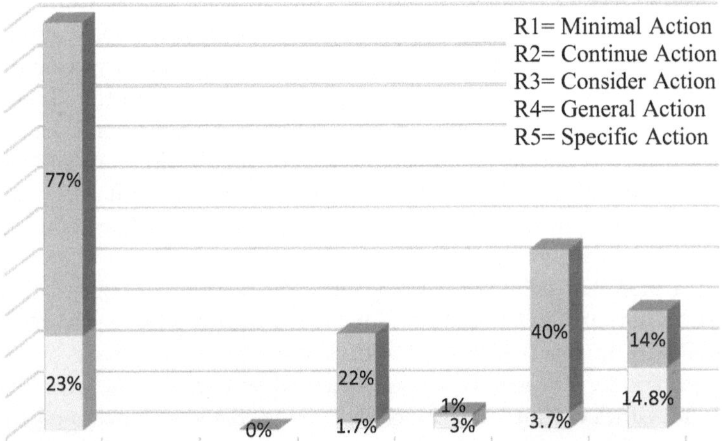

	Total Rec.		R1	R2	R3	R4	R5
Accepted	77%		0%	22%	1%	40%	14%
Rejected	23%		0%	1.7%	3%	3.7%	14.8%

Figure 7.5 South Africa—UPR III percentage of recommendations accepted by category

'continuing' action from South Africa. All UPR II recommendations in R2 and R4 were declared 'acceptable' by South Africa. In contrast, 92% of the recommendations that were declared 'not acceptable' by South Africa during UPR II were made by Western states. All rank 2 recommendations made by African states during UPR III were accepted by South Africa. Also, South Africa accepted 26 out of 28 'general' recommendations made by states within the African regional group during UPR III. This reinforces the theme of regionalism and highlights the diverging approach to cooperation in the UPR between African and Western states. In addition, the improvement in the response of South Africa across UPR I and II is an indication of evolving practice as states are increasingly providing clearer responses to their position on each UPR recommendation.

As noted in Chapter 5, the rank under which a recommendation falls presents a clearer picture of a state's level of receptiveness and plays a crucial role during implementation. General recommendations (R4) give the state under review greater autonomy to define the manner of implementation, but the more general a recommendation is, the harder it is to measure implementation. Unlike general recommendations, specific recommendations, when implemented, have the capacity to promote meaningful and measurable human rights changes on the ground.[79] As indicated in Figures 7.4 and 7.5, most of the recommendations rejected by South Africa across UPR II and III were specific recommendations. The majority of recommendations accepted by South Africa were 'general' recommendations, and this may pose problems in terms of measuring their implementation. Nevertheless, states can implement general recommendations through specific actions. In addition, the fact a recommendation is non-specific or less actionable does not necessarily mean it is qualitatively inferior or inconsistent with the ideals of the UPR. On the other hand, a specific recommendation (R5) may be more actionable but inconsistent with the ideals of the UPR by failing to 'take into account the level of development and the specificities of countries',[80] consider the capacity needs of the country[81] or aim to secure 'the improvement of the human rights situation on the ground'.[82] African states have generally adopted a 'soft' approach to cooperation, which in many cases results in non-specific recommendations.

As indicated in Table 7.1, the majority of the recommendations to South Africa during UPR I focused on violence against women and children, HIV/AIDS treatment, right to education and discrimination based on race or sexual orientation.[83] The issues that appeared predominantly in the recommendations to South Africa during UPR II included gender-based violence and gender equality

79 As pointed out in Chapter 5, a few general recommendations can translate into specific actions at the implementation stage.
80 See *Resolution 5/1,* UN Doc A/HRC/RES/5/1.
81 Ibid para 4(c).
82 Ibid para 4(a).
83 Ibid.

Table 7.1 List of the top 12 issues raised during South Africa's UPR I and II

UPR I				*UPR II*				*UPR III*			
Rank	*Issue*	*Total No. of Recom. (UPR I)*	*% of 22 Recom. (UPR I)*	*Rank*	*Issue*	*Total No. of Recom. (UPR II)*	*% of 151 Recom. (UPR II)*	*Rank*	*Issue*	*Total No. of Recom. (UPR III)*	*% of 243 Recom. (UPR III)*
1	Women's & Children's Right/ Gender Equality	5	23%	1	Women's Right and Gender Equality	24	16%	1	Racism and Xenophobia	46	19%
2	HIV/AIDS	3	13.6	2	Treaty Ratification	18	12%	2	Women's Right and Gender Equality	32	13%
3	Right to Education	3	13.6%	3	Health and HIV/ AIDS	17	11%	3	Treaty Ratification	25	10%
4	Treaty Ratification	3	13.6%	4	Racism and Xenophobia	15	10%	4	Rights of the Child	22	9%
5	Sexual Orientation	2	9%	5	Sexual Orientation	12	8%	5	Poverty and Development	20	8%
6	Racism and Xenophobia	2	9%	6	Freedom of Expression/ Information	11	7%	6	Health and HIV/ AIDS	16	7%
7	Human Rights Training	1	4.6%	7	Right to Education	9	6%	7	Right to Education	14	6%
8	Torture	1	4.6%	8	Poverty and Development	9	6%	8	Albinism and other Vulnerable Groups	14	6%
9	Poverty	1	4.6%	9	Torture, Detention and Rule of Law	8	5%	9	Torture, Detention and Rule of Law	14	6%

(*Continued*)

Table 7.1 (Continued)

UPR I				*UPR II*				*UPR III*			
Rank	*Issue*	*Total No. of Recom. (UPR I)*	*% of 22 Recom. (UPR I)*	*Rank*	*Issue*	*Total No. of Recom. (UPR II)*	*% of 151 Recom. (UPR II)*	*Rank*	*Issue*	*Total No. of Recom. (UPR III)*	*% of 243 Recom. (UPR III)*
10	Socio-economic Rights	1	4.6%	10	Migrants, Refugees and Asylum Seekers	8	5%	10	National and International Mechanisms	12	5%
11					Human Trafficking	5	3%	11	Human Trafficking	7	3%
12					Minorities/ Vulnerable Groups	4	3%	12	Privacy and Freedom of Express/ Information	6	2.5%
13					Right to Food and Water	4	3%	13	Sexual Orientation	6	2.5%
14					Rights of the Child	4	3%	14	Socio-economic Rights[1]	6	2.5%
15					Disability Rights	3	2%	15	Business, Environment and Human Rights	3	1%

[1] This only includes the right to food, water, housing and land.

(16% of the overall 151 recommendations), treaty ratification (12%),[84] HIV/AIDS (11%), racism and xenophobia (10%) and discrimination based on sexual orientation (8%).[85] These five issues accounted for about 57% of the overall 151 recommendations made to South Africa during UPR II. Similarly, Table 7.1 shows the issues of women and children's rights, racism and xenophobia and treaty ratification were among the top five recommendations made by states during UPR III and accounted for over 50% of the overall recommendations made to South Africa. There is a significant increase in the number of recommendations on these issues across the three cycles of the review. For example, the number of recommendations to South Africa addressing racism and xenophobia increased dramatically from two during UPR I to 15 during UPR II and 46 during UPR III.

In response to UPR I recommendations from its peers, South Africa stated that '[m]ost of the recommendations proposed for South Africa require serious contextualization . . . and have already been implemented through national legislation and programmes'.[86] For example, during UPR I, Slovenia made a specific recommendation that South Africa

> commit not only to removing the defence of reasonable chastisement but also to criminalizing corporal punishment with the concomitant pledges towards raising awareness and providing the necessary resource to support parents in adopting positive and alternative forms of discipline.[87]

The government of South Africa responded by stating that the issue of corporal punishment at home is being dealt with by the South African *Domestic Violence Act 1998*.[88] It further stated that it has outlawed corporal punishment at school by legislation but there are only 'isolated cases of non-compliance with legislation for which corrective measures are usually taken'.[89] However, NGOs such as Children Now, Global Initiative to End Corporal Punishment of Children and the SAHRC have repeatedly made recommendations for the government to ban corporal punishment at home and to remove the defence of 'reasonable

84 The two predominant treaties states recommended South Africa to ratify were the International Covenant on Economic Social and Cultural Rights and the Optional Protocol to the Convention Against Torture.

85 Twenty-four recommendations were made on Women's right and gender equality, 18 on treaty ratification, 17 on health and HIV/AIDS treatment, 15 on racism and xenophobia and 12 on sexual orientation.

86 *Report of the HRC on Its 8th Session*, UN Doc A/HRC/8/52 para 567.

87 *HRC UPR I Report—South Africa*, UN Doc A/HRC/8/32 para 67(1); see a similar recommendation from Mexico during UPR II for South Africa to prohibit and punish corporal punishment at home and in schools. See *HRC UPR II Report—South Africa—Addendum*, UN Doc A/HRC/21/16/Add.1 para 124.88.

88 *Report of the HRC on Its 8th Session*, UN Doc A/HRC/8/52 para 568.

89 Ibid. See a similar response by the government during UPR II—*HRC UPR I Report—South Africa*, UN Doc A/HRC/8/32 para 124.88.

chastisement'.[90] The special attention given to the issue of corporal punishment by various stakeholders during South Africa's UPR I underscores the relevance of the recommendations on corporal punishment. The relevance of these recommendations was reinforced by Mexico during UPR II when it recommended that the South African government should '[p]rohibit and punish corporal punishment both in the home, as well as in public institutions such as schools and prisons'.[91] Similar recommendations were made by Israel and Liechtenstein during UPR III which the South African delegation did not accept.[92] The following section examines the extent to which the South African government implemented these recommendations on corporal punishment.

On other issues, such as violence based on sexual orientation, racism and xenophobia, the government of South Africa responded by referring to the constitutional protection in place and to its international endorsement of LGBT rights at the HRC.[93] However, this undermines the commitment to increase domestic protection of the relevant human rights issues because the substance of many of the UPR recommendations raised concerns about the inadequacy and inefficacy of the existing protective measures. Examples of such UPR recommendations to South Africa include 'reinforce measures to combat and prevent xenophobia . . .',[94] enhance the prevention, investigation and prosecution of crimes of violence against individuals based on their gender or sexual orientation[95] and '[e]xert additional efforts to combat discrimination and xenophobia'.[96] In addition, despite the significant role played by South Africa in the establishment of the ICC, its UPR III delegation did not accept recommendations calling on South Africa to reconsider its decision to withdraw from the Rome Statute and in response cited perceptions of inequality and unfairness in relation to the Court's investigations and prosecutions.[97]

90 See Global Initiative to End All Corporal Punishment of Children, 'Corporal Punishment of Children in South Africa' (2015) 1–6 available at <https://bit.ly/2kIVDh4> accessed 12/09/2019; Global Initiative to End All Corporal Punishment of Children, 'South Africa: Briefing for the Human Rights Council Universal Periodic Review—1st session, 2007' (2007); SAHRC, 'NHRI Submission to the Universal Periodic Review Mechanism' (2007); Children Now, 'Alternate Report to the UN Committee on the Rights of the Child, Prepared for the Universal Periodic Review of South Africa, Scheduled for April 2008' (2008); Instituto Internazionale Maria Ausiliatrice et al., 'The Situation on the Rights of the Child in South Africa' (2011).

91 See *HRC UPR II Report—South Africa—Addendum*, UN Doc A/HRC/21/16/Add.1 para 124.88.

92 UN Human Rights Council, *Report of the Working Group on the Universal Periodic Review—South Africa*, 36th sess, Agenda Item 6, UN Doc A/HRC/36/16 (18 July 2017) ('*HRC UPR III Report—South Africa*) 139.233–139.234.

93 *Report of the HRC on Its 8th Session*, UN Doc A/HRC/8/52 paras 571–574.

94 See *HRC UPR II Report—South Africa—Addendum*, UN Doc A/HRC/21/16/Add.1 para 124.44.

95 Ibid para 124.82.

96 *HRC UPR III Report—South Africa,* UN Doc A/HRC/36/16 para 139.86.

97 Ibid para 93.

Nevertheless, it is observable, from an examination of South Africa as a state under review, that there has been an improvement in the UPR engagement of South Africa across UPR I, II and III. South Africa accepted a high percentage of the total UPR II and III recommendations. However, the receptiveness of South Africa to many UPR recommendations demonstrates the potential for rights ritualism. As I noted in Chapter 2, this concept in the context of the UPR relates to the participation of states in the UPR process but with reluctance about increasing the domestic protection of human rights.[98] The reluctance of the South African government to accept recommendations that raised concerns about the inadequacy and inefficacy of the existing measures for human rights protection limits the extent of the state's engagement at this stage of the review.

South Africa's implementation of UPR recommendations

The previous section highlighted the relevance of the UPR recommendations made during the review of South Africa on issues such as corporal punishment, violence based on sexual orientation, racism and xenophobia. The implementation of these recommendations could contribute to improving the human rights situation on the ground. Implementation of UPR recommendations is therefore a central component in evaluating the impact of the UPR mechanism. The implementation time frame for South Africa to implement its UPR I recommendations ran from April 2008 to May 2012 and UPR II from May 2012 to May 2017. It is important to consider these time frames when assessing implementation because the UPR is a dynamic and ongoing process and the human rights situation on the ground is constantly changing. As a result, the implementation of South Africa's UPR I and II recommendations are only analysed within the respective time frames. The analysis of implementation employs the IRI, which is based on an average of stakeholders' responses on the implementation outcome of each recommendation.[99]

At the conclusion of South Africa's UPR I, the South African government had fully implemented about 14% of the 22 recommendations, 46% were partially implemented and 32% were not implemented. About 9% of the recommendations were not assessed because the stakeholders did not provide any responses on

98 See Hilary Charlesworth and Emma Larking (eds), *Human Rights and the Universal Periodic Review: Rituals and Ritualism* (Cambridge University Press 2015) 16.

99 Commentary on South Africa's UPR I implementation was provided by stakeholders such as the SAHRC, the Government of South Africa, Ubuntu Centre, Community Law Centre (University of the Western Cape), Consortium for Refugees and Migrants in South Africa (CoRMSA), World Vision South Africa, and Child Welfare South Africa. Stakeholders who commented on UPR II implementation included SAHRC, the Government of South Africa, Legal Resource Centre, CIVICUS, Human Rights Institute of South Africa, UN Country Team for the Republic of South Africa, The Centre for the Study of Violence and Reconciliation, Edmund Rice International, UN High Commissioner for Refugees, Law Society of South Africa and Dullah Omar Institute for Constitutional Law, Governance and Human Rights.

implementation. In relation to UPR II, 17% of the total 151 recommendations were fully implemented, 43% partially implemented and 34% were not implemented. No information from stakeholders was available for about 5% of the recommendations to South Africa during UPR II. Some of the recommendations to South Africa during UPR I and II were vague, making it very difficult to assess their implementation outcome. An example is the recommendation by Sudan during UPR I that the South African government should 'give special attention to the role of international cooperation for the enjoyment of economic, social and cultural rights'.[100] The Legal Resource Centre in its commentary on South Africa's UPR II implementation criticised recommendations with the wording '[continue] in its efforts' as 'nebulous' and difficult to assess implementation.[101]

The UPR I recommendations stakeholders considered to be fully implemented only related to the issue of HIV/AIDS, while the partially implemented recommendations were mostly on the issues of poverty and education, xenophobia and discrimination based on race and sexual orientation. With regard to UPR II implementation, there was agreement among various UPR stakeholders that most of the recommendations concerning ratification of treaties (International Covenant on Social, Economic and Cultural Rights (ICESCR) and International Labour Organization (ILO) 189)[102] and human trafficking were fully implemented by the South African government. For example, SAHRC, UN Country Team for South Africa (UNCT–SA) and Law Society of South Africa[103] all agreed that recommendations for South Africa to ratify ICESCR and ILO 189 were fully implemented. There was also consensus that the recommendations calling for the enactment into law of the Prevention and Combating of Trafficking in Persons Bill were fully implemented.[104] Most of the UPR II recommendations considered to be partially implemented touched on issues including Health/HIV, socio-economic rights and torture. Many recommendations on issues involving violence against women and children, privacy and freedom of information, and racism and xenophobia were not implemented within the UPR II implementation time frame. Some of the recommendations which were not implemented during UPR I were repeated during UPR II and still not implemented. Three groups of issues that featured repeatedly in the review of South Africa across UPR I, II and III are examined below in relation to their implementation. These three

100 See *HRC UPR I Report—South Africa*, UN Doc A/HRC/8/32 para 18.

101 Legal Resource Centre, 'UPR Submission: Right to Adequate Food and Nutrition' (2016) 1 available at <https://bit.ly/2kdVli5> accessed 19/07/2019.

102 UN General Assembly, *International Covenant on Economic, Social and Cultural Rights* (16 December 1966), UNTS 993 (ICESCR); International Labour Organization (ILO), *Convention Concerning Decent Work for Domestic Workers* (16 June 2011), PRNo.15A (ILO 189).

103 Law Society of South Africa, International Bar Association Human Rights Institute and Southern Africa Litigation Centre, 'Joint Stakeholder Submission to the UN Human Rights Council Universal Periodic Review of South Africa' (2016) available at <https://bit.ly/2ku50RX> accessed 20/07/2019.

104 See *Prevention and Combating of Trafficking in Persons Act*, Act No. 7 of 2013 (South Africa) (29 July 2013) available at <https://bit.ly/2kJ1Jht> accessed 20/07/2019.

issues are corporal punishment, violence based on sexual orientation and gender identity, and racism and xenophobia. Many of these recommendations were relevant and addressed the inadequacy or ineffectiveness of the measures put in place by the government to address these human rights concerns.

Corporal punishment

The issue of corporal punishment featured among both state and NGO recommendations to South Africa during UPR I, II and III. The government of South Africa responded to these recommendations during the reviews by referring to existing legislation that outlaws corporal punishment at schools and stated that there were only 'isolated cases of non-compliance'.[105] The government provided a similar response in its comments on the implementation of the recommendation on corporal punishment and further stated that 'the country has experienced a significant reduction in regard to corporal punishment'.[106]

However, various UPR stakeholders were in consensus in their response that the government did not implement this recommendation. For example, the South African National Human Rights Commission responded that the South African government has not taken steps to implement the recommendation and repeated the exact wording of the recommendation made by Slovenia on this issue for South Africa during UPR II.[107] An NGO, Global Initiative to End Corporal Punishment of Children, stated that despite recommendations made to South Africa on this issue, 'the legality of corporal punishment of children in South Africa has not changed since the review in 2008' as corporal punishment continues to be lawful at home.[108] The South African Schools Act (1996) and other relevant laws expressly prohibit corporal punishment in schools. Section 10 of the South African Schools Act provides that '[n]o person may administer corporal punishment at a school to a learner'. The Constitutional Court of South Africa in the case of *Christian Education SA v Minister of Education* reinforced this.[109] However, there is no explicit prohibition of corporal punishment at home. According to another NGO joint report by Save the Child et al., the South African government did not implement the 2008 UPR recommendation on corporal punishment as the government continued to condone corporal punishment being practised at

105 See *UPR II National Report—South Africa*, UN Doc A/HRC/WG.6/13/ZAF/1, Annex 1.

106 Ibid.

107 SAHRC, 'NHRI submission to the Universal Periodic Review Mechanism' (28 November 2011) para 11.

108 Global Initiative to End Corporal Punishment, 'South Africa: Briefing for the Human Rights Council Universal Periodic Review—13th Session, 2012' (2011) para 1.3.

109 The appellants argued that the ban on corporal punishment violated the rights of the pupil's parents to freedom of religion that permits the use corporal punishment on children. The court did not find any violation of freedom of religion and upheld the ban on corporal punishment in schools as lawful. See *Christian Education South Africa v Minister of Education* 2000 (4) SA 757.

home, in schools and other social settings.[110] Additional recommendations were made on this issue during UPR III by Israel and Liechtenstein, and South Africa did not accept these recommendations.[111]

In addition, 2014 findings by the Centre for Child Law at Pretoria University suggest that there is an 'official ambivalence' towards the ban on corporal punishment.[112] The Centre found that approximately 2.2 million children were exposed to corporal punishment and that the phenomenon has been on a steady increase in certain provinces in South Africa.[113] Similar recommendations made by the UN Committee on the Rights of the Child, the UN Committee against Torture and by the African Committee of Experts on the Rights and Welfare of the Child have not been implemented.[114] They expressed concern at the continuous use of corporal punishment in schools. Their recommendations were that the government ensure that legislation banning corporal punishment is strictly implemented in schools and take effective measures to prohibit corporal punishment at home.[115] The response of the government that simply points to existing legislation on corporal punishment underscores its reluctance about increasing the domestic protection of human rights. In October 2017, the High Court of Guateng found that the common law rule established in the case of *R v Janke and Janke*[116] which allows parents to 'inflict moderate and reasonable chastisement on a child' was unconstitutional.[117] The failure of the government of South Africa to consider the inadequacy or ineffectiveness of the measures put in place to end corporal punishment at home demonstrates the potential for rights ritualism in its UPR engagement.[118]

110 Save the Child et al., 'Children's Rights Organisations Submission to the Universal Periodic Review of South Africa—13th Session in 2012' (2011) para 2.4.

111 *HRC UPR III Report—South Africa*, UN Doc A/HRC/36/16 para 139.233–234.

112 Centre for Child Law, *Promoting Effective Enforcement of the Prohibition Against Corporal Punishment in South African Schools* (Pretoria University Press 2014).

113 Ibid 11.

114 Committee on the Rights of the Child, *Concluding Observations of the Committee on the Rights of the Child, South Africa*, UN Doc CRC/C/15/Add.122 (2000) para 28; Committee Against Torture, *Concluding Observations of the Committee on the Rights of the Child, South Africa*, UN Doc CAT/C/ZAF/CO/1 (7 December 2006) para 25; African Committee of Experts on the Rights and Welfare of the Child, 'Concluding Recommendations by the African Committee of Experts on the Rights and Welfare of the Child (ACERWC) on the Republic Of South Africa Initial Report on the Status of Implementation of the African Charter on the Rights and Welfare of the Child' (2014) para 35 available at <www.acerwc.org/?wpdmdl=8754> accessed 12/09/2019.

115 Ibid.

116 1913 TPD 382.

117 YG v The State, High Court of Gauteng Local Division, Case No. A263/2016.

118 The existing enforcement mechanisms regulating the prohibition of corporal punishment in schools have been found to be inadequate and ineffective. See Global Initiative to End All Corporal Punishment of Children, 'Corporal Punishment of Children in South Africa' (2019) 1–12 available at <https://bit.ly/2mf49VP>; Centre for Child Law, above n 113.

Violence based on sexual orientation

Violence based on sexual orientation was one of the issues that featured prominently among state recommendations to South Africa across UPR I, II and III. Recommendations that states made to South Africa on sexual orientation include undertaking credible investigation and prosecuting perpetrators; enhancing prevention and monitoring capacity; training police and judiciary; and launching awareness-raising campaigns.[119] In some ways, South Africa is one of the few exceptions to the general criminalisation and discriminatory treatment confronting the LGBT community in Africa. Only seven of 54 Africa states have some form of protection against discrimination based on sexual orientation.[120] Article 9 (3) of the 1996 South African Constitution explicitly prohibits discrimination against anyone based on sexual orientation.[121] South Africa is the only UN member state from the African regional group to recognise same-sex marriage. At the international level, South Africa has achieved a milestone in advancing the rights of LGBT persons worldwide. In 2011, despite strong criticisms from its regional peers, South Africa tabled a draft resolution before the HRC that expressed concern at violence and discrimination against persons based on their sexual orientation.[122] South Africa was the only African state that voted in favour of a subsequent resolution on sexual orientation in 2014.[123] South Africa's response to state recommendations on this issue during UPR I and II and its comments on implementation simply made reference to the above domestic constitutional protection, government policy framework on combating hate crime and its international endorsement of the LGBT rights at the HRC.[124]

However, South Africa's role on the issue of sexual orientation lacks a consistent actual commitment domestically and internationally. According to various NGO reports, the domestic situation of LGBT individuals remained generally grim as they reportedly faced violence and intimidation because of their sexual orientation.[125] In 2011, Human Rights Watch published a report that found a

119 See for example *HRC UPR II Report—South Africa—Addendum*, UN Doc A/HRC/21/16/Add.1 paras 124.50, 124.51, 124.75–124.87.

120 International Lesbian, Gay, Bisexual, Trans and Intersex Association: Lucas Ramon Mendos, *State-Sponsored Homophobia 2019* (Geneva, ILGA March 2019).

121 *Constitution of the Republic of South Africa Act 1996* (South Africa) ch 2, art 9 (3).

122 UN Human Rights Council, *Human Rights, Sexual Orientation and Gender Identity*, UN Doc A/HRC/RES/17/19 (14 July 2011).

123 UN Human Rights Council, *Human Rights, Sexual Orientation and Gender Identity*, UN Doc A/HRC/RES/27/32 (2 October 2014).

124 *Report of the HRC on Its 8th Session*, UN Doc A/HRC/8/52 para 572; *HRC UPR II Report—South Africa—Addendum*, UN Doc A/HRC/21/16/Add.1, annex A para 124.51; See *UPR II National Report—South Africa*, UN Doc A/HRC/WG.6/13/ZAF/1, 23.

125 The Centre for Applied Psychology of the University of South Africa et al., 'Violate Hate Crimes in South Africa' (2012) 1–9 available at <https://bit.ly/2kIZmv4> accessed 12/09/2019; Human Rights Watch, '"We'll Show You You're a Woman": Violence and

dichotomy between the constitutional ideals and public attitude towards such individuals.[126] Furthermore, it found that despite the constitutional protection on the rights of the LGBT community, discrimination against them remained institutionalised in the communities, families and state institutions.[127] In 2016, a national research on LGBT discrimination and hate crimes found that 56% of LGBT South Africans experienced discrimination in schools at 24 or younger and 88% did not report instances of discrimination based on sexual orientation to the police.[128]

According to a joint report by the Centre for Applied Psychology of the University of South Africa and NGOs working on gay rights, state responses to violence based on sexual orientation have fallen short in many aspects.[129] They argue that there is lack of official monitoring and reporting because there is no effective system to monitor and collect data on such crimes.[130] The absence of such a system, they further argue, impedes policymakers from understanding the scope of the problem and developing adequate responses.[131] Moreover, there is the phenomenon of 'corrective' or 'curative' rape in South Africa, in relation to which Lea Mwambene argues that the government has failed to fulfil its constitutional mandate.[132] According to Mwambene, the government failed in its constitutional mandate by defining 'corrective' rape as a crime of rape instead of a hate crime and for the failure of the courts to resolve the conflict between the right to culture and the rights to equality in the context of 'corrective' rape.[133] Likewise, the UN Committee on the Elimination of All Forms of Discrimination against Women has expressed 'serious concern about the practice of so called "corrective rape" of lesbians' in South Africa.[134]

Nevertheless, various NGOs have commended several positive efforts by the South African government in responding to domestic violence based on sexual orientation, such as the increasing high-level government rhetoric in support of

---

Discrimination Against Black Lesbians and Transgender Men in South Africa' (2011) available at <https://bit.ly/2lSmgAk> accessed 12/09/2019.

126 Ibid 1.

127 Ibid 14–15.

128 Out LGBT, *Hate Crimes Against Lesbian, Gay, Bisexual and Transgender (LGBT) People in South Africa* (2016) 6.

129 See The Centre for Applied Psychology of the University of South Africa et al., above n 125, 7–8.

130 Ibid; UPR II recommendation made by The Netherlands to South Africa addresses this issue. See *HRC UPR II Report—South Africa—Addendum*, UN Doc A/HRC/21/16/Add.1 para 124.81.

131 The Centre for Applied Psychology of the University of South Africa et al., above n 125.

132 Lea Mwambene, 'Realisation or Oversight of a Constitutional Mandate? Corrective Rape of Black African Lesbians in South Africa' (2015) 15(1) *African Human Rights Journal* 58.

133 Ibid.

134 Committee on the Elimination of Discrimination Against Women, *Concluding Observations of the Committee on the Elimination of Discrimination Against Women—South Africa*, UN Doc. CEDAW/C/ZAF/CO/4 (4 February 2011) paras 39–40.

tolerance and non-discrimination and the advancement of a Hate Crime Bill.[135] But the rhetoric and strong conservative views about sexual minorities held by some other key public figures and those who design government policies in South Africa have not been helpful. For example, in 2012, Peter Holomisa, Chairperson of Parliament's Constitutional Review Committee, stated that 'homosexuality was a condition that occurred when certain cultural rituals have not been performed' and further said, 'when rituals are done, the person starts to behave like others in society'.[136] Jacob Zuma, former president of South Africa, was criticised in 2006 for publicly describing same-sex marriages as 'a disgrace to the nation and to God'.[137] Such statements and views by public officials undermined the commitment of the South African government to protect the rights of LGBT individuals.

At the international level, South Africa's commitment to protecting the rights of sexual minorities has also been inconsistent. As earlier noted, it made no recommendations on the issue to its regional peers during UPR I and II even though African states received the highest number of recommendations on sexual orientation. This demonstrates a reluctance to take a definite position at odds with the majority of African states. Graeme Reid has criticised South Africa for supporting a regressive HRC resolution on 'Protection of the Family' that infringed on the rights of the LGBT community.[138] He argued that reference to a singular 'family' in the resolution without acknowledging diversity could be used as precedent to oppose rights for LGBT couples in later negotiations.[139] Reid equally observed in 2014 that South Africa stopped attending meetings of the core group of LGBT-friendly states at the UNGA.[140]

South Africa's role in the advancement of LGBT rights is an important one. The cooperative framework of the UPR can facilitate the realisation of LGBT rights within Africa by prioritising recommendations that seek to transform the social and political culture against sexual minorities rather than recommendations for immediate decriminalisation. Many African states can perceive the latter

135 See The Centre for Applied Psychology of the University of South Africa et al., above n 125, 7; Consortium for Refugees and Migrants in South Africa et al., 'Republic of South Africa: Joint Report to the UN Universal Periodic Review (UPR)—13th Session of the UPR Working Group' (2011) para 5.4.

136 Deon De Lange, 'Call to Suspend ANC MP for Opening Fire on Gay Rights' *Cape Times* (Cape Town) (8 May 2012) 4; this statement was made during a submission made to the Constitution review committee calling for changes to section 9 of the constitution that protects against discrimination based on sexual orientation.

137 IRIN, 'South Africa: Zuma Slammed for Views on Homosexuality, Same-sex Marriage' (2006) available at <https://bit.ly/2lQoCQA> accessed 12/09/2019.

138 Graeme Reid is the Director of Lesbian, Gay, Bisexual, and Transgender Rights Programme at Human Rights Watch. See Graeme Reid, 'South Africa's Worrying Prevarication on LGBT Rights' (2014) *Policy Review* available at <https://bit.ly/2kiuFgi> accessed 12/09/2019.

139 Ibid.

140 Ibid.

as confrontational and in disregard of strongly held African cultural values. The government of South Africa has not been consistent in its commitment internationally or publicly taken the lead in engaging its regional peers on this issue that tends to be culturally sensitive within the continent. At the domestic level, the government has not addressed the inadequacies of the existing protective measures for the protection of the rights of sexual minorities. Enhancing prevention and monitoring capacity and launching awareness-raising campaigns as recommended by UPR stakeholders could help narrow the gap between the constitutional ideals and the attitude of the public towards the LGBT community.

Racism and xenophobia

Addressing racism and xenophobia against foreigners was a prominent issue in the review of South Africa with a dramatic increase from two recommendations during UPR I to 12 during UPR II and 46 during UPR III. Most of these recommendations required the government to 'reinforce measures to combat and prevent xenophobia' and to 'take all necessary steps to address the issue of xenophobia through legislation'.[141] Most of these recommendations focused on the ineffectiveness of existing measures to combat racism and reflected similar concerns raised by the human rights treaty bodies and other African regional mechanisms. For example, in August 2006, the UN CERD was concerned about the frequency of hate crimes in South Africa and the 'inefficacy of the measures in preventing such crimes'.[142] It recommended that the government 'adopt legislative and other effective measures to prevent, combat and punish hate crimes'.[143] In 2007, similar recommendations came from the APRM after observing that 'xenophobia . . . is currently on the rise and should be nipped in the bud'.[144] The similarity between the recommendations from various human rights mechanisms emphasises the relevance of these UPR recommendations to improving the human rights situation on the ground. Also, it underscores the potential for the UPR to create a synergy with other national, regional and international human rights mechanisms by amplifying and reinforcing their recommendations.

However, the recurrence of subsequent xenophobic incidents may be an indication that the South African government did not engage with the above recommendations to proactively prevent its recurrence. In May 2008, a spate of xenophobic violence in South Africa left more than 60 people dead, 342 shops looted and 213 burnt down, and about 100,000 people displaced.[145] During UPR I, Mauritania and Switzerland questioned the South African delegation on

141 *HRC UPR I Report—South Africa*, UN Doc A/HRC/8/32 paras 124.33–124.46.

142 *Report of the Committee on the Elimination of Racial Discrimination,* 61st sess, Supplement No. 18 (A/61/18), UN Doc A/61/18 (16 August 2006) para 390.

143 Ibid.

144 African Peer Review Mechanism (APRM), 'APRM Country Report for South Africa No. 4' (May 2007) para 3.134.

145 Jonathan Crush et al., *The Perfect Storm: The Realities of Xenophobia in Contemporary South Africa* (Cape Town 2008).

this incident, which had been described as xenophobic, during the adoption of South Africa's UPR I report in June 2008.[146] The government in its response at the eighth session of the HRC was hesitant to recognise the incident as xenophobic. It stated that '[t]he government of South Africa is on record as having publicly deplored the recent acts of violence against foreigners in the country by individuals and groups, ostensibly motivated by xenophobia'.[147] More than two major instances of xenophobic attacks continued in 2008 and 2011.[148] In April 2015, there was recurrence of major xenophobic violence in Durban with at least five people killed, about 2,000 displaced and several foreign-owned shops looted.[149] Similarly, in September 2019, three South Africans were reportedly killed during a xenophobic incident against foreign business in Gauteng, South Africa.[150] The recurrence of xenophobic incidents in South Africa underscores the ineffectiveness of the government's measures to combat xenophobia.

Nevertheless, various stakeholders in their commentary on implementation recognised the specific challenge of racism and xenophobia in South Africa and some of the steps taken by the government to address the problem. The joint report by the Centre for Applied Psychology of the University of South Africa and other NGOs, among other things, commended the periodic public denunciation of specific xenophobic incidents by President Jacob Zuma and the taking of steps to adopt specific legislation to address hate crime violence, such as the drafting of the Prevention and Combating of Hate Crimes and Hate Speech Bill.[151] In addition, the South African government in its comments on implementation referred to the substantive content of a draft NAP to Combat Racism, Racial Discrimination, Xenophobia and Related Intolerance, which was being finalised.[152] It also pointed to its leadership on resolutions against racism and xenophobia at the international level.[153]

146 *HRC UPR I Report—South Africa*, UN Doc A/HRC/8/32 paras 41, 58.

147 *Report of the HRC on Its 8th Session*, UN Doc A/HRC/8/52 para 574.

148 See reports of NGOs and other stakeholders for South Africa's UPR. The Centre for Applied Psychology of the University of South Africa et al., above n 125, 3; Human Rights Institute of South Africa (HURISA) et al., 'Joint Submission to the Universal Periodic Review' (28 November 2011) para 5.1; United Nations High Commission for Refugees (UNHCR), 'Submission by the United Nations High Commission for Refugees for the Office of the High Commissioner for Human Rights' Compilation report-Universal Periodic Review: South Africa' (2011) 3; Lawyers for Human Rights and Consortium for Refugees and Migrants in South Africa, 'The Situation of the Rights of Refugees and Migrant in South Africa: Follow-up since 2008' (2011) 9–10.

149 South African History Online, 'Xenophobic Violence in Democratic South Africa' (19 May 2016) available at <https://bit.ly/2XLScbT> accessed 12/09/2019.

150 Tom Head, above n 9.

151 See *Prevention and Combating of Hate Crimes and Hate Speech Bill 2016* (South Africa).

152 UN Human Rights Council, *Report of the Working Group on the Universal Periodic Review—South Africa—Addendum*, UN Doc A/HRC/21/16/Add.1 (12 July 2012) annex A para 124.36.

153 Ibid; while there has been a remarkable level of consultation on the draft plan, it has taken too long to finalise given that South Africa hosted the third World Conference against Racism in 2001 which adopted a resolution which urged 'states to establish and implement without delay' a national action plan against racism, xenophobia and related intolerance.

While South Africa has undertaken some measures to address the problem of racism and xenophobia, the ineffectiveness of these measures in preventing future recurrence in some parts of the country undermines the government's effort. The narratives constructed by some South African government officials and influential traditional leaders on the xenophobic attacks help to undermine the efforts of the government. Shortly after the April 2015 xenophobic attacks in Durban, the Small Business Development Minister, Lindiwe Zulu, stated that the businesses of foreign Africans based in township areas could not expect to co-exist peacefully with local business owners unless they share their 'trade secrets'.[154] The reluctance of the government to condemn the rhetoric of King Goodwill Zwelithini, King of the Zulu people in South Africa, undermines its commitment to addressing the problem of racism and xenophobia. King Zwelithini arguably played a role in inciting the 2015 xenophobic violence when he said at a public gathering that 'African migrants should take their things and go.'[155] The initial denial and ritual condemnation of such rhetoric and narratives undermine the government's commitment to combat racism and xenophobia. Recommendations on this issue, including to address the issue of xenophobia through legislation and to develop a NAP against racism and xenophobia, were not fully implemented within the UPR II implementation time frame.[156] Eight recommendations during UPR III reinforced this issue.[157] Nevertheless, in March 2019, the NAP to combat Racism, Racial Discrimination, Xenophobia and Related Intolerance was adopted by the South African government.[158] Moreover, the South African government has developed the Prevention and Combating of Hate Crimes and Hate Speech Bill which is a positive step towards addressing issues of racism and xenophobia.[159] During UPR III, ten recommendations were made to South Africa in relation to this bill, mostly in favour of passing the bill into law.[160]

See Department of Justice and Constitutional Development South Africa, 'Address by the Deputy Minister of Justice and Constitutional Development, the Hon John Jeffery, MP, at a Consultative Workshop on the National Action Plan to Combat Racism, Racial Discrimination, Xenophobia and Related Intolerance, 15 May 2015' (2015) available at <www.justice.gov.za/m_speeches/2015/20150515_NAP.html> accessed 12/09/2019.

154 Willian Gumede, 'South Africa Must Confront Root Causes of Its Xenophobic Violence' *The Guardian (online)* (20 April 2015) available at <https://bit.ly/1Dtj4GU> accessed 12/09/2019.

155 Ibid.

156 *HRC UPR II Report—South Africa—Addendum*, UN Doc A/HRC/21/16/Add.1 paras 124.37, 124.43.

157 *HRC UPR III Report—South Africa,* UN Doc A/HRC/36/16 para 139.43, 139.47, 139.52–139.57.

158 Republic of South Africa, *The National Action Plan (NAP) to Combat Racism, Racial Discrimination, Xenophobia and Related Intolerance* (13 March 2019) available at <https://bit.ly/2lLNIzU> accessed 20/07/2019.

159 Republic of South Africa, 'The Prevention and Combating of Hate Crimes and Hate Speech Bill' (2018) Government Gazette No. 41543 of 29 March 2018 available at <https://bit.ly/2kGjdv3> accessed 20/07/2019.

160 *HRC UPR III Report—South Africa,* UN Doc A/HRC/36/16 para 139.43–46, 139.48–52, 139.59.

Concluding remarks

South Africa has made statements of strong support for the UPR mechanism and increased the level of its participation as a reviewer and as a state under review across UPR I, II and III. Its participation as a reviewer across regional lines demonstrates the universality and non-selectivity of the UPR mechanism and contributes to enhancing the acculturation process. Moreover, the evidence of states implementing some of the UPR recommendations outside the implementation time frame underscores the potential value of a cooperative mechanism to over time contribute to human rights change within states. In addition, the South African government's commitment to provide a mid-term UPR implementation report, which it did, further indicates an increasing level of engagement with the UPR process. At the end of 2016, only 55 of the 193 UN member states submitted a UPR mid-term implementation report. By July 2019, this number had increased to 75 states.[161] This provides evidence of emulation and mimicry associated with the process of acculturation which can produce positive results over time.

However, the responses by the government to some of its UPR recommendations and the government's commentaries on implementation indicate the potential for rights ritualism. In its response to state recommendations during UPR I, the government of South Africa claimed that it had already implemented most of the recommendations made by its peers.[162] This underscores the reluctance of the government about increasing human rights protection especially as many of the UPR recommendations raised concern on the inefficacy or inadequacy of the existing measures for human rights protection. Another aspect of rights ritualism is evidenced in South Africa's support for HRC resolutions on sexual orientation and its unwillingness to recommend de-criminalisation of same-sex relations or at least sensitisation among its regional peers.

The ability of the UPR to move beyond ritualism and actually improve the human rights situation on the ground depends profoundly on effective NGO engagement. Unlike the case of South Africa, the NGOs in Kenya, despite some constraints, were proactive in engaging the Kenyan government in its UPR process. This was achieved through the formation of an NGO coalition and various awareness-raising, media and advocacy campaigns that contributed to influence state UPR recommendations to Kenya. It also followed up and monitored the implementation of the recommendations Kenya accepted and produced its own mid-term assessment of the government's implementation record. Moreover, coalitions can more effectively engage the state in the process of implementation than individual NGOs. Making effective use of these opportunities can help NGOs counter state ritualism in the UPR.

In terms of its engagement at the pre-review process, there was a general lack of substantial commitment to a broad and inclusive UPR national consultation

161 OHCHR, 'UPR Mid-Term Reports' (16 July 2019) available at <https://bit.ly/2n2J3aj> accessed 20/07/2019.

162 *Report of the HRC on Its 8th Session*, UN Doc A/HRC/8/52 para 567.

process. The South African government did not undertake any form of consultation during UPR I, and the national consultation for UPR II and III was only limited across government. The absence of an NGO coalition for the UPR limited the ability of domestic NGOs to proactively engage the government in a national consultation process. A state that undertakes an inclusive UPR national consultation process that seeks the views of domestic stakeholders and reflects those views in the final report would provide its peers with a reliable and realistic basis for reviewing the state's human rights situation and for making relevant recommendations. Nevertheless, the improvements in the quality of South Africa's UPR delegation that incorporated legal and judicial personnel and reflected a gender balance signalled an increasing level of commitment to the UPR mechanism. It indicated a potential transformation of the government's view of the UPR from a foreign affairs exercise to a process for the examination and improvement of human rights.

The UPR has attracted the full engagement of African states and there has been improvement across reviews, especially in terms of state representation and responses to recommendations. As has been evident in the case of Nigeria, Kenya and South Africa, their engagement with the UPR has contributed to enhance their treaty body engagement in terms of meeting their reporting obligations. In the case of South Africa, the UPR process has contributed to greater engagement of the South African government with the treaty bodies in terms of the committed efforts made by the government to meet many of its outstanding reports after its UPR II. Finally, the ability for the UPR to reinforce treaty body recommendations underscores the potential for the UPR mechanism to evolve into an effective cooperative mechanism that could complement other mechanisms for monitoring human rights implementation.

8 The Gambia and the UPR

Rhetoric, inaction and the effect of regime change

Background to The Gambia's UPR

The Gambia is the smallest country in mainland Africa with a population estimate of about 2.3 million people.[1] In the 1970s, The Gambia was considered a success for liberal democracy and commended for its adherence to international human rights principles and political tolerance.[2] The 1970s was a period where military coups were pervasive in Africa, human rights violations prevalent and over half of the countries on the continent were under some form of military dictatorship.[3] The Gambia's positive human rights record in the 1970s influenced the Organisation for African Unity to establish the African Commission for Human and Peoples' Rights (ACHPR) in 1986 in Banjul, capital of The Gambia. In 1989, for similar reasons, the Headquarters of the African Centre for Democracy and Human Rights Studies (ACDHRS), which was first established in the United Kingdom, was moved to The Gambia.[4] Between 1970 and 1994, under the pro-human rights and democracy government of The Gambia's first president, Dawda Jawara, The Gambia ratified several key human rights treaties, including the ICCPR, ICESCR, Convention on the Rights of the Child (CRC), International Convention on the Elimination of All Forms of Racial Discrimination, First Optional Protocol to ICCPR and the African Charter on Human and Peoples' Rights. Among many of The Gambia's human rights achievements during this period was the abolition of the death penalty in 1993.[5]

1 UN Department of Economic and Social Affairs, *World Population Prospects 2019* (United Nations 2019) 15.
2 Abdoulaye S M Saine, 'The Coup d'Etat in the Gambia, 1994: The End of the First Republic' (1996) 23(1) *Armed Forces & Society* 97–111.
3 Pat McGowan and Thomas Johnson, 'African Military Coups d'état and Underdevelopment: A Quantitative Historical Analysis' (1984) 22(4) *The Journal of Modern African Studies* 633–66.
4 ACDHRS is an independent and Pan-African regional human rights NGO based in Banjul.
5 This was reinstated in 1995 by the government of President Yahya Jammeh, see the Gambia Death Penalty (Restoration) Act, Decree No. 52 of 1995, Laws of the Gambia (2009), Vol. 3, Ch. 11:02; UN Human Rights Committee, 'Concluding Observations: Gambia' (12 August 2004) UN Doc CCPR/CO/75/GMB para 8.

In July 1994, President Jawara's government was overthrown in a bloodless military coup by the Armed Forces Provisional Ruling Council led by Yahya Jammeh, who was subsequently elected in 1996 as The Gambia's second president.[6] Between 1994 and 2017, there were serious human rights violations in The Gambia exacerbated by a failed coup attempt on 30 December 2014.[7] Several NGO and UN human rights reports documented widespread human rights abuses, including torture, arbitrary arrests and detention, enforced disappearance, restrictions on freedom of expression, discrimination and persecution of LGBT persons.[8] In October 2014, the government introduced a new offence of 'aggravated homosexuality' into the Gambian criminal law punishable with up to life imprisonment.[9] In 2015, the report of the Special Rapporteur on extrajudicial, summary or arbitrary executions observed serious disregard for the rule of law and noted that human rights protection in The Gambia 'was an illusion'.[10] Within the framework of Risse et al.'s spiral model of norm diffusion, The Gambia under President Jammeh between 1994 and 2017 can be considered as experiencing a regression from the 'prescriptive' phase of the model, marked by ratification of human rights treaties, to 'repression' and denial of the validity of human rights norms.[11] This is consistent with Eran Shor's argument on the role of security threats in hindering norm compliance and contributing to a regression in human rights protection.[12] The failed coup in December 2014 contributed in shaping the government's repressive policies and further hindering compliance with human rights norms.

It is within the above context that The Gambia undertook its UPR I in 2010 and UPR II in 2014.[13] On 1 December 2016, Jammeh lost the Gambian presidential election to Adama Barrow. Jammeh initially refused to cede power but eventually did so and went into exile in Equatorial Guinea following

6 Abdoulaye S M Saine, above n 2.

7 See Human Rights Council, *Report of the Special Rapporteur on Extrajudicial, Summary or Arbitrary Executions, Christof Heyns, on His Mission to the Gambia (3–7 November 2014): Mission to Gambia*, 29th sess, Agenda Item 3, UN Doc A/HRC/29/37/Add.2 (11 May 2015) 22.

8 See Amnesty International, 'Dangerous to Dissent: Human Rights Under Threat in Gambia' (2016) available at <https://bit.ly/2m9nJ5y> accessed 27/08/2019; Freedom House, 'Freedom in the World 2015—The Gambia' (10 July 2015) available at <www.refworld.org/docid/55a6447c3b.html> accessed 02/09/2019; Human Rights Council, above n 7; Human Rights Watch, 'Country Summary: The Gambia' (2016) 1–6 available at <www.hrw.org/sites/default/files/gambia.pdf> accessed 02/09/2019.

9 Criminal Code (Amendment) Act, 2014, Law No. 11 of 2014 (The Gambia), Section 144A.

10 Human Rights Council, above n 7 para 10.

11 Thomas Risse, Stephen Ropp, and Kathryn Sikkink (eds), *The Persistent Power of Human Rights: From Commitment to Compliance* (Cambridge University Press 2013).

12 Eran Shor, 'Conflict, Terrorism, and the Socialization of Human Rights Norms: The Spiral Model Revisited' (2008) 55(1) *Social Problems* 5–6.

13 This research was completed at the start of Gambia's UPR III. The analysis here is therefore limited to UPR I and II.

pressure from regional and international organisations.[14] Since taking power in January 2017, President Barrow began to reverse many positions taken by the previous government, including rescinding the notification of withdrawal to the Rome Statute submitted by the Jammeh government in October 2016.[15] The Gambia's interaction with various international mechanisms under President Jammeh was guided by hostility towards the West and a strategic defence of Islam and traditional African culture.[16] In a statement to the UNGA in 2013, Jammeh criticised the concepts of democracy, human rights and good governance as religious prescription by descendants of colonial powers, condemned economic sanctions and unilateral interventions, and identified homosexuality as a human existential threat and contrary to Islamic and African values.[17] This chapter examines the extent to which these positions by Jammeh's government were reflected in their engagement with the different stages of the UPR and the impact of the UPR on the human rights situation in The Gambia. It also considers the human rights rhetoric of the Jammeh's government and its impact on The Gambia's UPR engagement. The Gambia's engagement with the UPR can be viewed broadly from the perspectives of human rights rhetoric, inaction and the influence of regime change.

The Gambia's UPR national consultation and the quality of its UPR delegation

A broad-based UPR national consultation with domestic stakeholders has been identified as best practice when engaging with the pre-review stage of the UPR.[18] State engagement with NGOs in the preparation of its national report can help highlight human rights challenges, map out priorities and provide some level of credibility to the final state report submitted to the HRC for review. According to the Gambian government, the UPR I national report was prepared by a

14 See Economic Community of West African States (ECOWAS), 'Fiftieth Ordinary Session of the ECOWAS Authority of Heads of State and Government' (17 December 2016) para 33–39; Office of the UN Secretary General, 'Note to Correspondents—Joint Declaration on the Political Situation in the Gambia' (21 January 2017) available at <https://bit.ly/2jOyRSJ> accessed 02/09/2019.

15 See Manisuli Ssenyonjo, 'State Withdrawal Notifications from the Rome Statute of the International Criminal Court: South Africa, Burundi and the Gambia' (2018) 29(1) *Criminal Law Forum* 63–119.

16 In 2015, the Gambia cut ties with the EU and expelled its most senior diplomat, Agnes Guillard from the country See David Perfect, *Historical Dictionary of the Gambia* (Rowman & Littlefield 2016) 140.

17 See UN General Assembly, 'General Debate: Statement by H E Mr. Yahya Jammeh, President' (27 September 2013) available at <https://bit.ly/2kG8bpu> accessed 02/09/2019.

18 Universal Rights Group, *The Universal Periodic Review: Sharing National Experiences* (Universal Rights Group 2015) 3–12.

broad-based task force comprised of both government institutions and CSOs.[19] However, no information was provided on the type and number of CSOs that were consulted. According to the Media Foundation for West Africa, attempts to meet with the government during the preparation of its report failed.[20] The national task force set up for the preparation of the state's UPR II report did not include NGOs.[21]

The lack of extensive consultation with NGO stakeholders during the preparation of The Gambia's UPR reports can be explained by the hostility and repressive nature of the Jammeh government towards the media and various laws/statutes which restricted press freedom. The Newspaper Registration (Amendment Act),[22] the Criminal Code (Amendment) Act,[23] the Information and Communication Act[24] and the Official Secrets (Amendment) Act[25] were used by the government to create a culture of fear within the Gambian civil society through criminal prosecution, intimidation and censorship. There were several reported cases involving extrajudicial execution of journalists, journalists arrested and detained incommunicado, and media institutions banned from operating.[26] In 2018, the Court of Justice of the Economic Community of West African States (ECOWAS) in the case of *Federation of African Journalists & 4 Ors v The Republic of The Gambia* declared several provisions of the Criminal Code (Amendment) Act and the Information and Communication Act unlawful and a violation of The Gambia's obligation under the African Charter and the ICCPR.[27] The Court ordered the government of The Gambia to repeal these provisions which have been used to arrest, detain and convict journalists.[28]

The restrictive NGO environment which existed in The Gambia during UPR I and II may have also contributed to hamper NGO engagement at this stage of the review. Unlike in the case of Nigeria, Kenya and South Africa where there were several UPR events by NGOs, the establishment of a national NGO UPR

19 Working Group on the Universal Periodic Review, *National Report Submitted in Accordance with Paragraph 15 (a) of the Annex to Human Rights Council Resolution 5/1—Gambia*, 17th sess, UN Doc A/HRC/WG.6/7/GMB/1 (20 January 2010) ('*HRC UPR I State Report- Gambia*') para 1.

20 Media Foundation for West Africa, 'The Gambia: Submission to the Universal Periodic Review' (2010) 2 available at <https://bit.ly/2lQKcUK> accessed 05/08/2019.

21 Working Group on the Universal Periodic Review, *National Report Submitted in Accordance with Paragraph 15 (a) of the Annex to Human Rights Council Resolution 5/1—Gambia*, 20th sess, UN Doc A/HRC/WG.6/20/GMB/1 (24 July 2014) ('*HRC UPR II State Report- Gambia*') para 1.

22 The Newspaper (Amendment) Act of 2004 (The Gambia).

23 Criminal Code (Amendment) Act, Law No. 11 of 2014 (The Gambia).

24 The Information and Communication (Amendment) Act, 2013 (The Gambia).

25 Official Secrets Acts (Amended) Act of 2008 (The Gambia).

26 See Amnesty International, above n 8; Freedom House, above n 8; Human Rights Council, above n 7; Human Rights Watch, above n 8.

27 *Federation of African Journalists & 4 Ors v The Republic of The Gambia* [2018] ECW/CCJ/APP/13/14, 56–7.

28 Ibid.

coalition or several joint UPR submissions by NGOs, The Gambia lacked such level of strong NGO mobilisation for the UPR. During The Gambia's UPR I, there were no reported UPR events among domestic NGOs in Kenya and only one joint submission was made by two domestic NGOs to the HRC.[29] While there was an increase in the number of joint submissions by domestic NGOs in The Gambia during UPR II from one to seven, no domestic NGO in The Gambia was able to participate in the plenary session of the HRC and make oral statements during both cycles of the review.[30] The Gambian government's repressive media policies and hostile NGO environment has had a chilling impact on the ability of NGOs in The Gambia to engage with the UPR process.

The Gambian government submitted its UPR I and II state reports and participated in the review process in Geneva. With regard to its UPR delegation, there was a significant difference between its UPR I and II delegations in terms of both diversity and representation. The UPR I delegation comprised of 15 members led by the Attorney General and Minister of Justice.[31] There was representation from various government ministries, including Justice, Interior, Health and Social Welfare, Basic and Secondary Education and Foreign Affairs. However, there was no representation from parliament. A representation from parliament is important given that many of the recommendations from the UPR require legislative actions to implement. In contrast, the UPR II delegation was composed only of the Attorney General and Minister of Justice and the Minister of Interior. More so, The Gambia did not send any delegate to attend the adoption of its UPR II report during the plenary session of the HRC on 8 July 2015.[32]

The Gambia is one of the few states that did not make any recommendations to other states across UPR I, II and III.[33] Other small African states like Comoros and Seychelles have participated in some sessions of the UPR. Seychelles participated in the 17th and 22nd sessions of the UPR and made recommendations to Mauritius, China and Maldives.[34] Comoros participated in six sessions of UPR II

29 Gambian Press Union and the Coalition for Human Rights in the Gambia, 'Submission to the UN Universal Periodic Review' (1 September 2009) available at <https://bit.ly/2m6T0WL> accessed 05/08/2019.

30 See UN Human Rights Council, *Report of the Human Rights Council on Its Fourteenth Session*, 14th sess, Agenda Item 1, UN Doc A/HRC/14/37 (23 October 2012) para 610–613.

31 The only joint submission made by domestic NGOs in Kenya was by the Gambia Press Union and the Coalition for Human Rights in Gambia. See UN Human Rights Council, *Summary Prepared by the Office of the High Commissioner for Human Rights, in Accordance with Paragraph 15 (C) of the Annex to Human Rights Council Resolution 5/1: Gambia* 17th sess, UN Doc A/HRC/WG.6/7/GMB/3 (2 November 2009) 9.

32 UN Human Rights Council, 'Report of the Human Rights Council on Its Twenty-fifth Session' 28th sess, UN Doc A/HRC/28/2 (8 July 2015) para 469.

33 Other states include Belize, Dominica and Liberia—See UPRinfo, 'Statistics of Recommendations—'Recommending State Statistics' available at <www.upr-info.org/database/statistics/> accessed 09/08/2019.

34 See UN Human Rights Council, *Report of the Working Group on the Universal Periodic Review—Mauritius*, 40th sess, Agenda Item 6, UN Doc A/HRC/40/9 (27

and made 18 recommendations to 14 states.[35] Non-participation in the review of other states' human rights record may limit the ability of states to learn best practice within the UPR mechanism. Several factors may hinder state participation in UPR sessions, including limited financial resources and the lack of a permanent mission in Geneva. Unlike Seychelles and Comoros that have each benefitted from the Voluntary Fund for Participation in the UPR Mechanism, The Gambia did not receive any grant from this fund during UPR I and II.[36] The following section examines The Gambia's engagement as a state under review by considering the nature and receptiveness of the Gambian government towards UPR recommendations.

The Gambia as a state under review

The Gambia was reviewed by the HRC in February 2010 and October 2014 for UPR I and II respectively. The Gambia had three responses to the recommendations made—'accepted', 'noted' and 'rejected'. For the purpose of this analysis, the recommendations 'noted' were also considered to be 'rejected' or 'not accepted'; 48 states made a total of 153 recommendations to The Gambia during UPR I.[37] The Gambian delegation accepted 68 recommendations (44%). The majority of the recommendations (56%) were not accepted by The Gambian UPR I delegation. There was a slight improvement to the number of recommendations accepted during UPR II. Out of a total of 171 recommendations made to The Gambia during UPR II, it accepted 93 (54%) and rejected 78 (46%).[38] In response to several UPR recommendations, The Gambia delegation adopted a defensive attitude to justify its position by contesting the nature of the right, deferring to existing legislation as sufficient protection, referring to cultural values as justification for non-acceptance of certain recommendations or outrightly rejecting the recommendation as inconsistent with The Gambia's legislative or

December 2018) paras 115.63, 115.40; UN Human Rights Council, *Report of the Working Group on the Universal Periodic Review—China*, 40th sess, Agenda Item 6, UN Doc A/HRC/40/6 (26 December 2018) paras 28.66, 28.140; UN Human Rights Council, *Report of the Working Group on the Universal Periodic Review—Maldives*, 30th sess, Agenda Item 6, UN Doc A/HRC/30/8 (13 July 2015) paras 141.14, 141.109.

35 UPR Info, 'Statistics of Recommendation: Recommending State Statistics—Gambia' available at <https://bit.ly/2medg96> accessed 02/09/2019.

36 See Office of the High Commissioner for Human Rights (OHCHR), *Requests for Financial Assistance Under the Voluntary Fund for Participation in the UPR Mechanism* (As of 24 February 2012) available at <www.ohchr.org/EN/HRBodies/UPR/Documents/VPU FinancialRequest.pdf>.

37 See Human Rights Council, *Report of the Working Group on the Universal Periodic Review—Gambia*, 14th sess, Agenda Item 6, UN Doc A/HRC/14/6 (24 March 2010) paras 97–100.

38 See UN Human Rights Council, *Report of the Working Group on the Universal Periodic Review—Gambia*, 28th sess, Agenda Item 6, UN Doc A/HRC/28/6 (24 December 2014) paras 109–110; UN Human Rights Council, above n 32, 488.

policy framework. For example, in response to the 23 recommendations during UPR I and II to decriminalise same-sex relationship, the Gambian UPR delegation contested the existence of gay rights and rejected the recommendations based on cultural values, norms and practices.[39] A total of 19 recommendations on the death penalty during UPR I and II were rejected by The Gambia on the basis that 'the death penalty is provided for in the Laws of The Gambia and Constitution' to combat crime.[40] The Gambia UPR II delegation qualified its acceptance to some of the recommendations by adding the words 'subject to the laws of the Gambia'.[41] For example, the recommendation by Tunisia, France and Ireland for the Gambian government to create a safe environment for journalists and human rights defenders was accepted 'subject to the laws of the Gambia'.[42]

The above responses by the Gambian government to various UPR recommendations indicate an unwillingness to act on recommendations that require changes to The Gambia's legislative and policy framework. The response by the Gambian government to the UPR recommendations demonstrates a willingness to engage with the process but a reluctance to commit to recommendations that will strengthen the domestic human rights situation within The Gambia. By qualifying its acceptance of some of the recommendations, the Gambian government preserves its ability to justify any subsequent inaction on the relevant recommendations.

Figures 8.1 and 8.2 provide a general overview and compare The Gambia's responses to the recommendations made by its regional peers and those made by other groups of states to determine if there are any significant differences to its receptiveness to UPR recommendations across regional lines.

Figures 8.1 and 8.2 indicate that states within the WEOG made more recommendations to The Gambia (34%) than any other group of states. There was an observable decline in the number of recommendations requiring minimal action (R1) and a steady increase in specific recommendations (R5). During UPR I, 4% of the total 153 recommendations to The Gambia required minimal action to be taken by the state compared to 33% of the recommendations which required a specific action (R5). However, the majority of recommendations made to The Gambia during UPR I were general recommendations (R4). The number of R5 recommendations increased during The Gambia's UPR II to 44% and constituted the majority of recommendations made to The Gambia, whereas the number of R1 recommendations dropped to 1%. It is much easier to measure the implementation of specific recommendations than general recommendations which in some case can be vague. The Gambian government in its response to

39 See Human Rights Council, above n 37 para 63.

40 See UN Human Rights Council, *Report of the Working Group on the Universal Periodic Review—Gambia—Addendum: Views on Conclusions and/or Recommendations, Voluntary Commitments and Replies Presented by the State Under Review*, 28th sess, Agenda Item 6, UN Doc A/HRC/28/6/Add.1 (24 March 2015) para 2.

41 Ibid para 4, 47, 49–53.

42 Ibid para 50.

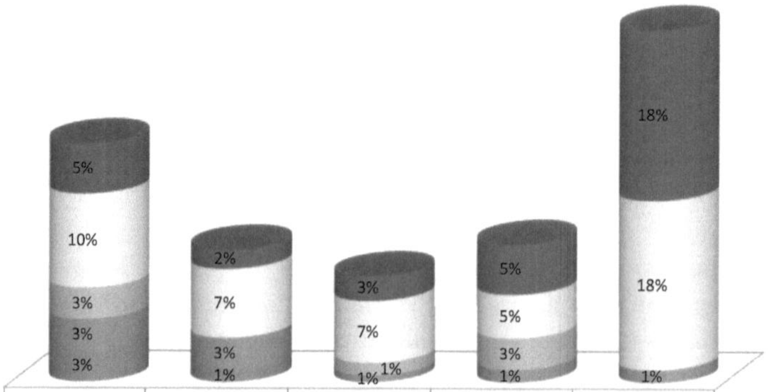

	Africa	Asia	EEG	GRULAC	WEOG
R5 - Specific Action	5%	2%	3%	5%	18%
R4 - General Action	10%	7%	7%	5%	18%
R3 - Consider Action	3%	0%	1%	3%	0%
R2 - Continue Action	3%	3%	1%	1%	1%
R1 - Minimal Action	3%	1%	0%	0%	0%

Figure 8.1 UPR I recommendations to Gambia

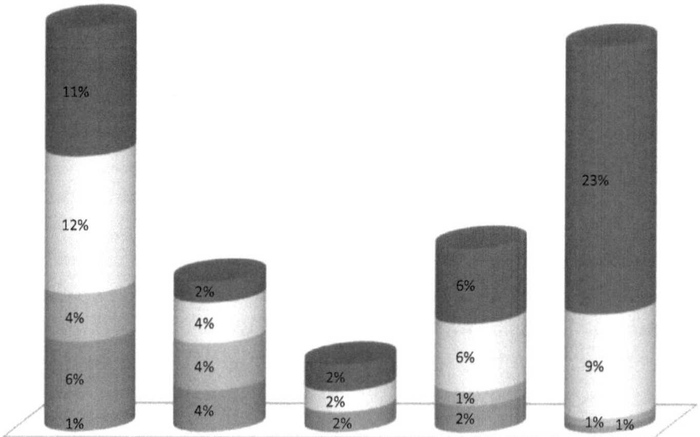

	Africa	Asia	EEG	GRULAC	WEOG
R5 - Specific Action	11%	2%	2%	6%	23%
R4 - General Action	12%	4%	2%	6%	9%
R3 - Consider Action	4%	4%	0%	1%	1%
R2 - Continue Action	6%	4%	2%	2%	1%
R1 - Minimal Action	1%	0%	0%	0%	0%

Figure 8.2 UPR II recommendations to Gambia

UPR recommendations showed a significantly higher level of opposition to recommendations made by Western states compared to other groups of states. The Gambian UPR I delegation rejected 82% of the total recommendations made by states within WEOG during UPR I compared to 37% and 4% from the African and Asian regional groups respectively. Similarly, during UPR II, it rejected 67% of the total recommendations by states from WEOG compared to 34% from Africa and 23% from Asia.

There are three possible explanations for The Gambia's generally negative response to UPR recommendations from Western states. In the first place, this attitude by The Gambian government under President Jammeh towards recommendations from states in WEOG appears to be consistent with its foreign policy which was guided by hostility towards the West and a strategic defence of Islam and traditional African culture.[43] Some specific actions taken by the Jammeh government in pursuit of this foreign policy included cutting ties with the EU, expelling its diplomat from The Gambia, describing the ICC as a 'Caucasian Court', withdrawing from the Rome Statute[44] and engaging in outright rejection of gay rights based on Islamic principles and traditional African cultural beliefs.[45] Second, The Gambia during UPR I and II was reluctant to accept specific recommendations. Fifty and 76 specific recommendations were made to The Gambia during UPR I and II respectively. The Gambia rejected 80% of the specific recommendations during UPR I and 74% during UPR II. The majority of these specific recommendations during UPR I and II were made by states within WEOG (54% and 51% respectively) and therefore contribute in accounting for the higher percentage of recommendations rejected from WEOG by The Gambia.

Third, the generally negative response by the Gambian UPR delegation towards recommendations from Western states can be explained by the rights priorities of the different regional group of states. Edward McMahon, in his evaluation of UPR I recommendations, found that WEOG made significantly more recommendations on civil and political rights than Africa or Asia.[46] The recommendations by Asia and Africa during UPR I were more focused on ESC rights.[47] As highlighted in Chapter 5, WEOG prioritised civil and political rights over socio-economic rights during Kenya's UPR I and II compared to African and Asian states, which prioritised socio-economic rights. In 2016, Philip Alston, Special Rapporteur on extreme poverty and human rights, criticised the limited attention given to socio-economic rights by states in their UPR recommendations.[48]

43 David Perfect, above n 16, 140.

44 See Manisuli Ssenyonjo, above n 15, 72.

45 UN Human Rights Council, above n 37 para 63.

46 Edward McMahon, 'The Universal Periodic Review: A Work in Progress, an Evaluation of the First Cycle of the New UPR Mechanism of the United Nations Human Rights Council' (2012) *Friedrich Ebert Stiftung* 21–2.

47 ibid.

48 Human Rights Council, *Report of the Special Rapporteur on Extreme Poverty and Human Rights*, 32nd sess, Agenda Item 3, UN Doc A/HRC/32/31 (28 April 2016) 16–17.

In the case of The Gambia, out of a combined total of 50 recommendations on ESC rights made during UPR I and II, Africa made 36% and Asia 30% compared to 16% by WEOG, 12% by GRULAC and 6% by EEG. In contrast, out of a combined total of 144 recommendations on civil and political rights made to The Gambia during UPR I and II, 47% was made by WEOG, 15% by GRULAC, 10% from EEG compared to 22% from Africa and 6% from Asia.[49] It is observable that there are significantly more recommendations made on civil and political rights across The Gambia's UPR I and II (144) than on ESC rights (50), with Western states focusing more on the former than African and Asian states. The Gambia rejected 67% of the recommendations on civil and political rights (with a higher percentage of 73% rejected from WEOG) compared to 14% rejection of recommendations on socio-economic rights. The majority of the civil and political rights recommendations were made by Western states on issues including the death penalty, torture, enforced disappearance and freedom of the press. By overwhelmingly focusing on civil and political rights, the domestic concerns within states wherein governmental policies have adversely impacted on the realisation of socio-economic rights are not being seriously considered by states in WEOG and GRULAC. Alston describes this phenomenon of prioritising civil and political rights over ESC rights as 'systematic marginalisation' of ESC rights.[50] This unequal treatment of rights within the UPR is seen to be a major shortcoming of the mechanism[51] and raises questions about the extent to which politics and regionalism influence the prioritisation of issues by states when making UPR recommendations.

The Gambia's progress on implementation of UPR recommendations: rhetoric versus action

The follow-up stages of the UPR process provide an opportunity for states to translate their UPR rhetoric and commitments into actions that will contribute to improving the human rights situation on the ground. As the UPR entered its third cycle in 2017, scholars and UPR stakeholders have raised key questions on the extent to which UPR recommendations from previous cycles were being implemented and how to share best practice in relation to the national implementation process for UPR recommendations.[52] HRC Resolution 16/21 recognises

49 The methodology used by the Center for Economic and Social Rights was adopted in analysing and categorising the recommendations. For details of this methodology please see Center for Economic and Social Rights, *The Universal Periodic Review: A Skewed Agenda? Trends Analysis of the UPR's Coverage of Economic, Social and Cultural Rights* (Center for Economic and Social Rights 2016) 12.

50 Philip Alston, 'Phantom Rights: The Systemic Marginalization of Economic and Social Rights' (2016) available at <https://bit.ly/2kwF740> accessed 20/08/2019.

51 Center for Economic and Social Rights, above n 49, 11.

52 See UPR Info, *Ensuring Sustainable UPR Implementation* (UPRinfo 2016); Gujadhur, Subhas and Marc Limon, *Towards the Third Cycle of the UPR: Stick or Twist? Lessons Learnt from the First Ten Years of the Universal Periodic Review* (Universal Rights Group 2016) 35–7.

that the implementation of UPR recommendations requires a collective effort by states, civil society, NGOs and other domestic stakeholders.[53] Examples of good practice have included the establishment of an inter-ministerial working group on the UPR, development of a UPR NAP in consultation with NGO stakeholders and NHRI, and the production of a mid-term implementation report.[54] At the end of UPR I, The Gambia had no NAP for the implementation of UPR recommendations.

Politics and a lack of genuine engagement with the UPR process have resulted in many states not giving serious consideration to the implementation of UPR recommendations. As Matthew Davies observed, while the HRC and its UPR mechanism were designed to depoliticise the UN human rights system and transition to a persuasive-based model, the UPR mechanism is not entirely free from politics.[55] This is consistent with the ethnographic study by Cowan and Billaud on the politics of human rights monitoring at the UPR and how histories of cooperation and antagonism between states manifest within the framework of the UPR.[56] According to Davies, the best way to conceive compliance within the UPR deliberative framework, in which politics continues to be relevant, is through Risse's approach termed 'rhetorical action'.[57] In his opinion, this approach involves the use of deliberative language to exchange information and preferences from one actor to another without the actors forgetting who they are or what their individual motivations may be in engaging with the deliberation.[58] This approach can be used to describe The Gambia's engagement with the deliberative process of the UPR as it involves arguing and deliberating about the validity of the rights subject to the review and is an approach which, arguably, can increase the influence of small and less powerful states like The Gambia.[59] However, Davies notes that for the UPR to achieve a successful outcome through rhetorical action, the deliberations must be meaningful and sustained and the participants must have a truthful commitment to the process.[60]

The argument to be developed from this point onwards is that The Gambia, in relation to its implementation of UPR recommendations, was trapped between

53 UN Human Rights Council, 'Follow-up to the Human Rights Council resolution 16/21 with regard to the universal periodic review' (19 July 2011) UN Doc A/HRC/DEC/17/119 para 17.

54 See *UPR Mid-term Reporting Optimising Sustainable Implementation: Good Practices for UPR Stakeholders* (UPR Info 2018) 1–34.

55 Mathew Davies, 'Rhetorical Inaction? Compliance and the Human Rights Council of the United Nations' (2010) 35(4) *Alternatives: Global, Local, Political* 449–68.

56 Jane K Cowan and Julie Billaud, 'Between Learning and Schooling: The Politics of Human Rights Monitoring at the Universal Periodic Review' (2015) 36(6) *Third World Quarterly* 1175–90.

57 Mathew Davies, above n 55, 449, 460.

58 Ibid.

59 Thomas Risse, '"Let's Argue!": Communicative Action in World Politics' (2000) 54(1) *International Organization* 1–39; see also Frank Schimmelfennig, 'The Community Trap: Liberal Norms, Rhetorical Action, and the Eastern Enlargement of the European Union' (2001) 55(1) *International Organization* 47–80.

60 Mathew Davies, above n 55, 449, 462.

rhetoric and action and its implementation of UPR recommendations has been influenced by politics, culture and regime change. This argument is developed by examining The Gambia's progress on implementation in relation to recommendations on cooperation with international mechanisms; freedom of expression and the press; the death penalty; and sexual orientation. These five categories of issues constituted more than 50% of the recommendations made to The Gambia during UPR I and II.

Cooperation with international mechanisms

The Gambia under President Jammeh consistently failed to cooperate with various international human rights mechanisms. A combined total of 108 recommendations were made to The Gambia during UPR I and II under this category.[61] These included recommendations to '[c]ooperate with international and regional human rights bodies . . .'; 'accept the visit of the special procedures of the human rights council . . .';[62] '[f]ollow-up on recommendations by CEDAW and the HRC . . .'; '[t]ake necessary measures to bring itself up to date with the reporting obligations to treaty bodies' and ratify various international human rights treaties.[63] The Gambia accepted 41% of the recommendations under this category. During the presentation of its UPR II state report before the Working Group on the UPR, The Gambian delegation stated that it had 'no objections to any visits to the Gambia by Special Rapporteurs of the HRC'.[64] This rhetorical commitment by The Gambian UPR delegation was inconsistent with its subsequent actions whereby the delegation rejected all five UPR II recommendations requiring The Gambia to accept visits by the Special Rapporteurs of the HRC.[65]

More so, The Gambia accepted UPR I and II recommendations to cooperate with international and regional human rights bodies and to fulfil its reporting obligations to the various treaty bodies.[66] However, in several instances between 1994 and 2017, The Gambian government failed to cooperate with the resolutions of the Banjul-based ACHPR, including Resolutions 134, 145 and 299,[67] and in 2016 had 11 overdue periodic reports pursuant to the African Charter on Human and People's Rights.[68] In 2010, The Gambia had only submitted two

61 See UPRinfo . . . This category was developed from UPRinfo database classification of issues and includes recommendations on 'treaty bodies', 'UPR process', 'technical assistance', 'special procedures' and 'international instruments' Recommendations calling for the abolition of the death penalty through treaty ratification are excluded from this number. See section 7.4.3 for a detailed discussion on the death penalty.

62 UN Human Rights Council, above n 38 paras 109.92, 109.141.

63 UN Human Rights Council, above n 37 para 99.30.

64 UN Human Rights Council, above n 38 para 28.

65 Ibid paras 109.91–109.95.

66 UN Human Rights Council, above n 37 para 99.21–99.30; UN Human Rights Council, above n 38 paras 109.88–109.95.

67 See Amnesty International, above n 8, 42–3.

68 Ibid 43.

of a total of 28 reports due under various UN human rights treaties, with some reports up to 23 years overdue.[69] The UN CERD, Committee on Economic, Social and Cultural Rights and the Human Rights Committee have at different times examined the situation of human rights in The Gambia in the absence of the state report and with no delegation sent to represent the state.[70] In fact, in 2009, the UN Human Rights Committee held The Gambia to be in violation of its obligation to cooperate with the Committee pursuant to Article 40 of the ICCPR and referred The Gambia to the UN High Commissioner for Human Rights.[71] The Gambia has on many occasions failed to cooperate with a number of treaty bodies by either failing to submit its periodic report or refusing to send any delegation to attend its review.

Furthermore, in 2008, 2010 and 2014, the government of President Jammeh refused to implement three legally binding decisions by the Court of Justice of the ECOWAS on issues relating to enforced disappearance of journalists,[72] torture[73] and murder.[74] In October 2016, the government of President Jammeh submitted to the UN Secretary General a written notification of The Gambia's withdrawal from the Rome Statute.[75] According to the then Minister of Information, Sheriff Baba Bojang, the withdrawal from the ICC was warranted because the ICC was an 'International Caucasian Court for the persecution and humiliation of people of colour, especially Africans'.[76] While there have been several legitimate criticisms of the ICC,[77] the timing of sending the notice of withdrawal was suspicious given the concern that the ICC Prosecutor could potentially open a preliminary investigation into the human rights situation in The Gambia under President Jammeh.

In contrast to the treaty bodies, The Gambia has at the minimum submitted its UPR reports, participated in the review sessions in Geneva and even engaged in human rights rhetoric. Several factors could account for the different levels of participation, including the perception of the UPR as a cooperative mechanism

69 Centre for Civil and Political Rights, 'Gambia's Non-Cooperation with UN Treaty Bodies' (2010) 1–4 available at <https://bit.ly/2lMVV6S> accessed 03/09/2019.

70 United Nations, 'Report of the Human Rights Committee' (11–29 October 2010) Supplement No. 40 (A/66/40) 15.

71 Ibid para 64.

72 *Manneh v Gambia*, Judgment, ECW/CCJ/APP/04/07 (ECOWAS, 5 June 2008).

73 *Musa Saidykhan v The Gambia*, Judgment, ECW/CCJ/JUD/08/10 (ECOWAS, 16 December 2010).

74 *Deyda Hydara and Others v The Gambia*, Judgment, ECW/CCJ/APP/30/11 (ECOWAS, 10 June 2014).

75 Manisuli Ssenyonjo, above n 15, 64.

76 Ibid 72.

77 See Catherine Gegout, 'The International Criminal Court: Limits, Potential and Conditions for the Promotion of Justice and Peace' (2013) 34(5) *Third World Quarterly* 800–18; Marieke de Hoon, 'The Future of the International Criminal Court: On Critique, Legalism and Strengthening the ICC's Legitimacy' (2017) 17 *International Criminal Law Review* 591–614; Max du Plessis, Tiyanjana Maluwa, and Annie O'Reilly, *African and the International Criminal Court* (Chatham House 2013) 1–13.

as opposed to confrontational or adjudicative, the state-led nature of the UPR as opposed to expert-led and the universality and equal treatment of all states in the UPR process. However, as the aforementioned analysis indicates, The Gambia's participation is trapped in this superficial engagement and has been reluctant to take actions to achieve specific outcomes that will result in the implementation of the relevant UPR recommendations. Charlesworth and Larking refer to this phenomenon as 'rights ritualism'.[78]

Nevertheless, since the dawn of a new political regime in The Gambia in 2017, there appears to have been a move towards greater cooperation with various international human rights mechanisms. The new government through various actions has signalled its willingness to renew cooperation with regional and international mechanisms. These included withdrawing The Gambia's notification of withdrawal from the Rome Statute,[79] renewing relations with the EU[80] and the ratification of two international human rights treaties.[81] In 2018, The Gambia participated in the periodic review of the Human Rights Committee notwithstanding the failure on the part of the previous regime to submit a State Report.[82] At the regional level, after 25 years of non-compliance and 22 outstanding reports, The Gambia, in 2018, submitted its periodic report pursuant to Article 62 of the African Charter on Human and Peoples' Rights.[83] It equally made a declaration under Article 34 (6) of the African Charter, granting NGO direct access to the African Court on Human and Peoples' Rights.[84] These actions are in line with several UPR I and II recommendations requiring the government to improve cooperation with UN treaty bodies and other regional and international mechanisms. However, there are still many treaty body recommendations and decisions by the ECOWAS Community Court which have not been implemented, although the new government has signalled a willingness to engage in institutional reforms that will further improve on its level of cooperation with these human rights mechanisms.

78 See Hilary Charlesworth and Emma Larking (eds), *Human Rights and the Universal Periodic Review: Rituals and Ritualism* (Cambridge University Press 2015).

79 United Nations, 'Gambia: Withdrawal of Notification of Withdrawal' (2017) UN Doc C.N.62.2017.TREATIES-XVIII.10 (Depositary Notification) available at <https://treaties.un.org/doc/Publication/CN/2017/CN.62.2017-Eng.pdf> accessed 23/08/2019.

80 European Commission, 'EU Partnership with the Gambia: Factsheet' (2018) available at <https://bit.ly/2IXVeln> accessed 23/08/2019.

81 These are the Second Optional Protocol to the ICCPR and the International Convention for the Protection of All persons from Enforced Disappearance.

82 UN Human Rights Committee, *Concluding Observations on the Gambia in the Absence of Its Second Periodic Report*, UN Doc CCPR/C/GMB/CO/2 (30 August 2018) paras 1–5.

83 The Republic of the Gambia, 'Combined Report on the African Charter on Human and Peoples' Rights for the Period 1994 and 2018 and Initial Report Under the Protocol to the African Charter on the Rights of Women in Africa' (2018) available at <https://bit.ly/2kh7q6g> accessed 23/08/2019.

84 African Court on Human and Peoples' Rights, *The Gambia Becomes the Ninth Country to Allow NGOs and Individuals to Access the African Court Directly* (23 November 2018) available at <https://bit.ly/2kG9Lrz> accessed 23/08/2019.

Freedom of expression, the press and the protection of human rights defenders

Between 1994 and 2016, The Gambia under President Jamal adopted repressive media policies and created a culture of fear within the Gambian civil society by means of criminal prosecution, banning of media institutions, censorship, arrests and detention of journalists and human rights defenders. Several domestic legislations were used by the government to curtail civil liberties, including the Newspaper Registration (Amendment Act),[85] the Criminal Code (Amendment) Act,[86] the Information and Communication Act[87] and the Official Secrets (Amendment) Act.[88] There were several reported cases of journalists arbitrarily arrested, closure of media outlets and journalists fleeing The Gambia as a result of threats, harassment and violence.[89] According to a 2016 Report of the Special Rapporteur on torture, there was no room in The Gambia for discussion on civil and political rights and any attempt at such discussion resulted in deprivation of liberty and possible torture or ill treatment.[90] In 2016, The Gambia ranked 145 out of 180 in the World Press Freedom Index.[91]

During The Gambia's UPR I in 2010, 18 recommendations were made in relation to civil society, freedom of expression and the press, and these included recommendations for the Gambian government to '[c]ease the harassment and intimidation of media institutions', '[g]uarantee the free exercise of activities of human rights defenders' and '[t]ake all necessary steps to strengthen the freedom of expression'.[92] Only one of these 18 recommendations was accepted by The Gambia. No African state made a recommendation under this category, further underscoring the influence of politics and regionalism in the prioritisation of issues in state recommendations. According to the Gambian UPR delegation, the allegations in these recommendations about the lack of protection for human rights defenders in The Gambia were 'unfounded'.[93]

During UPR II, out of a total of 19 recommendations made under this category, The Gambia outrightly rejected seven, accepted seven with the caveat 'subject to the laws of Gambia', noted four recommendations and accepted one. The recommendations that specifically required the Gambian government

85 The Newspaper (Amendment) Act above n 22.

86 Criminal Code (Amendment) Act above n 23.

87 The Information and Communication (Amendment) Act above n 24.

88 Official Secrets Acts (Amended) Act above n 25.

89 Amnesty International, above n 8.

90 UN Human Rights Council, 'Report of the Special Rapporteur on Torture and Other Cruel, Inhuman or Degrading Treatment or Punishment: Mission to Gambia' (16 March 2015) UN Doc A/HRC/28/68/Add.4 para 12 available at <http://ap.ohchr.org/documents/dpage_e.aspx?m=103> accessed 27/08/2019.

91 Reporters Without Borders, *2016 World Press Freedom Index* available at <https://bit.ly/1Vp6C9Y> accessed 11/05/2016.

92 UN Human Rights Council, above n 37 paras 99.49, 100.15, and 100.20.

93 UN Human Rights Council, above n 30 para 604.

to undertake legal and institutional reforms to protect the right to freedom of expression and the press were outrightly rejected.[94] These included recommendations to decriminalise press-related offences, amend the Criminal Code to ensure respect of the right to freedom of expression and reform the Information and Communication Act.[95] In response to some of these recommendations, the Gambian UPR delegation stated that human rights defenders and journalists can carry out their work in an atmosphere of freedom and security.[96] This is inconsistent with the findings in many NGO reports,[97] and in 2018, the ECOWAS Court of Justice in the case of *Federation of African Journalists & 4 Ors v The Republic of The Gambia*, declared several provisions of the aforementioned legislations to be unlawful and a violation of The Gambia's obligations under the ICCPR and the African Charter on Human and Peoples' Rights.[98] The responses from the Gambian government to these recommendations showed a lack of willingness to undertake actions that would bring about meaningful change at the domestic level.

By 2016, midway through The Gambia's UPR II, the recommendations under this category had not been implemented and there were reports of increasing crackdowns on opposing views to that of the government, including the arrests of several opposition leaders in April and May 2016.[99] According to reports by several NGOs, including the Commonwealth Human Rights Initiative (CHRI), Gambian Press Union, Reporters without Borders and International Service for Human Rights (ISHR), cases of censorship, harassment of journalists, and arbitrary arrest and detention of journalists in The Gambia increased between The Gambia's UPR I and II.[100] Between 2014 and 2016, several online news media

94 UN Human Rights Council, above n 40 para 14.

95 UN Human Rights Council, above n 38 paras 109.57–109.64.

96 Ibid para 52.

97 See Amnesty International, above n 8; Freedom House, above n 8; Human Rights Watch, above n 8; Access Now, Article 19 and the CPJ, 'Joint Submission to the Universal Periodic Review of the Gambia by Article 19, Access Now and the Committee to Protect Journalists' (2019) available at <https://bit.ly/2lJ5tQl> accessed 27/08/2019; International Service for Human Rights, 'The Situation of Human Rights Defenders in the Gambia' (18 March 2014) available at <https://bit.ly/2kIWZsb> accessed 03/09/2019.

98 *Federation of African Journalists & 4 Ors v The Republic of The Gambia* (2018) ECW/CCJ/APP/13/I4, 56–7.

99 Amnesty International, 'Gambia: Prison Sentences for Opposition Leaders Continues Downward Spiral for Human Rights' (21 July 2016) available at <https://bit.ly/2lRXGj3> accessed 04/09/2019; Article 19, 'Article 19 Individual Submission to the UN Universal Periodic Review of Gambia for Consideration at the 20th Session of the UN Working Group in October–November 2014' (15 March 2019) 1–6 available at <https://bit.ly/2lKa0lJ> accessed 03/09/2019.

100 Commonwealth Human Rights Initiative (CHRI), 'Commonwealth Human Rights Initiative (CHRI) Stakeholder Submission for the Universal Periodic Review of the Gambia' (2014) 1–5 available at <https://bit.ly/2kdQYDHf> accessed 03/09/2019; International Service for Human Rights, 'The Situation of Human Rights Defenders in the Gambia' (2014) available at <https://bit.ly/2kHBisG>; Gambian Press Union, 'Gambia Press

critical of the government were reportedly blocked and online journalists arrested.[101] There were reported cases of enforced disappearances of human rights defenders and journalists.[102] This hostile civil society environment was compounded by the harsh rhetoric by the Jammeh government against journalists and human rights defenders. President Jammeh is reported to have stated publicly that he will 'not compromise or sacrifice the peace, security, stability, dignity, and the wellbeing of Gambians for the sake of freedom of expression'.[103] Several newspapers, radio and TV stations were shut down or denied licenses.[104] Whereas the Jammeh government signalled a willingness to participate in the UPR process and even accept some recommendations on freedom of expression, it did not demonstrate any willingness to move beyond this ritualism as it considered freedom of expression and journalists as a threat to the survival of his regime.

However, since the dawn of a new regime in 2017, The Gambia has made progress towards implementing several UPR recommendations under this category. While a few incidents of the arrest of journalists have been reported, there is broad agreement among NGOs that the civil society space has improved, and the new regime has shown willingness to undertake institutional and legal reforms to protect freedom of expression and the press.[105] According to a joint report by Access Now, Article 19 and the Committee to Protect Journalists (CPJ), the actions by the new government, including the release of political prisoners and the public commitment to review the current regulatory framework on freedom of the press, have seen the return of journalists, human rights defenders from exile and media outlets previously banned were reinstated.[106] The government also enhanced collaboration with NGOs through the establishment of a National Media Law Committee aimed at advancing the agenda for the reform of laws on freedom of expression and the press in

---

Union Submission to the UN Universal Periodic Review Eight Session of the UPR Working Group' (2014) available at <https://bit.ly/2kiTFUI> accessed 03/09/2019; Reporters Without Borders, 'The Gambia—The State of Press Freedom' (2014) 1–5 available at <https://bit.ly/2kJjkpJ> accessed 03/09/2019.

101 Collaboration on International ICT Policy in East and Southern Africa (CIPESA) et al., 'Digital Rights in the Gambia: Submission to the 34th Session of the Universal Periodic Review, the Gambia' (2019) 1–6 available at <https://cipesa.org/?wpfb_dl=290> accessed 27/08/2019.

102 Commonwealth Human Rights Initiative (CHRI), above n 100, 3–4.

103 Collaboration on International ICT Policy in East and Southern Africa (CIPESA) et al., above n 101 para 17.

104 Niklas Hultin et al., 'Autocracy, Migration, and the Gambia's "Unprecedented" 2016 Election' (2017) 116(463) *African Affairs* 1–20.

105 The Association of Non-Governmental Organisations (TANGO), 'Submission for the United Nations Universal Periodic Review 3rd Cycle' (2019) 2–3; Collaboration on International ICT Policy in East and Southern Africa (CIPESA) et al., above n 101.

106 Access Now, Article 19 and the CPJ, above n 97; David Perfect, 'The Gambian 2016 Presidential Election and Its Aftermath' (2017) 106(3) *The Round Table: The Commonwealth Journal of International Affairs* 323, 326.

The Gambia.[107] This Committee, which was composed of representatives from the media, civil society, the National Assembly, government officials and regulatory bodies, completed its work in 2018 and made key recommendations in its report to the Ministry of Information and Communications Infrastructure. These recommendations included repealing Section 173A of the Information and Communications Act 2009 (as amended in 2013), Section 178 of the Criminal Code and Section 52 of the Criminal Code,[108] which were frequently used to arrest, detain and prosecute journalists. These recommendations were consistent with several UPR recommendations,[109] and although these recommendations are yet to be implemented by the government, the work of the National Media Law Committee signals a move towards greater cooperation between state and civil society for the protection of the right to freedom of expression and the press.

In addition, key decisions in 2018 by the national and regional courts have strengthened freedom of expression and the press. In *Federation of African Journalists & 4 Ors v The Republic of The Gambia* (2018), the ECOWAS Court of Justice declared the above provisions of Criminal Code (Amendment) Act and the Information and Communication Act unlawful and ordered the government of The Gambia to repeal the provisions.[110] Similarly, in May 2018 the aforementioned recommendations by the National Media Law Committee found support in the Gambian Supreme Court, which ruled in the case of *Bai Touray and Two Others v The Attorney General* that Section 173A of the 2013 Information and Communications (Amendment) Act was inconsistent with the rights and freedoms guaranteed under Section 25 (1) (a) and (b) and Section 207 of the Gambian Constitution.[111] The Gambian Supreme Court for similar reasons declared Sections 178, 179 and 180 of the Criminal Code to be unconstitutional.[112] While the repressive laws have not yet been repealed, the change in regime has, at the very minimum, had impact on the state's attitude towards freedom of expression and the press. These efforts by the new regime to change the media environment have contributed to significant improvement to The Gambia's ranking in the World Press Freedom Index. In 2017, The Gambia was the biggest global advancer in the World Press Freedom Index[113] and in 2019 was ranked 92 out of 180, moving up 53 places.[114]

107 See Article 19, 'Submission to the UN Human Rights Committee (Response to issues Raised in the Absence the Second Periodic Report of the Gambia)' (21 June 2018) para 11 available at <https://bit.ly/2kh8hnu> accessed 03/09/2019.

108 Ibid 2–4.

109 UN Human Rights Council, above n 38 paras 109.57–109.64.

110 *Federation of African Journalists & 4 Ors v The Republic of The Gambia* (2018) ECW/CCJ/APP/13/I4, 56–7.

111 *Emil Touray and 2 Ors v The Attorney General* (2018) Supreme Court Civil Suit No. 001/2017 para 54.

112 Ibid.

113 Article 19, *The Expression Agenda Report 2017/2018 The State of Freedom of Expression Around the World* (Article 19, 2018) 55 available at <https://bit.ly/2QDpBkH> accessed 03/09/2019.

114 Reporters Without Borders, '2019 World Press Freedom Index' available at <https://rsf.org/en/ranking> accessed 03/09/2019.

The death penalty

The use of the death penalty has witnessed a continuous decline globally over the last decade, and in 2018, a 30% decline in the number of known executions was recorded by Amnesty International.[115] At the end of 2018, 142 countries had abolished the death penalty in law and practice while 52 countries still retained the death penalty.[116] The Gambia is one of the countries that retained the death penalty for ordinary crimes, together with many other countries, including Nigeria, the United States of America, India, China and Japan.[117] Therefore, the imposition of the death penalty is a phenomenon which exists across different regions and cultures. According to Srini Sitaraman, the justification for the continuous imposition of the death penalty 'is deeply enmeshed in the religious and cultural values of many societies'[118] and has included arguments about deterrence, just retribution and the need for victim closure.[119] Some of these justifications have certainly been raised by states within the context of the UPR, which provides an appropriate platform to challenge these justifications and determine whether they are grounded in reality or in law. During UPR I, Benin expressed fears that abolishing the death penalty will create a haven for gangsters in Benin,[120] while Libya argued that the imposition of the death penalty was justified by Islamic values.[121] These arguments ignore the recognition of the death penalty as a human rights issue, and while this, historically, has not been without contention by states within the UN,[122] the interpretation of the imposition of the death penalty as justified by Islamic and Christian principles has been challenged by both Islamic and Christian scholars.[123]

Before 2012, the last public execution in The Gambia took place in 1985, and since 1995 there was a moratorium on the use of the death penalty. During UPR I and II, a total of 19 recommendations on the death penalty were made to The Gambia and none of them were accepted by the Gambian UPR delegation. One

115 Amnesty International, *Death Sentences and Executions in 2018* (Amnesty International 2019) 7 available at <https://bit.ly/2m6UqAz> accessed 29/08/2019.

116 Ibid 48.

117 Ibid 49.

118 Srini Sitaraman, *State Participation in International Treaty Regimes* (Ashgate Publishing 2009) 112.

119 Office of the High Commissioner for Human Rights, *Moving Away from the Death Penalty: Arguments, Trends and Perspectives* (United Nations 2015) available at <https://bit.ly/2lM1hPO> accessed 29/08/2019.

120 UN Human Rights Council, *Report of the Working Group on the Universal Periodic Review—Benin*, 8th sess, Agenda Item 6, UN Doc A/HRC/8/39 (28 May 2008) para 54.

121 Working Group on the Universal Periodic Review, *National Report Submitted in Accordance with Paragraph 15 (a) of the Annex to Human Rights Council Resolution 5/1—Great Socialist People's Libyan Arab Jamahiriya*, 9th sess, UN Doc A/HRC/WG.6/9/LBY/1 (24 August 2010) para 91.

122 Nigel S Rodley, 'The Death Penalty as a Human Rights Issue' in Office of the High Commissioner for Human Rights above n 119, 204–213.

123 Mario Marazziti, 'World Religions and the Death Penalty' in Office of the High Commissioner for Human Rights above n 119, 192–203.

of the arguments put forward by The Gambia during UPR I in March 2010 was that The Gambia was 'exercising a self-moratorium' and that 'no executions had been carried out'.[124] Other African states have raised similar arguments in the UPR, including Mali,[125] Tanzania[126] and Tunisia.[127] However, in October 2010, the Gambian parliament adopted legislation which made human trafficking, rape, violent robbery and some drug-related offences punishable by death.[128] This is consistent with the government's rhetoric during UPR I that it did not intend to abolish the death penalty in the near future[129] but contrary to its assertions during UPR II that the application of the death penalty is 'limited to murder and treasonable offences'.[130] Moreover, in 2012, the government executed nine death row inmates and some of the executed prisoners were reported to have been denied access to legal representation and not exhausted the judicial appeals process.[131] Therefore, the claim by the Gambian government during UPR II that a review by a higher tribunal must be observed before the death penalty can be applied in The Gambia was not consistent with the reality on the ground. The 2012 execution of death row inmates was condemned by several bodies, including the UN High Commissioner for Human Rights and the Commonwealth Secretary General who both requested the Gambian government to halt any subsequent executions.[132] Following these criticisms, the Gambian government announced putting back a moratorium on the use of the death penalty conditional on the future crime rate.[133]

The occurrence of a change in regime in January 2017 in The Gambia had two significant impacts on the issue of the death penalty in The Gambia. The first was

124 UN Human Rights Council, above n 37 para 57.

125 Working Group on the Universal Periodic Review, *National Report Submitted in Accordance with Paragraph 15 (a) of the Annex to Human Rights Council Resolution 5/1—Mali*, 9th sess, UN Doc A/HRC/WG.6/2/MLI/1 (14 April 2008) para 53.

126 Working Group on the Universal Periodic Review, *National Report Submitted in Accordance with Paragraph 15 (a) of the Annex to Human Rights Council Resolution 5/1—United Republic of Tanzania*, 12th sess, UN Doc A/HRC/WG.6/12/TZA/1 (19 July 2011) para 17.

127 Working Group on the Universal Periodic Review, *National Report Submitted in Accordance with Paragraph 15 (a) of the Annex to Human Rights Council Resolution 5/1—Tunisia*, 8th sess, UN Doc A/HRC/8/21 (22 May 2008) para 6(g).

128 The Drug Control Amendment Act 2010; Trafficking in Persons Amendment Act 2010; and Criminal Code Amendment Act 2010.

129 UN Human Rights Council, above n 30 para 600.

130 UN Human Rights Council, above n 38 para 23.

131 Amnesty International, 'The Gambia: Submission to the Universal Periodic Review 20th Session of the UPR Working Group' (2014) 6.

132 UN Office of the High Commissioner for Human Rights, 'Gambia Executions an Unfortunate Setback for Human Rights Protection—Pillay' (30 August 2012) available at <https://bit.ly/2kwn8e1> accessed 03/09/2019; UN Office of the High Commissioner for Human Rights, 'Death Row / Gambia: "Stop arbitrary stream of executions"' (28 August 2012) available at <https://bit.ly/2lRYrIV> accessed 03/09/2019.

133 UN General Assembly, *Report of the Special Rapporteur on Extrajudicial, Summary or Arbitrary Executions*, UN Doc. A/69/265 (6 August 2014) para 94.

the declaration of an official moratorium on executions and the commutation of all death sentences to life imprisonment in February 2018 by President Adama Barrow, as a first step towards abolition of the death penalty.[134] The second was the ratification of the second optional protocol to the ICCPR on 28 September 2018, aimed at the abolition of the death penalty.[135] These actions by the new regime in effect contributed to the implementation of the 19 recommendations made during UPR I and II on the abolition of the death penalty which were all previously rejected by the previous regime. These included recommendations to '[m]aintain the moratorium on executions with a view to abolishing the death penalty' and to '[a]bolish the death penalty sign and ratify ICCPR-OP2' made by Italy and Spain respectively.[136] Therefore, a change in regime in The Gambia has brought about a renewed sense of engagement with the recommendations of the UPR, but it is still too early to determine the impact it would have on The Gambia's UPR III and subsequent cycles of the UPR.

Sexual orientation

The criminalisation of same-sex relationships in most parts of Africa is a legacy of colonialism. Between 1700 and 1900, there were no countries in Africa with criminal codes or specific legislations criminalising consensual same-sex sexual conduct.[137] South Africa was the only country within this period that had common law criminalising consensual same-sex sexual conduct imposed by the Netherlands, which colonised South Africa between 1652 and 1795, and retained by the British, who occupied the land between 1795–1803 and 1806–1961.[138] This changed following the Berlin West African Conference in 1884 and the scramble for Africa whereby the desire to rid the colonies of what the colonisers considered as 'unnatural offences' contributed to the transplantation of criminal laws against consensual same-sex sexual conduct from the territory of the colonising power to the colonies.[139] While there is a debate on

134 Pap Saine, Aaron Ross, and Catherine Evans, 'Gambia Announces Moratorium on Death Penalty' *Reuters* (18 February 2018) available at <https://reut.rs/2kHBSXo>; Human Rights Council, 'List of Issues in the Absence of the Second Periodic Report of the Gambia—Addendum—Replies of the Gambia' UN Doc. CCPR/C/GMB/Q/2/Add.1 (11 June 2018) para 63.

135 United Nations, *Second Optional Protocol to the International Covenant on Civil and Political Rights, Aiming at the Abolition of the Death Penalty*, UN Doc C.N.465.2018. TREATIES-IV.12 (Depositary Notification) (28 September 2018) available at <https://treaties.un.org/doc/Publication/CN/2018/CN.465.2018-Eng.pdf> accessed 03/09/2019.

136 UN Human Rights Council, above n 38 para 109.101; UN Human Rights Council, above n 37 para 99.33.

137 See Amnesty International, *Making Love a Crime: Criminalisation of Same-Sex Conduct in Sub-Saharan Africa* (Amnesty International 2013) 14–16.

138 See Ibid 14–16; Erna Liver and Willem H Oliver, 'The Colonisation of South Africa: A Unique Case' (2017) 73(3) *Herv Teol Stud* 1–8.

139 See Amnesty International, above n 137, 14–16.

whether same-sex behaviour was acceptable in pre-colonial African society, it is observable that majority of the existing laws criminalising same-sex conduct in Africa are a reflection of the laws of the colonising power.[140] Whereas many of the colonial powers have over time repealed the laws criminalising same-sex conduct, many of their former colonies in Africa have continued to adhere to them and, in some cases, expanded the scope of the laws.[141] John Ambani describes this expansion as a 'second wave of criminalisation of homosexuality' and a reaffirmation of the colonial heritage.[142]

The Gambia is an example of a British colony that continued the legacy of the British colonial law that criminalised same-sex sexual conduct, inspired by repressive Victorian-era laws on homosexuality.[143] Section 144 of the 1965 Gambian Criminal Code penalises as a felony with imprisonment of up to 14 years 'a person who has carnal knowledge of any person against the order of nature . . . or permits any person to have carnal knowledge of him against the order of nature'.[144] This was amended in 2005 to penalise women who engaged in lesbianism.[145] A further amendment in 2014 introduced a new offence of 'aggravated homosexuality' in Section 144A which attracts a penalty of life imprisonment.[146]

The above criminal provision of the law provided a cover for President Jammeh's harsh rhetoric against members of the LGBT community which was displayed through numerous statements at the domestic level and within the UN. During The Gambia's 49th Independence anniversary, President Jammeh reportedly stated:

> The coercive and dictatorial pressures by some foreign powers aimed at imposing on us their ungodly and decadent cultures like homosexuality and

140 See S Ekine, 'Contesting Narratives of Queer Africa' in S Ekine and H Abbas (eds), *Queer Africa Reader* (Pambazuka Press 2013); Busangokwakhe Dlamini, 'Homosexuality in the African Context' (2006) 67(2) *Agenda: Empowering Women for Gender Equity* 128–36; Enze Han and Joseph O'Mahoney, 'British Colonialism and the Criminalization of Homosexuality' (2014) 27(2) *Cambridge Review of International Affairs* 268–88.

141 For example, England and Wales abolished the law criminalising consensual same-sex sexual conduct in 1967, but the former British colonies such as Uganda, Kenya and Gambia did not. France decriminalised same-sex sexual conduct in 1791; some of its colonies, including Cameroon, have continued to adhere to the law.

142 See John O Ambani, 'A Triple Heritage of Sexuality: Regulation of Sexual Orientation in Africa in Historical Perspective' in Sylvie Namwase and Adrian Jjuuko (eds), *Protecting the Human Rights of Sexual Minorities in Contemporary Africa* (PULP 2017) 16; See also Solomon T Ebobrah, 'Africanising Human Rights in the 21st Century: Gay Rights, African Values and the Dilemma of the African Legislator' (2012) 1 *International Human Rights Law Review* 120; Kenya, Uganda and Gambia are examples of British former colonies that have expanded the scope of the offence and prescribed harsher penalties.

143 Sexual Offences Act 1956 (United Kingdom), section 13.

144 Criminal Code, 1965 (The Gambia).

145 Criminal Code (Amendment) Act, 2005. No. 3 of 2005.

146 Criminal Code (Amendment) Act, 2014 (No. 11 of 2014).

> unbridled freedoms that endanger the peace and welfare of the majority, will never be accepted in this country.[147]

Jammeh is reported to have compared homosexuality to be as 'deadly' and 'heinous' as murder or terrorism and was vocal about not accepting the rights of sexual minorities in The Gambia.[148] Within the context of the UPR, The Gambia received 23 recommendations across UPR I and II on the issue of sexual orientation, including recommendations to '[r]epeal laws that provide for the criminalization of LGBT . . .' and '[d]ecriminalise same-sex activities in accordance with international human rights standards'.[149] The Gambia rejected all 23 recommendations and used culture and religion as justification for its position on these recommendations. In relation to the argument on culture, The Gambia stated during UPR I it 'did not recognise sexual orientation as a universal human right' and that it had 'cultural values, norms and practices that were different from those of other countries'.[150] This contributes to the perception that calls for decriminalisation of same-sex conduct are a form of Western cultural imperialism.[151] On the issue of religion, Jammeh stated that homosexuality is 'immoral', 'satanic' and a 'declaration of war on both [r]eligions and [h]uman existence'.[152] These arguments are consistent with the position adopted by the African Group at the HRC arguing gay rights is not a universally defined and accepted concept in international human rights law and described the calls for decriminalisations as 'obsession by other regions or groups to impose their own value system on other regions'.[153] While these arguments were consistent with those echoed during the review of The Gambian and other African states, they contradicted various resolutions of the HRC and decisions of other judicial and quasi-judicial bodies.[154] The 23 recommendations on sexual orientation made to The Gambia during

147 AllAfrica, 'Gambia: Jammeh Vows to Fight Homosexuals the Same Way As Mosquitoes' (19 February 2014) available at <https://allafrica.com/stories/201402191598.html> accessed 03/09/2019.

148 Amnesty International, 'Gambia: Amnesty International Submission for the UN Universal Periodic Review 20th Session of the UPR Working Group, October–November 2014' (2014) available at <https://bit.ly/2m3HLhL> accessed 02/09/2019.

149 UN Human Rights Council, above n 38 para 109.53; UN Human Rights Council, above n 37 para 100.13.

150 UN Human Rights Council, above n 37 para 63.

151 See Rahul Rao, 'Echoes of Imperialism in LGBT Activism' in Kalypso Nicolaïdis, Berny Sebe, and Gabrielle Maas (eds), *Echoes of Empire: Memory, Identity and Colonial Legacies* (IB Tauris 2015) 355–72; Katerina Dalacoura, 'Homosexuality as Cultural Battleground in the Middle East: Culture and Postcolonial International Theory' (2014) 35(7) *Third World Quarterly* 1290–306.

152 Amnesty International, above n 148, 2.

153 See *Statement by Mr. Ositadinma Anaedu, Representative of the Nigerian Delegation to the United Nations on Sexual Orientation on Behalf of the African Group (minus South Africa)* (22 March 2011) www.djibouti.ch/mission/uploads/MissionPermanente.LesDeclarations/MS122011.pdf

154 Amnesty International, above n 131, 1–18; See UN General Assembly, above n 17.

UPR I and II were not implemented, and the changes in The Gambian political regime have had no impact on the decriminalisation of same-sex sexual conduct in The Gambia.

Concluding remarks

The Gambia's engagement with the UPR presents a case study which questions the effectiveness of the UPR mechanism in improving the human rights situation on the ground. The participation of The Gambia in UPR I and II on many significant human rights issues did not immediately translate to implementation within the state. The fact that many of the recommendations were not accepted or were accepted with qualifications showed the reluctance of the Gambian government to reflect on its domestic human rights situation and to undertake meaningful improvement. Politics, culture and religion impacted on The Gambia's engagement with the UPR process. The hostility of the Jammeh government towards the West and Western values in many ways informed the government's receptiveness to UPR recommendations. The impact of politics in the UPR process is a phenomenon which has been examined by many scholars, and this has implications for the effectiveness of the UPR mechanism.[155] While regime change in The Gambia has positively impacted on human rights issues, including freedom of expression, the press and the abolition of the death penalty, there has been no observable change on other issues, including the decriminalisation of same-sex relations. There is also the risk that if the position on gay rights adopted by the African regional group in the HRC is not challenged from within the regional group, this could provide international legitimation for discrimination against sexual minorities within the region and dilute international human rights norms. Therefore, the UPR as a human rights mechanism may be more or less effective, depending on the political regime in the relevant state with other contextual factors, and it is yet to be examined if the change in regime in The Gambia will result in greater engagement with UPR III.

155 See Rochelle Terman and Erik Voeten, 'The Relational Politics of Shame: Evidence from the Universal Periodic Review' (2018) 13(1) *The Review of International Organizations* 1–23; Sara Bertotti, 'Separate or Inseparable? How Discourse Interpreting Law and Politics as Separable Categories Shaped the Formation of the UN Human Rights Council's Universal Periodic Review' (2019) 23(7) *The International Journal of Human Rights* 1140–65; Jane Cowan and Julie Billaud, above n 56, 1175–90.

Index

Page numbers in *italic* indicate a figure. Page numbers in **bold** indicate a table.